THE LATER PHILOSOPHY
OF R. G. COLLINGWOOD

Oxford University Press, Amen House, London E.C.4

GLASGOW NEW YORK TORONTO MELBOURNE WELLINGTON
BOMBAY CALCUTTA MADRAS KARACHI LAHORE DACCA
CAPE TOWN SALISBURY NAIROBI IBADAN ACCRA
KUALA LUMPUR HONG KONG

THE LATER PHILOSOPHY
OF R. G. COLLINGWOOD

BY

ALAN DONAGAN

OXFORD
AT THE CLARENDON PRESS
1962

PRINTED IN GREAT BRITAIN
AT THE UNIVERSITY PRESS, OXFORD
BY VIVIAN RIDLER
PRINTER TO THE UNIVERSITY

CONIVGI

DILECTISSIMAE

D. D. D.

AVCTOR

PREFACE

COLLINGWOOD discouraged discussion of his work. Those who disapproved of it he begged to write, not about it, but about its subject; and those who approved he charged to show their approval by attending to work of their own (*A*, 118–19). I have disregarded his injunction, because it seemed to me that I could not economically proceed with my own work until I had taken stock of his.

Of the English-speaking philosophers whose work between the two great wars deserves to be remembered, Collingwood alone has not been 'placed'. While widely read, his books have seldom been thoroughly mastered; nor do I pretend to have mastered them. This book is little more than an impression of how Collingwood's philosophy developed after he had completed his *Essay on Philosophical Method*. At most, I hope that it may persuade some of my readers to abandon the injurious preconceptions with which Collingwood's later books are often read; and to read at least his masterpieces, *The Idea of History*, *The Principles of Art*, and the first three parts of *The New Leviathan*, as together expounding a coherent philosophy.

Every serious student of Collingwood is deeply indebted to his literary executor, T. M. Knox, the Principal of St. Andrews. Yet, much as I owe to his editorial preface to *The Idea of History*, I am disquieted by the awareness that this book would have been improved if I had succeeded in owing more. Mr. R. B. McCallum, Master of Pembroke, Professor I. A. Richmond, and Professor W. H. Walsh very kindly answered my questions about Collingwood, and gave me much other information. Dr. Alda Croce has graciously provided me with a typed copy of the original text of five of Collingwood's letters to her father, Benedetto Croce: I thank both her, and Professor G. N. G. Orsini of Wisconsin, who wrote to her on my behalf, after drawing my attention to Croce's references to Collingwood in *Nuove Pagine Sparse*. I regret that Professor Orsini's *Benedetto Croce: Philosopher of Art and Literary Critic* appeared too late for me to use it.

Besides allowing me to reproduce portions of a letter which Collingwood wrote to him, Professor Gilbert Ryle generously read about two-thirds of my manuscript, and expelled from it some blunders and much bad writing. Professor William Kneale and Mr. G. A. Paul read Part I and a portion of Part II. Mrs. J. L. Ackrill, as well as verifying my quotations from *Faith and Reason*, commented on an early draft of Chapter VIII. Professor R. E. Allen read parts of Chapters III and XI, Professor H. E. Mason part of Chapter VII, and Professor May Brodbeck all of Chapters VIII and IX. What I owe them for this labour, much as it is, is as nothing to what I owe to them, and to my teachers and fellow-students at Melbourne, Minnesota, and Oxford, for their guidance and example. My wife has read the whole manuscript, in every one of the transformations through which it has passed; and her acuteness in detecting faults has been matched only by her dexterity in proposing remedies. To all I offer my thanks. For the manifold errors that remain, I alone am responsible.

By awarding me a research grant for summer 1958, and research leave for fall quarter 1959, the University of Minnesota provided me with the leisure I needed for study, and later for writing. A grant-in-aid from the American Council of Learned Societies defrayed the expenses of a visit to Oxford in the autumn of 1959. I owe three special debts: at the Council of Learned Societies, to Dr. Frederick Burkhardt; and at the University of Minnesota, to Theodore C. Blegen, formerly Dean of the Graduate School, and to E. W. McDiarmid, Dean of the College of Science, Literature, and the Arts. To them, and to the institutions they represent, I am grateful.

A. D.

Eynsham—Minneapolis
October 1959–April 1961

CONTENTS

PART III. METAPHYSICS

ABBREVIATIONS

The titles of Collingwood's works are abbreviated as follows:

A	*An Autobiography* (London, 1939).
EM	*An Essay on Metaphysics* (Oxford, 1940).
EPM	*An Essay on Philosophical Method* (Oxford, 1933).
IH	*The Idea of History* (Oxford, 1946).
IN	*The Idea of Nature* (Oxford, 1945).
NL	*The New Leviathan* (Oxford, 1942).
PA	*The Principles of Art* (Oxford, 1938).
SM	*Speculum Mentis* (Oxford, 1924).

Except to *The New Leviathan*, all references in the text to these works are to page numbers; those to *The New Leviathan* are to its numbered paragraphs. Hence '*A*, 126' means '*An Autobiography* (London 1939), p. 126'; and '*NL*, 4. 13' means '*The New Leviathan* (Oxford, 1942), paragraph 4. 13'.

I

INTRODUCTION

§ 1. Collingwood's Philosophical Development: His Own Interpretation

THE first obstacle to understanding Collingwood's later philosophy is his own narrative of its development, which beyond doubt is untrue. The Principal of St. Andrews, T. M. Knox, his literary executor, first drew attention to this.[1] Collingwood's narrative, which may be found in his *Autobiography*, affords melancholy evidence of the power of an intellectual temptation he had himself exposed. Only two years before he wrote it, he had warned autobiographers that in reconstructing their past thoughts, 'recollection is a treacherous guide'; and had sighed over politicians writing their memoirs, who 'remember very well the impacts and emotions of a crisis, but are apt, in describing the policy they then advocated, to contaminate it with ideas that belonged in fact to a later stage in their career' (*IH*, 295–6).

The story of Collingwood's philosophical thought, as he himself recollected it, is as follows. After a thorough training in the 'realist' principles and methods of Cook Wilson and his school, he came to doubt their soundness. While yet an undergraduate he had found time to serve an apprenticeship in archaeology under Haverfield, and he soon discovered that realist epistemology did not assort with scientific history. The realists took knowing to be a simple act of 'apprehension' which a mind would perform of itself when placed in 'compresence with' what was to be known; but you cannot get historical knowledge so. An historian cannot place his mind in compresence with what he wants to know, because it is past; nor will compresence with relics of the past by itself enable him to 'apprehend' the facts of which they are evidence (*A*, 25–26).

---

[1] *Proc. Brit. Acad.* xxix (1943), pp. 472–3; *IH*, x–xiii.

B

Nor was that all. Realism was essentially critical: its principles were for the most part negations of those of idealism. Yet the realists' historical technique was so weak that again and again they spent their shot on positions which were not held by those against whom they set up as adversaries. Cook Wilson, for example, 'constantly criticized Bradley for views which were not Bradley's' (*A*, 22). The results were calamitous. The better realists unwittingly stole more and more from idealism; the worse 'little by little destroyed everything in the way of positive doctrine that they had ever possessed' (*A*, 45, 49).

The impacts and emotions of his emancipation from realism thrust into the back of Collingwood's mind other memories of his early career as a philosopher; and in crediting that emancipation almost entirely to his progress in historical understanding he did his other interests scant justice. Although as a young man he had done serious work on the relations between theology and philosophy, which bore fruit in his first book, *Religion and Philosophy*, he had no more to say of it in his *Autobiography* than that it had revealed to him the incapacity of psychology to justify or condemn any belief (*A*, 93–95).

For information about his work on the philosophy of art, he was content to refer his readers to his *Principles of Art*. He had been reared in a family of artists. As a child he had written incessantly, in verse and in prose, 'lyrics and fragments of epics, stories of adventure and romance' (*A*, 3). At school he learned to play the violin, and although he came to think of his compositions there as 'a great deal of trash', he continued to play (*A*, 7, 13). He painted. It was from experience of this kind, not looking at pictures and reading books about them, but spending time and trouble in the actual practice of the arts, that in 1925 he wrote his lively *Outlines of a Philosophy of Art*.

A year earlier he had published his first comprehensive philosophical treatise, *Speculum Mentis*. It is a philosophical analysis of five 'forms of experience', Art, Religion, Science, History, and Philosophy, in an endeavour to ascertain the proper character and limitations of each, and the relations between them.

Collingwood's writings on religion and art held no interest for his realist colleagues; and he despaired of bringing them to understand his criticism of their position. When Cook Wilson's pupils, notably Joseph,[1] tried to debate non-Euclidean geometry and the theory of relativity out of existence, although Collingwood saw that their tactics belonged not to the academy but to the hustings, he was more enraged than amused: as debaters they were too successful. The pages in his *Autobiography* in which he recorded his decision to refrain from controversy and pursue his investigations in solitude betray how bitter that decision had been (*A*, 53–55).

Looking back from the vantage-point of his fiftieth year, he saw his life's work as 'in the main an attempt to bring about a *rapprochement* between philosophy and history' (*A*, 77). The war had left him the only resident in Oxford whom Haverfield had trained as a Romano-British specialist, and in 1919 Haverfield himself had died. Collingwood therefore considered himself obliged to transmit to others the training he had received, and to carry forward the re-searches Haverfield had been unable to complete (*A*, 120). Even had he been capable of pursuing a theoretical activity without reflecting on it, he would have been provoked to vindicate scientific history by his realist colleagues' open scepticism towards its results, a scepticism which he put down to their complacent ignorance. Besides, he had a further motive. He ascribed both the outbreak of war in 1914, and the bungled peace which concluded it, to a failure of intellect rather than of will; and he came to suspect that what the European intellect had lacked was relevant historical knowledge (*A*, 89–91). For the sake of the future, a thorough investigation of the nature and methods of scientific history could no longer be put off.

History can be of use in controlling the present, because the past, so far as it is the subject of historical inquiry, is not dead: relics of it survive and are in a measure understood (*A*, 96–97). This prin-ciple, which Collingwood recorded that he had fully grasped by about 1920, cannot stand alone. The past may not be dead, but how is it kept alive? On the evidence of his own manuscripts, Colling-wood confessed that he did not contrive to answer this question until the summer of 1928, during a vacation near Die in France, and

[1] Members of the school of Green as well as Cook Wilson's pupils did so. For example, Professor J. A. Smith (see *A*, 18) stood up with Joseph to assail the Theory of Relativity, in a celebrated exchange with Professor F. A. Lindemann, later Lord Cherwell. See R. F. Harrod, *The Prof* (London, 1959), pp. 17–27.

that he took two more years to work out its implications (*A*, 107,
115). Nothing that is past can live in the present but past thoughts.
History proper is therefore concerned with thought. Hence, since
natural events neither are nor express thoughts, narratives of past
natural events are not history but pseudo-history. Geologists,
palaeontologists, and astronomers are not historians, even though
they investigate past events. A past thought can live only because
it can be rethought. When one man thinks again something he
thought yesterday, or something someone thought before he was
born, he performs literally the same act of thought over again, not
another act of thought like it (*A*, 111); and he can know that he
has done so, provided that he has evidence which excludes every
other possibility. Although he came to think that history differs
from natural science in its subject-matter, Collingwood continued
to protest that it is 'Baconian' in method (*A*, 133–4).

The philosophical conclusions which he professed to have drawn
from his new conception of history are even more daring. Past
thoughts are about past problems; for no problem is eternal. Moreover, the evidence from which an historian reconstructs a past
thought is normally what remains of an attempt to solve it. A piece
of ancient pottery is a relic of an ancient attempt to produce something that would fulfil a certain purpose; and it may be the only
evidence that an historian has that a past craftsman had that purpose. The same point holds in intellectual history. A philosopher
tries to state not a problem but its solution; and, if a past philosopher
had been 'so confused in his mind as to make a complete mess of the
job of solving his problem, he was bound at the same time to mix
up his own tracks so completely that no reader could see quite
clearly what his problem had been' (*A*, 69–70).

It follows that there are not two separate sets of questions to be
asked, one historical, 'What did so-and-so think was the answer to
such-and-such a question?' and the other philosophical, 'What is the
answer to that question?' If the historical question can be answered
at all, then the answer to the corresponding philosophical question
must be contained in it. It also follows that there is no difference
between an historical study of a past philosophical problem and a
philosophical study of it (*A*, 72; see below, Ch. X, § 2).

Soon after he had (so he claimed) reached these results, Colling-wood planned to place them before the public in a series of books (*A*, 117). His health, however, had become precarious. Fortunately, illness did not prevent him from writing. The first book in his series, *An Essay on Philosophical Method*, was written during a long illness in 1932 (*A*, 118). Although in his *Autobiography* he gave the impression that on completing it he for a time turned away from philosophy in order to settle accounts with his archaeological studies (*A*, 118), his editor has recorded that from August 1933 to September 1934 he worked hard at the history of natural science and cosmology, and elaborated a cosmology of his own (*IN*, v).

Nevertheless, in 1934 and 1935 his work was predominantly historical. During that time he revised the book on *Roman Britain* which he had originally written in 1921 and enlarged in 1931; he wrote the British section in Tenney Frank's *Economic Survey of Ancient Rome*; and, setting the crown upon a lifetime's effort, he wrote the brilliant and daring sections on prehistoric and Roman Britain in the first volume of the *Oxford History of England* (*A*, 121). His only philosophical publication during this period was his Inaugural Lecture in the Waynflete Chair, *The Historical Imagination*, in which he expounded some of the principles upon which he had carried out his historical researches.

When he returned to philosophy, it was to the philosophy of art. In 1937 he wrote his *Principles of Art*, intending it to take the place of his earlier *Outlines*, which, he informs us in his Preface, the Delegates of the Clarendon Press had invited him to revise or replace (*PA*, v). Although he described the *Principles of Art* as 'the second book of my series', it is not clear whether in 1930 he had planned it as such. Before he had seen it through the press (it was published in 1938) he was again overtaken by illness. This time he did not attempt to continue with his series, but wrote his *Autobiography*, whose purpose was to put on record a brief account of the work he had not been able to publish, in case he should not have been able to publish it in full (*A*, 118).

Collingwood plainly implied that he had reached the principal doctrines of his *Autobiography* before he wrote his *Essay on Philosophical Method* (*A*, 117). Not only did he not acknowledge any important change of opinion after he wrote the *Essay on Philosophical Method*, he even affirmed the continuity of his later views with those he had advocated in *Speculum Mentis*. Of that early work he wrote that while 'much of it needs to be supplemented and qualified', not a great deal 'needs to be retracted' (*A*, 56 *n*.). By 1938, then, Collingwood had convinced himself that when he wrote the *Essay on Philosophical Method* he already held that philosophy and history are identical (*A*, 72). Now, as Knox has pointed out, it is impossible to reconcile Collingwood's recollection with the text of the *Essay* itself.

§ 2. *Collingwood's Conversion to Historicism: Knox's Interpretation*

Knox did not deny that the *Essay on Philosophical Method* arose out of Collingwood's long endeavour to connect philosophy with history. Indeed, Knox's very reason for describing the book as 'a philosophical landmark' was that it advocated and in a measure exemplified 'an interfusion of philosophical and historical thinking'.[1] What he denied was that in the *Essay* and the *Autobiography* Collingwood gave the same account of the relation between philosophy and history.

The conception of philosophy presented in the *Essay* is difficult to describe. According to it the subject-matter of philosophy is Being itself, as opposed to any special kind of being; and, since *omne ens est unum verum bonum*, Being itself must be considered under the philosophical concepts of *unity*, *truth* (or *reality*), and *goodness* (*EPM*, 33; cf. *IH*, xi).

Unlike the concepts of classificatory mineralogy or biology, the specific forms in which each of these philosophical concepts is exemplified are ordered in a scale: thus it has long been customary to specify goodness in the forms of pleasure, utility, and duty. But pleasure, utility, and duty do not all exhibit their generic essence, goodness, in the same degree. Utility is good in a higher degree than pleasure, and duty is good in a higher degree than utility. Moreover, the classes of goods which exhibit these different specific forms

---

[1] *Proc. Brit. Acad.* xxix (1943), p. 471.

overlap. What is ordained by duty is often both expedient and pleasant. Collingwood considered such overlaps to be essential to the specific classes which fall under any philosophical concept; and he reconciled them with his doctrine of the scale of forms, by arguing that the higher forms in which a philosophical concept is specified, differ from the lower in kind as well as in degree. The higher pleasures, therefore, do not differ from the lower in intensity only but in kind: a pleasure of a higher kind is not only pleasant but useful as well. The pleasure of intellectual achievement is of a higher kind than bodily pleasure, because intellectual achievement is useful as well as pleasant.

The chief difficulty in the doctrine of the scale of forms is that unity, truth, and goodness have opposites. While an adequate theory of goodness must account for its opposite, evil, the doctrine that the concept of goodness is the concept of a scale of forms seems to abolish evil altogether; for the lowest form on the scale of goods is still a good. Collingwood's solution was in the Platonic tradition. Absolute diversity, falsity, and evil are fictions. Everything diverse hangs together in some way, every genuine thought has some truth, and every act some goodness. Mere diversity, or falsehood, or evil only exists when a low degree of unity is affirmed to be a higher one, or a lower truth is believed to be both true and incompatible with a higher, or a lower good is chosen in preference to a higher.

A higher form on a philosophical scale is therefore not only of the same genus as a lower, differing from it as a more adequate embodiment of their generic essence, it is also both distinct from the lower and opposed to it 'as a higher specification to a lower, a relatively adequate to a relatively inadequate, a true embodiment of the generic essence to a false embodiment'. As true, it beats its opposite on its own ground. A higher good is not only better than a lower, it also includes it. 'The higher thus negates the lower, and at the same time reaffirms it: negates it as a false embodiment of the generic essence, and reaffirms its content, that specific form of the essence, as part and parcel of itself' (EPM, 88).

Between philosophy so conceived and history Collingwood discerned two connexions. First, philosophy as the science of Being is pursued by reflecting on the various special sciences, which treat of

the various departments of being. Philosophy therefore rests on experience, but experience of a special kind. 'If . . . we say that the
initial knowledge on which philosophy rests as its data is arrived
at by way of experience, we must add that the term experience in
this case carries a special meaning: not the experience of a perceiver,
but the experience of a thinker' (*EPM*, 169). However, most philosophers who reflect on natural science or politics or any other special
field of knowledge are not themselves natural scientists or politicians. Their scientific and political thinking is largely historical: a
rethinking of the thoughts of others.

A second connexion between philosophy and history is that a
critical written history of philosophy and a systematic philosophical
treatise ought largely to coincide. The successive philosophical systems, so far as each begins where its predecessors left off, themselves
constitute a scale of forms, each of which exemplifies the generic
essence of a philosophical system, and sums up that part of the scale
which came before it. Although every philosopher is in error inasmuch as he cannot identify or solve all the problems to which his
own work has given rise, or to which further progress in first degree
thinking will give rise, the steps forward that he has taken are true
and final, in the sense that they have solved, once for all, the problems they were meant to solve (*EPM*, 190–1).

It goes without saying that the higher forms of philosophy are
developed later in time than the lower; for a problem cannot be
solved until it has been set, and it is the lower forms of philosophy
that set some of the problems for the higher. Yet it does not follow
that an historical narrative of what philosophical theory came after
what will be the same as a critical account of what philosophical
theory is a genuine development from what. The history of philosophical systems may diverge from that of philosophical thought;
for philosophical systems, like other human creations, express
thought less often than the lack of it.

This conception of how philosophy has developed is excellently
illustrated in Collingwood's introductory comparison between
Descartes's work and Kant's. Descartes had reflected well and
accurately on his experience as a mathematician, and, disgusted
with the dialectic of the schools, turned to mathematics for a guide

in the two other sciences he recognized, natural science and meta-physics. Although, as his practice showed, Descartes knew that natural science and metaphysics were not at all points identical with mathematics, he overlooked or implicitly denied it in his philo-sophical theory of them. Consequently, when Kant entered into his heritage, he found that the three Cartesian sciences had not profited equally from Descartes's work.

The Cartesian mathematics had stood firm, and continued to advance; the Cartesian natural science had undergone a good deal of criticism, notably at the hands of Newton; and the Cartesian meta-physics had worked itself into a blind alley. The inference was that Descartes' method, as stated by himself, was adequate to the case of mathematics, but required modification in natural science, where it showed insufficient grasp of the significance of experiment, and still more modification in the case of metaphysics. (*EPM*, 19–20.)

A philosophical system can be an advance on its predecessors only if at least one of two conditions is fulfilled: either the 'experience' on which it rests, the experience of scientific thinking, must be more advanced than that on which its predecessors rested; or it must re-present a deeper understanding of the experience on which both rest. In major advances in philosophical thinking, like Descartes's over his medieval predecessors, or Kant's over the eighteenth-century rationalists, both conditions are fulfilled.

Although Collingwood, in propounding this conception, obvi-ously connected philosophy far more closely with history than most of his contemporaries were willing to do, it is plain that he did not identify them. Even if he did not think that any philosophical system had yet arisen, or would ever arise, which is completely true, he unquestionably implied that some are nearer to the truth than others (*EPM*, 189–90). He therefore believed that it makes sense to ask of any two philosophical systems, 'Which is nearer to the truth?' Such a question is philosophical, not historical. Even if an historical inquiry into a philosophical system inescapably gives rise to the question, 'Is it true?' (cf. *IH*, 300), an answer to that question is not a matter of history. Philosophy is therefore 'a dis-tinct and living form of thought', and not 'an appendage of natural science or . . . a part of history' (*EPM*, 5).

Accordingly, Knox was certainly right in denying that Collingwood's analysis of philosophy in his *Essay on Philosophical Method* is
compatible with his analysis of it six years later in his *Autobiography*.
Between 1932 and 1938 Collingwood abandoned the conception of
philosophy as a form of thought distinct from history for the doctrine that in its primary form, metaphysics, it is nothing but an
historical investigation into what is absolutely presupposed in the
special sciences as pursued in different societies at different times.
Furthermore, he declared that in his reformed historical metaphysics no question about the truth or falsity of any absolute presupposition could even arise; for absolute presuppositions, as he
took them to be, are neither true nor false (*A*, 65–66; see below,
Ch. X, § 2).

Collingwood's conversion to 'historicism' can be dated more precisely than the period 1932–8. In a later chapter (X, § 1) evidence
will be presented that he adhered to the position of his *Essay on
Philosophical Method* as late as June 1935; and Knox has referred to
'documentary evidence' that Collingwood clung to his conception
of metaphysics as a non-historical science of the One, the True, and
the Good, that is, of Being itself, as late as 1936 (*IH*, x).

Between June 1936 and the autumn of 1938, when he wrote his
Autobiography, Collingwood wrote only two philosophical works, a
paper on causation for the Aristotelian Society, on which he drew
in Part III of his *Essay on Metaphysics*, and *The Principles of Art*. The
paper on causation is equally compatible with the position of the
Essay on Philosophical Method and that of the *Autobiography*. *The Principles of Art* is harder to judge. Yet, although it traverses the distinction between poetry and prose that is drawn in the *Essay on
Philosophical Method* (*PA*, 296–8; cf. *EPM*, 212–15), and contains
occasional asperities in his later manner (e.g. *PA*, 198–9, 327), its
design accords perfectly with the conception of philosophy he had
expounded in 1932. The philosophy of art rests on experience in the
arts, whether as original creator or as critic. Its fundamental problem is to define the word 'art', as aesthetically used. While it is an
historical question when and how the word 'art' came to be used
aesthetically, and also whether its usage in a given passage is or
is not aesthetic, the distinction between the aesthetic and the

non-aesthetic usages of the word is not historical but critical (*PA*, 5–9). In *The Principles of Art*, then, Collingwood took for granted the legitimacy of a philosophical investigation of the nature of art which would not be 'a part of history' (cf. *EPM*, 5). However, he said nothing of the relation between the philosophy of art and metaphysics. His *Autobiography* shows beyond doubt that during or soon after the composition of *The Principles of Art* he ceased to believe that a distinct philosophical science of Being itself was possible, and came to hold that metaphysics should be reformed as an historical science (*A*, 65–66).

In the light of these facts, Knox has rejected Collingwood's own division of his work into juvenilia (before his discoveries in the period 1928–30) and mature works, and replaced it by a division into three groups.

The first consists of what he came to regard as juvenilia, *Religion and Philosophy* (1916) and *Speculum Mentis* (1924). The second begins with the *Essay on Philosophical Method* (1933) and continues with *The Idea of Nature* (which dates, except for its Conclusion, from 1934) and much (1936) of *The Idea of History*. The last comprises the *Autobiography* (1939), the *Essay on Metaphysics* (1940), and *The New Leviathan* (1942). *The Principles of Art* (1938) is akin in part to the second group, in part to the third. (*IH*, vii.)

While confessing that in each group Collingwood's work was 'many-sided', and that his discussion of it 'is mainly confined to only one of its facets, namely to Collingwood's conceptions of the relation between philosophy and history', Knox seems to have considered that 'facet' fundamental, at least to the works of the second and third groups (*IH*, vii–viii).

According to Knox's verdict, in the works of the second group Collingwood succeeded in effecting a *rapprochement* between philosophy and history, in which the independence of philosophy as a distinct form of thought was safeguarded (*IH*, vii, ix–x). In the works of the third group, however, Knox believed Collingwood to have come to think that 'philosophy as a separate discipline is liquidated by being converted into history' (*IH*, x). This position is so pressed with difficulties that 'it is sometimes hard enough to make the later works consistent even with themselves' (*IH*, xviii–

xix). Consequently, it is not surprising that in them Collingwood's
style degenerated. Although they 'contain passages of outstanding
worth', they 'lack serenity', unlike the works of the second group,
and are 'marred by febrility' (*IH*, xxi).

How came Collingwood to fall from the heights of the *Essay on
Philosophical Method* to the depths of his *Autobiography*? Holding that
where the later work differed from the earlier it was essentially
unsound, Knox could suggest no good or even plausible reason for
it. He pointed out that in his first period Collingwood anticipated
some of the doctrines of his *Autobiography*. However, that does not
show us why he reverted to them. For that, Knox offers only one
explanation: ill health. Soon after Collingwood completed his *Essay
on Philosophical Method*, 'tiny blood-vessels began to burst in [his]
brain, with the result that the small parts of the brain affected were
put out of action' (*IH*, xxi). This culminated in a series of strokes
which eventually left him helpless. It was during his recovery from
the first of those strokes that he wrote his *Autobiography*.

§ 3. *Collingwood's Later Works: a Third Interpretation*

Knox's demonstration that between 1936 and 1938 Collingwood
radically changed his mind about the relation of philosophy to history must be the foundation of any interpretation of his later works.
Yet, although Knox's principal conclusions are firmly established,
neither his explanation of Collingwood's change of mind, nor his
division of Collingwood's later works into two distinct groups, a
non-'historicist' and an 'historicist', is beyond question.

No doubt an illness as grave as Collingwood's might easily have
led to a far more serious decline in his intellectual powers than Knox
supposes to have occurred. Yet even if it were true that Collingwood would not have abandoned the conception of philosophy he
had expounded in his *Essay on Philosophical Method* had he not fallen
ill, his change of mind would not be explained. By disordering his
judgement, illness may cause a man to mistake bad reasons for good,
but it will not cause him to change his mind on a philosophical
question for no reason at all. At the very least, Knox's explanation of the late triumph in Collingwood's thought of sceptical and

dogmatic trends, which he had temporarily defeated between 1932 and 1936 (cf. *IH*, xi), must be supplemented by identifying Collingwood's reasons for allowing them to triumph, even if those reasons would not have imposed on him in his prime.

It is natural to look to the *Autobiography* and *Essay on Metaphysics*, in which Collingwood first expounded his later views, for his own statement of his reasons. If you do, however, you will be disappointed. In his *Autobiography* Collingwood did not even concede that anybody but a realist would imagine a non-historical study of the One, the True, and the Good to be possible, much less let slip that he had himself advocated such a study five years earlier; and although in the *Essay on Metaphysics* he did formally refute the conception of metaphysics as 'the science of pure being', what he demolished was a mere caricature of his earlier position in the *Essay on Philosophical Method*. Whatever his reasons were for renouncing that position, he did not reveal them.

Sceptical arguments against the possibility of an independent philosophical science of pure being abound; and, lacking other evidence, historians of Collingwood's later thought would be obliged to ascribe his rejection of that science to the influence of such arguments. Fortunately, other evidence is not lacking. In the *Essay on Philosophical Method*, he had distinguished the logical form of philosophical propositions from those of the various special theoretical sciences, namely, mathematics, the natural sciences, and history. Mathematics and the natural sciences he had taken to be concerned to establish 'hypothetical universal' propositions, and history 'categorical singular' ones; philosophy, however, he had maintained, could rest content with nothing less than propositions which were both categorical and universal (*EPM*, 133–6). This doctrine directly descended from his idealist position in *Speculum Mentis* that the special sciences, along with art and religion, are all forms of error, that 'every error is a lapse from concreteness into abstraction, and [that] all abstraction is dogmatism' (*SM*, 288). Philosophy escaped this comprehensive condemnation because it is a concrete study of the concrete. In 1937, however, Collingwood began to undermine this position.

In writing *The Principles of Art* he had to analyse the concept of imagination, and to distinguish imagining from thinking. The distinction he drew was simple: unlike imagining, thinking is essentially analytic and abstract (*PA*, 254). Later, in *The New Leviathan*, he elaborated this conception of thought, arguing that all forms of thinking, from the highest to the lowest, are conceptual, and that all concepts are abstract (*NL*, 7. 63, 7. 22). If, as I shall contend (see Ch. X, § 5), these conclusions are incompatible with his earlier position that philosophical propositions are both universal and categorical, then one of his reasons for abandoning that position is plain: he could not reconcile it with his new analysis of conceptual thinking. That this reason did weigh with him is made probable by a curious fact which otherwise must be put down to sheer effrontery. Although in the *Essay on Philosophical Method* he had repudiated the conception of the science of Being itself as a science of anything abstract (*EPM*, 33; cf. *SM*, 299), in the *Essay on Metaphysics* he assumed without question that ontology could only be a science of abstract being (*EM*, 11–16). He could not have made this assumption as a matter of course, unless he had ceased to believe that a non-abstract concept of being was even possible.

Nevertheless, Collingwood's adoption of the theory that concepts are essentially abstract does not explain how he came to the conclusion that 'philosophy as a separate discipline [must be] liquidated by being converted into history' (*IH*, x). Metaphysics may take other forms than an investigation of a chimerical non-abstract concept of being; and even if metaphysics in all its forms should prove impossible, it has not been shown that philosophy as a separate discipline must be metaphysical.

Knox has pointed out that Collingwood was often tempted to identify a special subject he happened to be studying with philosophy itself. Being conscious that 'it was the same questioning mind at work, whatever its object', he seems to have been 'inclined to draw the conclusion that philosophy was simply identical with whatever he happened to be studying most intensively at the time' (*IH*, xv). His absorption in history during 1935 and 1936 would have afforded a strong temptation to identify history with philosophy.

The *Essay on Metaphysics* provides a further clue. It shows that Collingwood had studied A. J. Ayer's *Language, Truth and Logic*, which was first published in 1936, and that he had come to endorse Ayer's view that the propositions of traditional metaphysics are unverifiable (*EM*, 163–5). Yet he could not bring himself to believe that traditional metaphysics had been a waste of energy, or that at least some of its conclusions approximated to the truth. His hypothesis that the affirmations which Ayer took to be unverifiable propositions were not propositions at all, but absolute presuppositions, which are neither true nor false, naturally pointed to the further hypothesis that metaphysics is not a futile inquiry into what absolute presuppositions are true. What then remains? One thing would be to inquire into what absolute presuppositions have been held, by whom, and why; and, prima facie, these questions are historical.

Although Knox has conclusively demonstrated that Collingwood's proposed reform of metaphysics as an historical science is inconsistent with his earlier position in the *Essay on Philosophical Method*, some doubts remain whether he was right in dividing Collingwood's later philosophical writings into two radically distinct groups (*IH*, vii). Undoubtedly, such a distinction may be made on grounds of style, especially of tone. All his books from *The Principles of Art* to *The New Leviathan* are disfigured by hectic and bombastic passages which he would not have permitted himself in the period of calm before his illness. Yet Knox's division was made on grounds not of style, but of content. He pointed out that in Collingwood's writings after 1936, irreconcilable strains of scepticism and dogmatism emerged, which between 1932 and 1936, before his illness, he had been able to master. The central topic concerning which those strains emerged was that of the relation of philosophy to history (*IH*, x–xv, xvii).

My reasons for hesitating to accept Knox's division of Collingwood's later writings are two. First, except on the question of what philosophy is, and of how it is related to history, I do not think that what Collingwood wrote after he began *The Idea of Nature* in 1934 contains any major reversal of opinion. On minor questions he did indeed change his mind: sometimes for the better, as when in *The New Leviathan* he revised the classification of the emotions he had made in *The Principles of Art* (see below, Ch. V, § 3); and sometimes for the worse, as when he abandoned the doctrine that sensation has objects as well as modes (see below, Ch. II, § 2). His historicist speculations about the nature of philosophy occasionally led him to repudiate conclusions he had arrived at in the philosophy of history, as when he denied that it was possible for historians to rediscover mistaken or unsuccessful thoughts (*A*, 69–70; cf. *IH*, 300–1, 312–14). Even then, however, he seldom gave up the repudiated conclusion, but inconsistently allowed it to survive elsewhere in the very work in which he had denied it (*A*, 62–63, 130–2; cf. *IH*, xii). His fundamental work in the philosophy of mind, and the superstructure he erected on it of philosophy of art, of natural science, and of history, seem to have been little, if at all, affected by his abortive attempts to produce an acceptable theory of the nature of philosophy. Except for the passages which contain those ill-starred attempts, it is impossible to divide Collingwood's writings from *The Idea of Nature* to *The New Leviathan* into two distinct groups. The analysis of natural science in *The New Leviathan*, for example, is directly developed from that in *The Idea of Nature*.

A second reason for hesitating to accept Knox's division is that it may be doubted whether Collingwood, when he wrote *The New Leviathan*, still believed that philosophy could be converted into history. It is true that he declared that the first three parts of *The New Leviathan* were 'all constructed on what Locke called "the historical plain method"' (*NL*, 9. 1), and that what he had to say in the first Part was 'entirely matter of history' (*NL*, 9. 23). Nevertheless, despite this perfunctory deference to the *Autobiography* and the *Essay on Metaphysics*, the first three Parts of *The New Leviathan*, although nourished by Collingwood's historical knowledge, are emphatically not history, according to his own analysis of scientific history in the *Autobiography* itself. *The New Leviathan* exemplifies philosophy as a form of thought distinct from history no less than the *Essay on Philosophical Method*.

In *The New Leviathan* Collingwood was significantly silent about what philosophy is. He appears to have resolved not only to put aside the question of the relation between philosophy and history which had engaged him in the *Autobiography* and *Essay on Metaphysics*, but even to eschew the very word 'philosophy'. He left it to his readers to determine what conception of philosophy *The New*

Leviathan exemplifies. However, in declaring that his aim was to bring Hobbes's masterpiece up to date 'in the light of the advances made since it was written, in history, psychology, and anthropology', he implied that it was not a work of history, psychology, or anthropology, but one of a kind that was only possible 'in the light of' such work (*NL*, iv). The phrase recalls his description of philosophy, in the portion of *The Idea of History* which he had written in 1936, as 'thought of the second degree, [that is,] thought about thought' (*IH*, 1).

Hence, while on one side the works placed by Knox in his second group are not sharply distinct from those of his third group, except on the question of the relation between philosophy and history; on the other, the last and greatest of the works of the third group neither exemplifies nor endorses the doctrine of the relation of philosophy to history which is supposedly characteristic of that group. This suggests the possibility of a third interpretation of Collingwood's writings after 1930, which would do justice both to Knox's demonstration that between 1936 and 1938 Collingwood radically changed his mind about the relation of philosophy to history, and to Collingwood's own impression that the *Essay on Philosophical Method*, *The Principles of Art*, and the other works which he projected when he wrote his *Autobiography*—presumably his incomplete *Idea of Nature*, *The Principles of History*, the *Essay on Metaphysics*, and *The New Leviathan*—all belonged to a series which he had planned before he wrote the *Essay on Philosophical Method* (*A*, 117; cf. *NL*, v).

That third interpretation is as follows. By 1932 Collingwood had planned a series of philosophical books. It was to begin with an essay on method, which would be followed by works on the philosophy of natural science, of art, of history, and of politics; and possibly the whole series was to culminate in a metaphysical treatise on Being itself: the One, the True, and the Good. In 1932 he completed the first book of his series, the *Essay on Philosophical Method*; then, having seen it through the press, he turned to the philosophy of natural science, and wrote, in the academic year 1933–4, the first version of *The Idea of Nature*. After an interlude of two years, in which he was preoccupied with history, but in which he nevertheless found time to write the bulk of his great philosophical study of it, *The*

Idea of History, in 1937 he wrote the second book of his series, *The Principles of Art*. Since the theory of conceptual thinking which he developed in that book was incompatible with the conception of philosophy he had advanced in the *Essay on Philosophical Method*, he was compelled to reconsider that conception. This he did, in his *Autobiography* (which also contains progress reports on his work in philosophy of history, ethics, and politics), the *Essay on Metaphysics*, and the unpublished and incomplete *Principles of History*. He then returned to his series, revising and augmenting *The Idea of Nature*, and carrying through a major study of political theory from philosophical first principles, *The New Leviathan*. This last work, however, shows that the 'historicist' conception of philosophy he upheld in the *Autobiography*, the *Essay on Metaphysics*, and the *Principles of History* satisfied him as little as his earlier conception in the *Essay on Philosophical Method*.

His major philosophical work in *The Idea of Nature*, *The Idea of History*, *The Principles of Art*, and *The New Leviathan* forms a largely consistent whole, which should not be divided into historicist and non-historicist groups. Of this whole Collingwood offered two distinct interpretations: an 'idealist'[1] one in the *Essay on Philosophical Method*, and an 'historicist' one in the *Autobiography* and the *Essay on Metaphysics*. Neither interpretation was adequate to his philosophical achievement.

§ 4. *Design of this Book*

This book is divided into three Parts. In the first two Parts I shall analyse Collingwood's major philosophical works, and in the third Part his speculations on the nature of philosophy, and his projected reform of metaphysics. In all three Parts, I shall arrange the topics Collingwood considered in a systematic order, and not in the chronological order in which Collingwood himself took them up.

Collingwood's work can only be understood in the light of his philosophy of mind, which he first expounded in full in *The New*

---

[1] Collingwood repudiated the description 'idealist'; but no other is so little misleading. On the jacket of *EPM* his publishers quoted a reviewer who described it as a restatement of 'a Platonic and Hegelian metaphysic viewed from a modern standpoint'.

Leviathan, although he had anticipated parts of it in *The Principles of Art*. Since all of his philosophical work on the various departments of human activity, from art to theoretical science, grew out of his general philosophy of mind, *The New Leviathan* is the best key to his whole later philosophy. Accordingly, I have followed the major subdivisions of the first part of *The New Leviathan* in the first part of this book. I begin with the principles of Collingwood's philosophy of mind, whether he himself expressed them or not, and go on to examine, in turn, his distinction between feeling and perception, his theory of concepts and propositions, and his analyses of practical and theoretical thinking. In my chapter on his theory of concepts and propositions I investigate the revolution in logic which he proposed in his *Autobiography*, but which in his later works he seems to have thought better of; and in my chapter on practical and theoretical thinking I consider the theory of presuppositions which underlies his proposed reform of metaphysics. In both cases, my findings are adverse to his innovations. I conclude the first Part by investigating Collingwood's analyses of imagination, emotion, and expression, and his application of them to the philosophy of art.

Many readers will be surprised by some of my conclusions. Even of those who acknowledge that he decisively repudiated his earlier theory of conceptual thinking, some will be reluctant to accept the plain evidence that he denounced introspection as a method in the study of mind, and revived Hobbes's doctrine that, since all consciousness involves the use of language, the philosophy of mind and the philosophy of language are two sides of a single study. Of those who suspect me of foisting upon Collingwood views that are fashionable among our own contemporaries, I can only beg that they consult the sixth chapter of *The New Leviathan* with an open mind.

In deferring my examination of Collingwood's philosophy of art until after I have expounded his theory of consciousness, I have departed from Collingwood's division, and have separated what he, rightly as I think, considered to be inseparable. He held that every fresh linguistic act was a work of art, no matter at what level of consciousness, although he acknowledged that the word 'art' is customarily reserved for self-conscious creations. Had I followed Collingwood, I should have discussed the expressive or artistic side of language at every level of consciousness. In separating my discussion of consciousness from my discussion of expression, I hope to have simplified both; but it must be borne in mind that the activities I discuss separately are not separable in fact. In saying that art was expressive Collingwood did not deny that it was cognitive.

In the second Part I treat of Collingwood's philosophical analysis of the three great branches of theoretical science: natural science and the two sciences of mind; namely, psychology, the science of feeling, which he considered an 'apanage' of mind; and history, which he considered to be the science of mind proper. While this Part largely rests on *The Idea of Nature*, *An Essay on Metaphysics*, *The Idea of History*, and parts of the *Autobiography*, there is evidence in *The New Leviathan* that to the end of his days he continued in the main to accept the account of theoretical science he had given in those works.

According to the definition in the *Essay on Philosophical Method*, while the second-degree study of the special sciences is a part of philosophy, it is not the whole of it. What, in general, is the relation between the thinking mind and its objects? Can philosophy judge, as well as interpret, the scientific principles it is its business to examine? Above all, what is the relation between philosophy and history? Is philosophy 'as a separate discipline . . . liquidated by being converted into history' (*IH*, x)?

In the first chapter of the third Part I try to reconstruct and explain the various answers to these questions which Collingwood gave or took for granted in his books from the *Essay on Philosophical Method* to *The New Leviathan*. In the *Essay on Philosophical Method* he held not only that philosophy was a genuine form of thought, distinct from history, but also that it had a distinct subject-matter, Being itself, which was related to the subject-matters of the various special sciences as reality is to its appearances (*EPM*, 123, 86–88). In his statements of what philosophy is in *The Idea of Nature* and *The Idea of History*, he refrained from making this extreme claim. Instead of asserting that the philosophy of history is about a reality, and history itself about an appearance of that reality, he made only the more moderate claim that the philosophy of history is a critical study of historical thought: it is thought of the second degree. In the *Autobiography*, the *Essay on Metaphysics*, and *The Principles of History*, however, he proposed to reform metaphysics on the ground that thought of the second degree can only be historical. Unfortunately, the reasons he gave for this conclusion were varied and inconsistent with one another, and his conclusion itself was inconsistent with his practice in his last book, *The New Leviathan*.

In the final chapter I consider what Collingwood had to say in his *Autobiography* and in *The New Leviathan* about two perennial metaphysical problems: that of the realist theory of knowledge, and that of the relation of mind and body. I conclude by investigating his account of the bearing of philosophy on the claims of religion.

I have chosen to confine my attention to Collingwood's theoretical philosophy, and to pass over his ethical and political philosophy except when they have a theoretical bearing. That my interpretation is true could only be demonstrated by explaining every passage in his writings, both published and unpublished, which appears to conflict with it. I must confess that I have not attempted such a demontration. My method has been impressionistic rather than encyclopaedic. I have reconstructed Collingwood's thought by reflecting on what I have read and re-read in his books; but although, as my reconstruction became more definite, I looked more and more for evidence against it, I do not try to cite or discuss all that evidence. Nor do I attempt to refute interpretations offered by others which disagree with my own. However, I do cite evidence for such of my conclusions as I foresee will be controversial, and I try to meet any serious objections to them of which I know.

As Collingwood observed in *The Idea of History*, it is impossible to reconstruct another man's philosophy without passing judgement on it. 'What is required, if I am to know Plato's philosophy, is both to rethink it in my own mind and also to think other things in the light of which I can judge it' (*IH*, 301). Knowledge of another man's philosophy that does not enable you to judge it critically is not philosophical, but simply a parrot-like capacity to recall what he said or wrote. Accordingly, in presenting what I believe to have been Collingwood's thought, I have tried to be critical; and on all major questions to which I think his answer was wrong I give my reasons for thinking so. When I think he was right or largely right I do not usually say so, but simply give his reasons in the hope that others will be as convinced by them as I have been. If matters on which I agree with Collingwood did not far outnumber those on which I do not, I should not have written about him.

PART I

MIND AND LANGUAGE

PART I

MIND AND LANGUAGE

II

FEELING AND CONSCIOUSNESS

§ 1. *The Fundamental Principles of Collingwood's Philosophy of Mind*

IN his philosophy of mind Collingwood was fundamentally anti-Cartesian; for he held that mind, as it is in itself, cannot be studied at all, but only 'man as mind'. And although he defined 'man as mind' as '*whatever he is conscious of being*' (*NL*, 1. 84), he repudiated Descartes's doctrine that acts of consciousness are, as it were, self-illuminating. A man may be conscious of being something, and yet not aware that he is conscious of it. To become aware of any of his acts of consciousness he must perform an additional act (*NL*, 5. 91), and no act of consciousness is analogous to seeing or to any other form of sensation (cf. *NL*, 11. 36; *PA*, 222). You cannot know your own mind by turning an inner eye on its operations, because introspection can do no more than bring to mind something of which you have already become aware (*EM*, 43).

Collingwood did not wish to deny that if you have contrived to become aware of one of your own acts of consciousness, your consciousness of it is immediate, but only to expose the fallacy of inferring, when you are immediately aware of something, that you must be aware of it by observing or 'introspecting' it. It would be equally fallacious to infer that, because consciousness is immediate, you cannot mistake what you are conscious of, although it is true that argument about it would be misplaced (*NL*, 4. 71–4. 73). If you profess to admire Napoleon, it must be reasonable for somebody to try to persuade you that you ought not; but he would make himself ridiculous if he tried to argue that you do not. Yet in saying you admired Napoleon, you could be mistaken. You must express your beliefs about what you are aware of, if you express them at all, in propositions; and, while there are mistakes that people do not make, any proposition may theoretically be mistaken (*NL*, 11. 35).

A man may make mistakes about his own mind from two causes: conceptual confusion and inattention. The propositions in which he expresses his beliefs about his mind, like all propositions, involve the use of concepts. The proposition that you admire Napoleon, for example, involves the concept of admiring; and if you were uncertain or confused about that concept, your opinion on the question of whether or not you admire Napoleon might be unsound. Although he was fully persuaded that on many questions about their own minds people do not make mistakes, Collingwood believed that even exceptionally clear-headed men like Hobbes and Spinoza had been led, by conceptual confusions, to misdescribe such elementary states of mind as being angry (*NL*, 10. 4–10. 43).

You may be careless or inattentive in becoming aware of one of your conscious acts as well as in any other activity; and when you are, your judgement is impaired. One way of detecting careless errors of this kind is to contrast them with what others believe about their minds. The philosophy of mind is not about the peculiarities of individuals: it has to do only with what is common to all minds, or at least to all that share in a given civilization. Although *The New Leviathan* was largely a study of Collingwood's own mind, because he could be directly conscious of no other, he believed that his own mind and many of his readers' minds were representatives of what he called 'the modern European mind'. Whether or not his belief was well founded is an historical question; for what other European minds were and are can only be ascertained historically. That is why he described his conclusions about the mind as 'matter of history' (*NL*, 9. 21–9. 25).

Many philosophical analysts today consider that Collingwood's programme was fundamentally misconceived. He took it for granted not only that the concept of consciousness is not confused, but also that it is clear enough to work with. Yet Professor Ryle has thought it necessary to preface his examination of the Cartesian conception of consciousness by distinguishing five ways in which the words 'conscious' and 'consciousness' are used in ordinary discourse.[1] Even

---

[1] Gilbert Ryle, *The Concept of Mind* (London, 1949), p. 156.

more stringently, Professor Austin has recommended that philosophers forbear to pronounce upon the meaning of the more abstract
terms they are wont to use until they have investigated the homely
expressions by which the concrete activities which fall under those
terms are commonly talked about.[1] Because he neglected these
precautions, Collingwood is not seldom dismissed without a
hearing.

That summary verdict would not be unjust if he had employed
the words 'conscious' and 'consciousness', and their synonyms
'aware' and 'awareness', in a private or technical way, or had
attempted to analyse their meaning off-hand. But he did not. His
use of them, which is quite untechnical (cf. *NL*, 4. 24–4. 29), coincides with a use the negative form of which Ryle has described as
follows. '... [A] person can be said to be unconscious of a sensation,
when he pays no heed to it. A walker engaged in a heated dispute
may be unconscious, in this sense, of the sensations in his blistered
heel, and the reader of these words was, when he began this sentence, probably unconscious of the muscular or skin sensations in
the back of his neck, or in his left knee.'[2] It is true that Ryle went on
to say that ' "Conscious" in this sense means "heeding" ', which
Collingwood would have denied; for while he agreed that you
become conscious of what you feel by heeding it or attending to it,
he thought that heeding was not the same thing as consciousness,
but only its 'practical aspect' (cf. *NL*, 4. 33). On that point I think
he was right. Now provided that a word is employed in a familiar
way, as Collingwood employed 'conscious' and 'consciousness', it
may be presumed to be free from confusion until reasons are given
to the contrary. No philosopher is obliged to begin by analysing
the familiar words he employs.

Throughout *The New Leviathan* Collingwood evidently presupposed two principles, neither of which he expressly stated. The first
was that if a man is conscious, he must be conscious of something
(cf. *NL*, 5. 26). I shall call it the Principle of Intentionality. If 'consciousness' be taken in the familiar sense of 'result of heeding', this
principle is necessarily true; for in that sense you can no more be

---

[1] J. L. Austin, 'A Plea for Excuses', *Proc. Aris. Soc.* lvii (1956–7), pp. 4–7.
[2] Ryle, op. cit., p. 157.

conscious but conscious of nothing than you can heed but heed nothing.

The second, which I shall call the Principle of Order, is that if a man is conscious of one of his own acts of consciousness, then it is not by that act itself, but by another act of consciousness which may be said to be of a higher order (cf. *NL*, 4. 31, 5. 92). This principle is rejected out of hand by those who hold that, since all mental acts are selfconscious, a man makes himself conscious of his own mental acts merely by performing them. Yet, although it is not implausibly supposed that whenever you think something you must be aware that you think it, at least part of its plausibility derives from a confusion. The order which Collingwood's principle affirms, as he was careful to point out, is not temporal but logical. It may be true that you do not usually think of something without being aware that you are doing so; and it may even be true, although I do not think so, that you cannot; but it does not follow that your thought and your simultaneous awareness of it are not distinct acts of consciousness, one of which is prior to the other as its object. That there is a distinction between being conscious of something, and being conscious that you are conscious of it, appears to me self-evident; and I know of no philosopher who, having got the matter clear, has denied it.

These principles have a corollary, which Collingwood called the Law of Primitive Survivals. His own extremely elliptical statement of it runs: 'When A is modified into B there survives in any example of B, side by side with the function B which is the modified form of A, an element of A in its primitive or unmodified state' (*NL*, 9. 51). The word 'function' here is an ellipsis for 'mental function' or 'function of consciousness', by which Collingwood meant 'type of conscious (or mental) activity' (cf. *NL*, 9. 3). The symbols 'A' and 'B' must be understood to stand for mental functions. So understood, the law amounts to this. When a function of consciousness (B) is brought into existence having a lower-order function (A) as its object, unless the lower-order function (A) continues to exist in its primitive state, the higher-order function (B) cannot exist at all; for, by the Principle of Intentionality, no act of consciousness can exist without its object (*NL*, 9. 54). This extremely abstract law has a practical application. Although Collingwood, as we shall see, was persuaded by Spinoza that any lower-order mental function may be controlled by attaining a higher, he abominated the ascetic inference that the higher-order functions annihilate or transform the lower. Reason neither annihilates nor transforms desire, nor desire appetite (*NL*, 9. 55).

Collingwood's doctrine that acts of consciousness are as it were stratified in logically distinct orders led him to break with the theory held by some Idealists that the lower-order mental functions give rise to the higher by logical or dialectical necessity. He dignified his counter-proposition that 'the earlier terms in a series of mental functions do not determine the later' with the title of the Law of Contingency (*NL*, 9. 48). Here 'earlier' and 'later' are synonymous with 'of a lower order' and 'of a higher order', and 'determine' means 'logically determine'. The point of the law is simply that it does not follow, because a man has performed mental acts of a given type, that he will go on to perform acts of the next higher type. To ask why a man has taken the step from one order of consciousness to another is illegitimate; for he was under no necessity to do so. Occasions arise when it becomes possible for this person or that to take such a step, but it is never necessary; whether he takes it or not depends entirely on his 'practical energy' (*NL*, 7. 25–7. 29; cf. 13. 4).

An act of consciousness either has some other act of consciousness as its object, or it does not. If it does not, it belongs to the first, or lowest, of the orders of consciousness. In principle, there may be an infinite series of higher orders. Acts of the second order are those by which you become conscious of your acts of first-order consciousness; acts of the third order are those by which you become conscious of those of the second, and so forth. This classification is purely logical. Nothing whatever follows from it about the order of consciousness that any given person has attained, or about the concrete character of the acts by which he attained it.

In the first part of *The New Leviathan* Collingwood set out to answer two questions of this kind. Taking himself to be a representative modern European, to what order of consciousness had he attained? And what were his mental functions at each of those orders? His procedure was to take an inventory of his various mental functions, sorting the items inventoried each according to its order. This he likened to taking soundings at points marked on a mariner's chart. The points at which he would take his figurative soundings were to be determined by his logical classification of the orders of consciousness; but whether he would find anything when he took a sounding, and what he would find, could not be settled *a priori*. They were 'matter of history' (*NL*, 9. 23–9. 4).

§ 2. *The Status of Objects of First-order Consciousness*

That acts of first-order consciousness have objects follows from the Principle of Intentionality; and that their objects are not other acts of consciousness is true by definition. What, then, are their objects? Philosophical tradition and reflection on 'the normal usage of the word "conscious" ' concur in the answer that they are whatever is 'felt' (*NL*, 4. 24–4. 26). Consciousness dawns in an infant when he becomes aware of something he sees, hears, feels, tastes, or smells, together with what Collingwood called its emotional charge. The immediate object of first-order consciousness is not merely 'a sensuous element such as a colour seen, a sound heard, or an odour smelt', but that together with its emotional charge: 'the cheerfulness with which you see the colour, the fear with which you hear the noise, the disgust with which you smell the odour' (*NL*, 4. 1). Feeling is thus a complex consisting of a sensuous element together with its emotional charge.

The verb 'to feel' and the various specific verbs of sensation take grammatical objects, which are naturally presumed to stand for objects felt. However, although in his earlier book *The Principles of Art* Collingwood did not question this presumption, when he wrote *The New Leviathan* he had come to think it highly dubious and probably false. Feeling may be conceived as having no objects at all, but only modes. Both the object theory and the modal theory concur in holding that feeling has modes, that it may be strong or weak, clear or confused; they differ in that the modal theory asserts that even when feelings apparently differ in their objects, they really differ only in mode. It holds that 'the grammar of the sentence "I see a blue colour" is not like the grammar of "I kick a bad dog" but like the grammar of "I feel a transient melancholy" or "I go a fast walk". The colour, the melancholy, the walk are not objects of an action, they are *modes* of an action; their names have an *adverbial* function . . .' (*NL*, 5. 35).

Collingwood considered that either the object theory or the modal theory could be true, on the ground that neither was self-contradictory and both fitted the facts (*NL*, 5. 38). That two theories of feeling should have identical empirical consequences does not seem to have struck him as odd. However, he did think that there was a reason for preferring the modal theory: a methodological one. The object theory asserts that feeling has objects and modes, the modal theory that it has only modes; therefore, by Ockham's Razor, according to which it is bad method to suppose the existence of more entities than you must, the object theory ought to be rejected (*NL*, 5. 39).

This would be well enough if both theories did fit the facts. But is it not incredible that two incompatible theories of feeling should not be empirically testable? Prima facie it would seem that if it should make no difference which is true, then they cannot be genuinely incompatible. Fortunately it does make a difference. Collingwood himself acknowledged that 'feeling as we are actually conscious of it is a *field*, a here-and-now extended in space and time . . .' (*NL*, 5. 61). Now, recurring to Collingwood's examples of modes, it makes sense to say that 'a transient melancholy' stands for a mode of my feeling and 'a fast walk' for a mode of my gait; but it makes no sense whatever to say that a field is a mode of anything. The field of my walking today is a region, i.e. an object; it would be ridiculous to describe it as a mode of my walking, or as a mode of the wider region which comprises it. In short, the modal theory of feeling entails that what is felt is not a field; the object theory does not. Experience therefore shows that the object theory is true.

Since feeling has objects, Berkeley's question cannot be dodged, 'Is their *esse percipi* or not?' It is hard not to suspect that Collingwood's desire to dodge it was one reason why in *The New Leviathan* he embraced the modal theory (cf. *NL*, 5. 38). Certainly, his position in *The Principles of Art* will not do.

There, he had endorsed Berkeley's answer. He appears to have held that the objects of feeling, the existence of which he had not yet come to question, were sensuous. As in *The New Leviathan*, he analysed feeling into two elements, one sensuous and one emotional (*PA*, 161). To overcome the lack in ordinary English of a pair of generic terms to cover all the specific forms that the sensuous element in feeling may take, he had recourse to the Latin verb *sentire* and its English derivatives. *Sentire* in Latin is a generic term for seeing, hearing, feeling by touch, smelling, and tasting (*PA*, 160). Accordingly, he used the derivative verb 'to sense' and its noun 'sensation' as equivalents of *sentire* and *sensatio*. As a generic term for the objects of sensation he retained the Latin participle *sensum*. However, he added a refinement. In ordinary English a distinction is drawn between seeing a bright light and either imagining one, or having an after-image or an hallucination of one. Like most of his generation Collingwood conceived these 'experiences' as generically identical but specifically different. As experiences taken by themselves, seeing a flash of light and having an hallucination of one are similar; and it might be that they could only be discriminated by considering their relations to other experiences. Both experiences may therefore be classified generically as sensations, and the objects of both as sensa. Thus sensa may be either real or imaginary; and imaginary ones are as truly sensa as real ones (*PA*, 173).

Armed with this analysis of the term 'sensum', Collingwood made short work of Berkeley's question. He summed up his conclusions as follows: 'We found in Chapter VIII that sensation must be regarded as a flux of activity in which, however few or however many distinct sensory acts are going on together at any one time, each is no sooner achieved than it gives place to another. In each act we sense a colour, a sound, a scent or the like, which can be present to us only in our performance of the corresponding act. As soon as the act is over the sensum has vanished, never to return. Its *esse* is *sentiri*' (*PA*, 198).

I cannot discuss Collingwood's arguments in Chapter VIII of *The Principles of Art* for the conclusion that the *esse* of a sensum is *sentiri*, because I have not found any.[1] It is true that he asserted it there

---

[1] The relevant passages are *PA*, 160-1, 165-6, 168-70. In none of them do I find it demonstrated that the *esse* of a sensum is *sentiri*.

(*PA*, 168–70), but he appears to have been confident that, in context, assertion alone would prove irresistible.

One of his reasons for confidence was certainly mistaken. Of Moore's view, in 'The Nature and Reality of Objects of Perception', that sensa may exist unsensed, he had produced the following summary refutation. 'The only way in which a sensum can be present to us is by our sensing it; and if there is anything which enables us to speak of "sensa" not now being sensed, this cannot be strictly sensation, and the sensa in question cannot be strictly sensa. This is an obvious truth; but the denial of it has become an orthodoxy . . .' (*PA*, 200). That he believed this to be an 'obvious truth' goes far to explain his unsupported assertions of Chapter VIII.

In fact, what he took for an 'obvious truth' is a howler. Consider a parallel. A parliamentary candidate is by definition one who is standing for election to the House of Commons. Before he was nominated he was not a candidate, although he may have been a 'prospective' one, because he was not then standing; after the declaration of the poll, whatever his lot, he will no longer be one, for he will no longer be standing. Does it, then, follow that the *esse* of a parliamentary candidate is *munus petere*?

Quite obviously not. Standing for election is only an episode in a candidate's life, even though it is his very essence as a candidate. In the same way, it is not at all obvious that being sensed may not be merely an episode in the history of a sensum, even though it is its very essence as a sensum. Collingwood seems to have confounded the obvious truth that only while it is sensed does a sensum exist as a sensum with the pleasantry that when it is not being sensed it cannot exist as anything whatever. While the former is compatible with the common-sense view that the moon is your sensum (i.e. what you see) whenever you see it, the latter is not; for although the moon ceases to exist as your sensum when you stop looking at it, it does not cease to exist as the moon.

It is not enough, however, to repel Collingwood's attack. Some positive evidence must be found for maintaining that the *esse* of a sensum is not *sentiri*. Can it be shown that such things as the moon are genuinely 'sensed'? To believe it merely because it is logically possible would be what Collingwood once dubbed 'an excellent example of "metaphysics" in the sense in which that word has at various times become a term of merited abuse' (*PA*, 198–9). On the same ground you could justify belief in fairy-tales.

Sensation itself cannot provide evidence for the doctrine that sensa may exist unsensed; for, in the nature of the case, it can only present what is sensed. To escape phenomenalism help must be sought in another quarter. It is surprising that Collingwood did not anticipate what that quarter would be. The strongest argument for asserting that most of our sensa are physical objects, and so can exist unsensed, is that every natural language in which men speak of what they see, hear, feel, taste, and smell is a physical-object language. It does not seem to be possible to think in any sustained way about more than a fraction of what you 'sense' except in terms of physical objects. The reason for believing that the greater part of what you 'sense' consists of physical objects in a physical world is not that physical objects are data of sensation, but that the only coherent general account of what you sense that can be given is in terms of physical objects.

Berkeley was unable to forestall this argument, and Collingwood fared no better. He recognized that it was necessary for him to attempt a non-physical analysis of the objects of perception, but the best he could do was to adopt John Stuart Mill's phenomenalist doctrine that 'in the case of all the thinking that is called empirical . . . we seem in the last resort to be expressing our thoughts about the relations between sensa, actual and possible' (*PA*, 165–6). Here, of course, he supposed sensa to be 'fleeting' entities which 'neither persist nor recur', whose whole existence is to be 'sensed' (cf. *PA*, 169).

Applying it to an actual case, Collingwood obtained the following result. 'When I say that this is my hat, I am stating certain relations between certain [sensa] that I now have (for example, if I am merely looking at my hat, certain colour sensa arranged in a certain way) and other [sensa] which I remember having in the past, for example the [sensa] to which I should refer by speaking of the "look" of my hat as I remember it hanging on a peg in my own hall; and I am saying that these relations are of such a kind that the hat at which I am now looking cannot be other than mine' (*PA*, 165, substituting 'sensum' for 'feeling' throughout). Collingwood excused himself for the complexity of such analyses by pleading that although even 'the roughest analysis is almost intolerably complicated, and no analysis, however complicated would be exhaustive' this shows 'not that the analysis is mistaken, but that thought is quick' (*PA*, 166).

The defect of Collingwood's analysis (and of any phenomenalist analysis whatever) is neither that it is too complicated nor that it is not exhaustive. If the facts are complex, analysis must be complicated; and nobody would ask for an exhaustive inventory of everything that somebody has sensed at some time. What is wanted is an analysis of the real constituents of some selected object of sensation; and that is what Collingwood in fact tried to provide in his phenomenalist analysis of the object, my sensing of which I describe in physical object terms (and so, Collingwood believed, misdescribe) by saying, 'That is my hat'. An analysis of an object of sensation into 'relations between sensa, actual and possible' must identify those relations without referring to physical objects. Collingwood began by evading this obligation. 'When I say that this is my hat', he remarked, 'I am stating certain relations between certain [sensa] that I now have (for example . . . certain colour sensa arranged in a certain way) and other sensa . . .'; but since he did not tell us what those relations are, or between what sensa how arranged they hold, he did not identify them. When he came to deal with the sensa to which the 'certain [sensa] that I now have' are so indefinitely related, he did indeed offer something definite; for he described them as 'the [sensa] to which I should refer by speaking of the "look" of my hat as I remember it hanging on a peg in my own hall'. Here, however, instead of identifying the class of sensa he meant without referring to physical objects, he located them in physical space by reference to two physical objects! No phenomenalist reduction of objects of sensation to sensa whose *esse* is conceived as *sentiri* can escape this difficulty: the class of sensa to which the objects of sensation are reduced can only be identified by reference to physical objects.

Out of this wreckage, does anything remain of Collingwood's two theories? We have found no reason to doubt the fundamental doctrine of *The New Leviathan* that the object of first-order consciousness is what is felt; and what is felt in all cases consists of something sensed, together with the emotional charge it bears. At the level of first-order consciousness, a man will be conscious of how what is felt looks, sounds, feels, tastes, and smells, and of its corresponding emotional charges. So much appears to be secure. But both the theory in *The New Leviathan* that what is felt consists simply of modes of feeling, and not of objects, and the theory in *The Principles of Art* that the *esse* of objects of feeling is *sentiri*, must go. Feeling has objects; and since it appears to be impossible to form any intelligible notion of what are most of the objects that anybody feels, except the common-sense one that they are parts of his body and its physical surroundings, it is reasonable to conclude that most of the objects of feeling are physical.

§ 3. *Perception as an Achievement*

Even as corrected, Collingwood's theory of feeling would be rejected by many philosophers as irreconcilable with the ordinary concepts of seeing, hearing, feeling, tasting, and smelling. Collingwood would not have dismissed such criticisms on the ground that as a philosopher he was entitled to use words as he pleased. He did not aspire to write in a language of his own, and he despised the work of those who did.

The objection his theory has to meet is that a statement that a man sees, hears, feels, tastes, smells something is normally understood to entail that he is aware of his seeing, hearing, feeling, tasting, or smelling. Collingwood was obliged to deny this; for, by his Principle of Order, feeling something is an act of a lower order than any act of consciousness, and, by his Law of Contingency, an act of a lower order does not necessarily bring about an act of a higher.

It is easy to misunderstand Collingwood here. He did not for a moment deny that anybody who said and meant 'I smell smoke' would be aware that he was smelling. But that does not entail that 'to smell' stands for an act of consciousness. The Principle of Intentionality implies that the expression of any act of consciousness will contain words for its object; but the Principle of Order implies that it will not contain words for the act itself; for, if it did, it would express an act of a higher order. The statements 'I see a fire', 'I smell smoke', just because they contain words for feelings, express a function of a higher order than feeling, namely consciousness of feeling. In the same way the statement, 'I am aware that I see a fire', expresses an act of a higher order than consciousness of a feeling, namely, consciousness of that consciousness.

The question at issue is not whether a man who truly says 'I smell smoke' is conscious of smelling smoke, but whether a man who has said nothing about smelling, even to himself, but of whom it is truly said, 'He smells smoke', is conscious of the smell of smoke. Even on this question, an off-hand verdict would go against Collingwood. If you say of somebody that the smoke is so thick he must be smelling it, you will undoubtedly be taken to imply that he is aware of smelling it. As Professor Ryle has observed, the 'see', 'hear', 'feel', 'taste', and 'smell' are in their typical uses achievement words;[1] and the achievements they signify are achievements of consciousness.

Nevertheless, Collingwood's position is not irretrievable. There is a group of examples, though not a large one, which supports him. It makes sense to speak of seeing but not noticing. If you visit a friend and, deep in conversation, are conducted into a newly papered room, you may look full at his striking new paper without noticing it, and be embarrassed to find, when asked your opinion of it, that you are not even aware of its colour. You cannot in such a case plead either that you have not seen the paper, or that you cannot remember it: you can only say that you did not notice it. In the same way, if you eat a well cooked breakfast while absorbed in your morning newspaper, you cannot say that you did not taste what you ate, but only that you did not notice its taste.

The specific verbs of sensation are only used in this way in conjunction with a disclaimer of consciousness, like the clause 'but he did not notice it'. Without such a disclaimer, they invariably stand for achievements of consciousness. It is a thousand pities that Collingwood failed to recognize it. In distinguishing seeing, hearing, and so forth as achievements of consciousness (e.g. seeing and

[1] Ryle, op. cit., p. 223.

noticing) from the sensuous element of feeling which is the foundation of those achievements (e.g. seeing without the implication of
noticing) Collingwood was not flying in the face of ordinary usage;
for his distinction is sanctioned by such expressions as 'He saw it
but did not notice it'. His fault was not in the distinction he drew,
but in the way he expressed it. In using the specific verbs of sensation, without a modifying disclaimer, to stand for the sensuous
element in feeling, he risked seriously misleading his readers.

There is a non-technical way of marking the distinction which
escapes this objection. The expression 'the visual field', although
not in the diction of labourers, is not at all esoteric. When I look
down as I write, my shirt-cuff and the blotter on which my hand
rests are within my visual field; but since I pay no attention to
them, I do not see them, in the sense in which 'see' stands for an
achievement of consciousness. The statement that something is in
your visual field does not entail that you are aware of it, but only
that you would be aware of it, without refocusing your gaze, if you
were attending to it. When Collingwood spoke of seeing a red
patch, or having a visual sensation of it, he meant having a red
patch in your visual field.

Although each of the senses has a field that corresponds to it as
does the visual field to the sense of sight, ordinary educated speech
lacks expressions for them. Yet I do not think that the terms
'auditory field', 'tactual field', 'field of taste', and 'field of smell'
would be misunderstood if they were introduced as counterparts
to 'visual field'; or even that the term 'sense-field' would baffle anybody if it were proposed as a generic term applying to all fields of
the specific senses. If that is so, Collingwood's misleading statements
about the sensuous element in feeling can be unambiguously rendered. '*A* sees fire' and '*A* smells smoke' become 'Fire is in *A*'s
visual field' and 'Smoke is in *A*'s field of smell'; and the generic
statements '*A* has a sensation' and '*A* has a feeling' become 'Something is in at least one of *A*'s sense-fields' and 'Something is in at
least one of *A*'s sense-fields, and has for him some emotional
charge'.

§ 4. *Consciousness and Attention*

Collingwood's distinction between feeling and consciousness has a philosophical consequence of the very last importance. Many of his contemporaries, especially those who were inclined to use the expression 'sense-datum', thought of seeing, hearing, feeling, tasting, and smelling not only as achievements of consciousness, as ordinary usage entitled them to do, but also as simple achievements, each brought about by the straightforward exercise of a single receptive mental faculty. Now the fact that 'see', 'hear', and the rest, as commonly used, stand for achievements of consciousness entails nothing whatever about the simplicity or complexity of those achievements. Because they are for the most part effortless, it is tempting to conclude that acts of perception are simple and as it were transparent. Familiarity with those acts has bred not so much contempt as oblivion (cf. *A*, 26). That it is a mistake so to conclude becomes manifest as soon as you reflect on the place of attention in perception.

If you allow your attention to wander while your sense-organs remain as before, what you see, hear, feel, taste, and smell will vary with it. Yet attention does not create objects of perception out of nothing (*PA*, 207; *NL*, 5. 13–5. 14). Unless feeling provides something to attend to, you would perceive nothing. Acts of perception are therefore complex, consisting of acts of feeling and something else. In *The Principles of Art* Collingwood described the additional element as 'attention', which he took to be selective; in *The New Leviathan*, since he perceived that first-order consciousness is not selective, he did not use the word 'attention' (*PA*, 207; *NL*, 6. 2–6. 21).

I shall call this something else 'attention', without presupposing that all attention is selective. Like the acts of consciousness they bring into existence, acts of attention are ranged in an ordered series. The attention which brings first-order consciousness into existence is directed to a whole sense field, which Collingwood called a 'here-and-now' (*NL*, 4. 4–4. 46). A here-and-now is not a point instant: it is spatially and temporally extended, and qualitatively diverse, although it would be absurd to inquire minutely how long it lasts, or exactly how wide it is. Because it has a focus and a penumbra, it can have no definite edge. Again, although qualitatively diverse, it is not cleanly divided into distinct regions. To grasp what a here-and-now yielded by first-order consciousness is, you must penetrate through the sorting out accomplished by higher-order acts of consciousness. Impressionist painters have tried to record the visual field as first-order consciousness is aware of it: a field of diverse colours 'pervaded all over by a sort of vibratory or "dazzling" quality of a peculiar kind' (*NL*, 4. 56).

First-order attention determines not the content, but the focus of first-order consciousness. It presupposes a diverse here-and-now of feeling, and it achieves a diffused consciousness of it (*NL*, 4. 5). Only when first-order consciousness has been achieved is attention of a higher order possible.

Anybody who has become conscious of his here-and-now of feeling, with its focal and penumbral regions, may, without varying its focus, attend now to this and now to that in it. If the visual field that forms part of that here-and-now includes a friend's face with his nose as focus, he may attend now to the shape of his nose, and now to its colour. This selective attention is of a higher order than first-order attention, because it presupposes first-order consciousness, which is brought into being by first-order attention (*NL*, 4. 5, 7. 24).

Although in *The Principles of Art* Collingwood maintained that feeling is raised to consciousness by attention, he did not distinguish first-order attention from selective second-order attention. That is why he made the mistake of regarding all attention as selective: 'We attend, for example, only to this red patch out of all the variegated field of vision; but what we attend to is the red patch as it presents itself to us, a concrete individual' (*PA*, 204). This led him to a further error, that 'Attention divides, but it does not abstract' (*PA*, 204). How he corrected it in *The New Leviathan* (7. 38–7. 39) we must now consider.

§ 5. *Attention as a Linguistic Act*

Feeling as such is, in Freud's terminology, preconscious: it is not raised to consciousness until it is attended to (*NL*, 4. 22, 5. 9–5. 92).

What then is attention? Is it a sort of inner sense, for example intro-spection, or is it something else?

On Collingwood's principles, no form of consciousness can be brought into existence by an act of feeling, whether outer or inner. No act of feeling is an act of consciousness. You cannot become conscious of your visual field by mentally seeing within, or of your auditory field by mentally hearing within. All that introspection could do would be to reproduce your visual field in a second 'inner' visual field; and there is no reason to suppose that having a second visual field or a second auditory field would make you conscious of your first one. Something altogether different from feeling is needed (*NL*, 4. 17–4. 19; 11. 36).

The solution Collingwood reached, the idea of which he acknow-ledged he had found in Hobbes, is one of his more striking anticipa-tions of philosophical thought after his death. Hobbes had argued that you cannot think scientifically except in words.

A naturall foole that could never learn by heart the order of numerall words, as *one*, *two*, and *three*, may observe every stroak of the Clock, and nod to it, or say one, one, one; but can never know what houre it strikes. . . . So that without words, there is no possi-bility of reckoning of Numbers; much lesse of Magnitudes, of Swift-nesse, of Force, and other things, the reckonings whereof are neces-sary to the being, or well-being of mankind. (*NL*, 6. 46, quoting *Leviathan*, ch. 4.)

Reason is therefore the child of language. Collingwood extended Hobbes's theory to all functions of consciousness. Mind itself is the child of language (*NL*, 6. 5–6. 59).

At first sight, Collingwood's theory is paradoxical. Mind invents language; and, if it does, it would seem impossible that language should beget mind. Collingwood knew that this rejoinder had been made to Hobbes, but it did not deter him. ' "Instinct" ', he scorn-fully remarked, 'may say if it likes that you must first be conscious of a feeling before you can fit it with a name; experience teaches that this is a vulgar error' (*NL*, 6. 56).

Collingwood had shown that inner sense cannot explain atten-tion. He had now to show that what inner sense cannot do, lan-guage can. He began by defining language or discourse as 'any system of bodily movements, not necessarily vocal, whereby the men who make them *mean* or *signify* anything' (*NL*, 6. 1); and protested that it must not be identified with its bodily vehicle. 'To discourse is to *mean something* by the sounds (or what not) you make. A language is not a system of sounds or the like; it is a system of sounds or the like as having meanings' (*NL*, 6. 18). A mere bodily vehicle of meaning, whether a sound, a movement, a visible sign, or any other, may be called an utterance (cf. *PA*, 235–6).

Collingwood's theory, then, comes to this: you attend to your here-and-now of feeling, and so become conscious of it, by making a significant utterance. Its truth cannot be determined by argument, but only by reflection on experience, and 'the experiment . . . is not easy to make, because normally the act of naming is preconsciously done'. Nevertheless, Collingwood claimed to have carried out the 'experiment', and to have found that it bore Hobbes out; and he believed that his readers would obtain the same result (*NL*, 6. 56; cf. 6. 24–6. 28).

There is a plausible but false analogy which he feared might prevent some of his readers from putting the question clearly to themselves. It is certainly true that an explorer may first see (in the ordinary sense) an unrecorded mountain, and then find a name for it; or that a man out for a walk may first see a little pink flower, and then wonder what its name is. These cases are not analogous with those in which the step is taken from feeling to consciousness, because seeing an unrecorded mountain or a little pink flower is a conscious act. The fact that you may see a mountain without being aware that it is named 'Mont Blanc', or a little pink flower without being aware that it is named 'snapdragon', does not entail that you may do so without knowing the words 'mountain' or 'little pink flower', or their equivalents (*NL*, 6. 26).

Wittgenstein was later to make what I take to be the same point. He remarked that there are cases in which it is right to say, 'First I am aware of it as *this*; and then I remember what it is called'. For example, you are aware of it as *this* little pink flower; and then you remember that it is called snapdragon. But it is not right to say such a thing in all cases. Wittgenstein gave the following example.

'How do I recognize that this is red?—"I see that it is *this*; and then I know that that is what this is called". This?—What?! What kind of answer to this question makes sense?'[1] Manifestly no answer would make sense except a description, e.g. 'the same colour as a sunset', 'a colour I know whose name escapes me', which would be appropriate if you had forgotten that the name of the colour described is red. You cannot, in such cases, get behind language.

For the little it is worth, my own reflection corroborates Collingwood's. Whenever my attention shifts from one thing to another, it seems to me that I invariably form some conception, either in words or in some other form of utterance, first of the one and then of the other. If such shifts of attention do not consist in forming, by means of language, successive conceptions of the things attended to, I am at a loss to know what they are. Although attention of this kind, like that in Collingwood's and Wittgenstein's examples, is selective and so not first-order, a fact which Collingwood neglected to make clear,[2] evidence that it is linguistic supports his doctrine that first-order attention is linguistic.

But for brief periods, first-order consciousness exists in adults only as a primitive survival in higher-order acts of consciousness; it does not endure for any length of time except in infants and probably in animals. The language in which it is expressed is therefore difficult to isolate and study. Collingwood described that language as 'the mere "register" of feelings, as wild and mad as those feelings themselves; irrational, unorganized, unplanned, unconscious' (*NL*, 6. 58). It cannot but be very primitive, illogical, and ejaculatory (*NL*, 7. 24). How does it come about at all? In particular, how does an infant come to utter a cry that means what he feels?

§ 6. *The Language of First-order Consciousness*

Since Collingwood did not discuss the origin of the language of first-order consciousness in *The New Leviathan*, it is necessary to fall back on what he wrote about it in *The Principles of Art*. There he had already advanced his theory that feeling has both a sensuous

---

[1] Ludwig Wittgenstein, *Philosophical Investigations* (Oxford, 1953), i, §§ 379–80.
[2] *NL*, 6.23–6.26; Wittgenstein, ibid.

and an emotional element. While feeling remains mere feeling, both are preconscious; nevertheless they have effects. Babies show their feelings before they are conscious of them; and when adults relapse into preconscious feeling, as in panic or mass emotion, they involuntarily express their emotions in bodily movements. That is why a man may fly in panic, or leap in exultation, without being aware of what he is doing. In *The Principles of Art* Collingwood's rather unhappy epithet for such involuntary expressions of preconscious feeling was 'psychical': 'preconscious', the Freudian term he adopted in *The New Leviathan*, is much better; and I shall employ it henceforth (*PA*, 228–9).

Every preconscious feeling has its counterpart in some change in the muscular or circulatory or glandular system, which involuntarily or preconsciously expresses it. Collingwood believed that preconscious expression of that kind is the source of language, and vividly described how language springs from it.

Everyone who is accustomed to looking after small children [he declared] in addition to distinguishing the cry of pain from the cry of hunger and so forth—various kinds of [preconscious] expression—learns to distinguish the automatic cry of uncontrolled emotion from the self-conscious cry which seems (through a certain exaggeration on the listener's part) deliberately uttered in order to call attention to its needs and to scold the person to whom it seems addressed for not attending to them. The second cry is still a mere cry; it is not yet speech; but it is language. . . . The crucial difference lies in this, that the child, instead of making a certain noise automatically and involuntarily, has learnt to make it, as we say, 'on purpose'; by which we mean, not that it has a purpose in the strict sense, a plan *propositum sibi*, . . . but that its action is controlled instead of being automatic. (*PA*, 236–7.)

Language begins at that point in infancy when children deliberately repeat the movements of preconscious expression; by doing so they convert involuntary preconsciously expressive cries and the like into deliberate expressive utterances (*PA*, 237). Children become aware of more and more of what they feel as they differentiate their utterances more and more. That is how language develops. When highly developed, it has left preconscious expression far behind. 'The merely [preconscious] expression of emotion is already highly differentiated; but this is nothing to the differentiation achieved by language' (*PA*, 237). Here, however, Collingwood spoke of language in general. There is no reason to suppose that the language of first-order consciousness is more highly differentiated than preconscious expression; for it does no more than differentiate one here-and-now of feeling from another. A higher degree of differentiation is not achieved until attention becomes selective and language conceptual.

Collingwood's doctrine that the language of first-order consciousness is derived from preconscious expression resembles Wittgenstein's suggestion that words are connected with primitive or natural expressions of sensation and are used in their place. 'A child has hurt himself and he cries; and then adults talk to him and teach him exclamations and, later, sentences. They teach the child new pain-behaviour.'[1] Collingwood, however, would certainly have denied that a child could pass at a jump from preconscious behaviour to learning his mother-tongue. Unless he were already conscious of pain, he could not learn how to express it in an artificial or conventional language. In order to learn the new pain-behaviour of his mother-tongue, he must therefore be able to express it in a language of his own.

Although this appears to traverse Wittgenstein's powerful arguments against the possibility of an essentially private language, I do not think that Collingwood would have denied what I take to be their cardinal point: that if any utterance is to mean anything, there must be some assurance that it means the same thing on different occasions. This is readily assured in a language that is in fact used by several persons in communicating with one another; but at first sight it seems to be impossible to assure it of the individual expressive utterances of a baby.

Nevertheless, Collingwood's solution is not hard to divine. He had maintained not only that preconscious expressions are uniform enough to be interpreted by a skilled observer, but even that 'nothing but lack of this skill prevents us from reading like an open

---

[1] Wittgenstein, op. cit. i, § 244.

book the [preconscious] emotions', and so the sensa on which they are a charge, 'of everyone with whom we have to do' (*PA*, 230). It is not by comparing his usage with that of others that a child connects his utterances with the feelings they express. Those connexions were established between his involuntary cries and movements and the feelings they preconsciously expressed. That is what ensures that the utterances which bring first-order consciousness into being shall mean the same thing on different occasions. They are no more difficult to interpret than the preconscious expressions from which they grew.

Collingwood's theory of first-order consciousness is now complete. In any act of first-order consciousness, a whole here-and-now of feeling is raised to consciousness by a linguistic act. That act consists in deliberately performing the bodily movements by which that feeling would be preconsciously expressed. In children, first-order consciousness is the first stage of mental life. Although it is seldom found in adults by itself, Collingwood was committed by his Law of Primitive Survivals to maintaining that it is an element in all higher-order functions of consciousness (*NL*, 9. 54). What holds for consciousness holds for language. In its higher forms, language becomes remote from deliberate performances of the gestures of preconscious expression, yet such performances are an element in even the most abstract and intellectualized utterances. Although mathematicians, natural scientists, historians, and philosophers are not primarily concerned to express what they feel when they think, they cannot help doing so if they express their thoughts at all. No sooner has the symbolism of any of the higher-order functions of consciousness been mastered and put to good use than it regains the expressiveness of the language of children (cf. *PA*, 268).

III

CONCEPTS AND PROPOSITIONS

§ 1. *Selective Attention as Conceptual*

FOLLOWING his plan of 'taking soundings' at each of the orders of consciousness, in order to find what functions belong to it, Collingwood's next task was to investigate second-order consciousness, that is, consciousness of first-order consciousness. No step from a lower order of consciousness to a higher would ever be taken but for the spur of practical need; and the need for the step from first-order to second-order consciousness is plain. Nobody could procure for himself the coarsest food or the most rudimentary shelter unless he could discriminate between at least some of the many things that fill his here-and-now of feeling. In order so to discriminate he must selectively attend now to this element in what he feels, and now to that. Yet he could not selectively attend to some element in what he feels unless he were first conscious of his whole here-and-now of feeling. He might indeed fasten on an item out of it at random without being aware of the whole from which he took it, but that would not be a selection. Furthermore, he could not select one as opposed to the other unless he were distinctly aware of both, as he would not be if he were merely now conscious of feeling one, and now conscious of feeling the other. The two acts of consciousness must be combined; and they can only be combined, while remaining distinct, in a higher-order act which has both of them for its object. Selective attention therefore requires not only consciousness of feeling, but consciousness of that consciousness. It is 'the second stage of mental life' (*NL*, 4.5, 7. 24).

The step from the first stage of mental life to the second is taken in infancy by normal human beings, and may even be taken by brutes (*NL*, 7. 22, 7. 68). The following example would be typical. Suppose that a baby, while dry and warm in a comfortable cot, suffers, owing to lack of food, a gnawing sensation at his stomach, accompanied by general organic sensations of weakness and lassitude, these carrying an unpleasant emotional charge (cf. *NL*, 7. 4). Provided that his pangs are mild, his whole here-and-now of feeling will not be unpleasant, but mixed; and his expression of it in the primitive language of first-order consciousness will be equivocal. Now suppose that he begins to utter cries which express his pangs of hunger alone. To do so he must single those pangs out of their pleasurable background, and that, as we have seen, presupposes that he is aware of his consciousness both of his pangs of hunger and of their background. He has reached second-order consciousness.

As lately as when he wrote *The Principles of Art*, Collingwood believed that selective attention precedes conceptual thinking, and accordingly that 'attention divides, but it does not abstract'. On this view, you could not abstract from a red patch its quality of redness unless you had already selected it for attention from your variegated field of vision; and, when you did abstract it, it would be 'not by attending, but by thinking' (*PA*, 204). The baby whom in our former example we supposed selectively to have attended to his pangs of hunger would not have needed to abstract from them their specific painful quality. Four years later, when he wrote *The New Leviathan*, Collingwood retracted all of these opinions.

The foundation of his later position was his revised conception of first-order consciousness. In *The Principles of Art* he had maintained that selective attention brings about the step from feeling to consciousness (*PA*, 204–5, 207). Since he knew that conceptual thinking is not the most primitive form of consciousness, he was therefore constrained to separate selective attention from conceptual thinking. But when he came to see that first-order consciousness is not discriminatory (*NL*, 4. 5), he was freed from that constraint. It became clear that his earlier view was impossible.

How can even the simplest object be selected from even the simplest background? Collingwood's own example of such an object was a red patch against a green background—say, a red blanket on a lawn as seen from a window. The answer that presumably he had in mind when he wrote *The Principles of Art* was that you circumscribe the red patch in your mind, that is, you draw an imaginary line around it (cf. *PA*, 204). In *The New Leviathan*, however, he pointed out that circumscribing the red blanket in your mind is not the same as attending to the red patch you see; for you can circumscribe it without attending to it as a red patch, as you might if somebody asked you to look at the old blanket on the lawn. In order to select the red patch for attention as a red patch, which is what selectively attending to it is, you must 'clarify' to yourself what you are attending to (*NL*, 7. 3–7. 31, 7. 38); and this clarification can be nothing but distinguishing its character as red, and abstracting that character from the others it bears (*NL*, 7. 22).

Abstraction is the essence of conceptual thinking (*NL*, 7. 22). To form the concept *red* is to abstract what being red is, as distinct from being something else; and you show that you have formed it by such acts as telling whether a rose or a blanket or the like is red or not, and perceiving that if pearls are white all over they cannot be red even in part. These acts are inescapably linguistic, although neither the word 'red' nor the English language need be employed. Unless you employed some sign or gesture that means what the English word 'red' means, you could not employ the concept *red*, even in your head. The idea that it is possible to form a pure wordless concept of red, whose glassy essence may be contemplated by a mind alone with itself, is only not refutable because it is vacuous. If a concept can only be expressed in words or by reference to them, e.g. in obeying commands, and if nobody can be recognized as possessing a concept unless he can express it, it is idle to assert that concepts are wordless. The prevalent conviction that they are arises from a misunderstanding. As Collingwood pointed out, language is not a physical phenomenon. An utterance is not linguistic unless it has meaning, and having meaning is not a physical property (*NL*, 6. 1). Anybody who mistakenly held that language was a physical phenomenon would not unreasonably infer that concepts were not linguistic.

Conceptual or abstract thinking necessarily involves universals and is predicative. A universal is something which may characterize various individual things (cf. *NL*, 7. 65, 11. 35). It is impossible to attend to a red patch as a red patch without recognizing that things other than that patch may also be red, that is, without thinking in terms of the universal property *red*. Universals need not, however, be qualities like red, or even properties of any kind whatever. Not only relational properties like *being on the lawn*, but also concepts like being of a sort or kind, e.g. *being a blanket*, may characterize various individual things, and so be universals.

By being predicative, that is, predicable of various expressions that denote individual things, the linguistic expressions that signify universals reflect the fact that universals may characterize various individuals. Since Collingwood used the term 'abstraction' synonymously with 'concept' and 'universal', he naturally enough called predicative expressions 'abstract terms' (*NL*, 6. 58, 7. 22).

§ 2. *The Development of Conceptual or 'Intellectualized' Language*

Collingwood did not think that many truly primitive 'abstract terms' are to be found in any common spoken language. We must not forget that he considered that second-order consciousness begins in the cradle, when a baby begins to select some of his feelings for attention rather than others. Children attain to second-order consciousness before they learn their mother-tongues (cf. *PA*, 237); and although Collingwood did not ask the question how they do so, what he would have answered can be plausibly conjectured, in the light of his discussion of the language of children in *The Principles of Art*.

Selective attention, like the first-order attention which brings first-order consciousness into being, is a linguistic act; and, since selective attention involves conceptual thinking, the language employed in performing it must be conceptual. It accords both with common experience and with Collingwood's principle that the lower orders of consciousness provide materials for the higher (*PA*, 232–4), to suppose that conceptual language would originally at least make use of the language of first-order consciousness. Let us return to the example of a child selectively attending to pangs of hunger. He has an expression ready-made for them in the cries which express first-order consciousness of grievous hunger, that is, hunger the pains of which are severe enough to colour his entire here-and-now of feeling. A baby can express that he feels a little hungry by crying as though he feels nothing but hungry. In the same way, in order to express to somebody, whose language you do not know, that you have a pain in the foot, you may clasp your foot and groan. Unless you were in great pain, your behaviour would be absurd as an expression of first-order consciousness, but the person to whom it is addressed would be unlikely to misinterpret it. Speaker and hearer, as both babies and parents have found from time immemorial, soon come to a very fair understanding.

According to the system of *The New Leviathan* cries and gestures of the kind we have been considering are abstract terms. Parents soon distinguish between the cry of hunger and the cry of being too hot; and they know that when the cry of hunger is uttered on different occasions it means the same thing. What adults can express by gestures is far more differentiated. You can say that you have a pain in your head by clasping your head and groaning, as easily as you can say that you have a pain in your foot by varying the gesture and clasping your foot. Taking the acts of clasping the head and groaning, and clasping the foot and groaning in abstraction from any particular person's performing them, they correspond exactly to the predicative expressions '. . . has a pain in the head' and '. . . has a pain in the foot', except that they can, as it were, only take subjects in the first person.

The most serious lacuna in Collingwood's theory is not about how a primitive conceptual language is developed, but about how the primitive conceptual language of the cradle is first supplemented and then replaced by an intellectualized spoken language. Unless this further step were taken, conceptual thought could not be extended beyond the narrow confines of our physical feelings and needs; yet in *The New Leviathan* Collingwood remained silent about how it is taken, and in *The Principles of Art* he volunteered a theory which beyond doubt is wrong.

There, not recognizing that selective attention is conceptual, he classified the genus language into two species: the expressive but non-conceptual, and the conceptual but conventional. Then, presuming that expressions acquire conceptual meaning only by convention, and that the existence of linguistic conventions presupposes a language in which the convention was made, he concluded that such a language would belong to his expressive but non-conceptual species. 'Symbolism or intellectualized language', he wrote, 'thus presupposes imaginative language . . .' (*PA*, 226).

However, since the conclusion that a language may be both non-conceptual and one in which conventions about conceptual language can be reached is not only self-contradictory, but also incompatible with the Principle of Order, which underlies his system in *The New Leviathan*, it is not surprising that Collingwood forsook it and the assumptions that had led him to it. We have already seen that in *The New Leviathan* he reclassified as conceptual many of the childish utterances which he had described in his *Principles of Art* as purely expressive, and that, in doing so, he abandoned his classification of all conceptual language as conventional.

But that was not enough. Since a convention that an expression shall signify a certain concept can only be laid down by somebody who is conscious of both the expression and the concept, by the Principle of Order the act of laying such a convention down is of a higher order than any act of consciousness in which the concept is merely employed. The ordinary use of conceptual expressions is to say something about an object; and, when they are so used, the person who uses them may not pay any attention either to the conceptual expressions he uses or to their meaning. A geometer who says that the intersection F of the line AB with the circle FGH has position but no magnitude is conscious of the intersection of a certain line with a certain circle, not of the expression 'has position but no magnitude' and its meaning. But he is in a different case when he lays down the convention that 'point' is to mean that which has position but no magnitude. There he is not thinking of lines and points, but of words and concepts. It follows that concepts cannot be introduced into language by convention. Convention can do no more than assign more convenient expressions to concepts that have been expressed already.

The collapse of the theory that spoken conceptual language is conventional left Collingwood without any theory whatever about how conceptual language is developed. He had already implicitly renounced the most obvious and popular alternative: the theory of ostensive definition. According to that theory concepts are learned by being shown examples. Thus, the concept *red* would be learned by hearing the word 'red' pronounced while being shown red things. The fatal objection to any such theory is that having a red object pointed out to you, or 'circumscribed' for you, does not ensure that you will pick it out as red. A red blanket on a lawn, even when pointed out and circumscribed by your teacher running his hand around it, may be picked out as rectangular, or dark, or flat, or rumpled, or any number of other things. Attending to a red object as red requires more than looking at it when it is pointed out to you. But, whatever more is required, the theory of ostensive definition does not provide it (*NL*, 7. 3–7. 31).

Perhaps Wittgenstein was the first philosopher to show what was needed. In his *Philosophical Investigations* (I, § 29 et seq.) he argued that concepts are learned not by ostensive definition, but by training. You learn what red is by being expected to use the word 'red', after you have witnessed others doing so, and by being corrected when you misuse it. You learn its meaning, not before you use it, but as you use it. Even after you have learned to use it correctly, you may be quite unable to define your use or even to explain it; but you will be able to pass on its use in the way you acquired it yourself, by training others. It might appear that this does not solve the problem but only puts off the day of reckoning. Who trained the original trainer? Yet reflection will show that this is not a serious difficulty. A man may simply invent a use of a word; and his invention may consist merely in that he has become able to use it in a new way, and to correct others when they try to use it in that way and fail. In some of his imaginary 'language-games' Wittgenstein has shown how even to its originator a new use of a word may be no more than something he is able to do and which he can train others to do. It is true that nobody could invent out of nothing any of the highly developed natural languages which children learn as their mother-tongues. Such languages, however, have presumably been developed from far simpler origins. There is no plausible alternative to the theory that the complex uses of words in natural languages have developed as games develop, by players making modifications as they play or practise, and, after their modifications have excited interest, training others in them.

§ 3. *Collingwood's Lapse into Associationism*

Although it is neither complete nor free from error, Collingwood's theory of language and consciousness, as far as we have followed it, was a considerable achievement. *The New Leviathan* shows how keenly he had scrutinized the impressive results he had obtained in *The Principles of Art*, and how sharp was his eye for faults; even where, as in his theory of sensa, owing to illness and haste, he was unable to amend them. Such of his changes of opinion as we have recorded were almost all for the better; and for those few that were not, he at least had good reasons. The disagreeable task now confronts us of examining a regression. We have traced how, from an uneven beginning in *The Principles of Art*, he developed a powerful if incomplete theory of conceptual thinking; and we must now show how he squandered part of the fruit of his labours.

He had described concepts as abstractions, and had emphatically declared that in selectively attending to something felt it was necessary not only to 'circumscribe' it, but also to 'clarify' it, i.e. to get clear what you were selecting it *as* (*NL*, 7. 22, 7. 38). He had thereby grasped a fundamental truth: that a concept is not what is selected, a feeling or an object felt, but something created in order to make the selection. It is what the selected thing is clarified or selected *as*. When you select a red patch for attention, you must clarify it as red, or, putting it more cumbersomely, as falling under the concept *red*; but it does not follow that the red patch selected and the concept *red* are the same thing.

Yet that was the blunder Collingwood was to commit. He had prepared the way for it, possibly under the influence of Hobbes,[1] by persuading himself that in selectively attending to something you arouse in yourself 'feelings you do not find as "given" in yourself . . .

---

[1] Cf. Thomas Hobbes *Leviathan* (ed. Michael Oakeshott, Oxford, no date), chs. 2–4, esp. p. 13: 'The imagination that is raised in man, or in any other creature endued with the faculty of imagining, by words, or other voluntary signs, is what we generally call *understanding*; and is common to man and beast.'

[which] form a *context* inseparable from any selection and [which] are connected with it by logical relations . . .' (*NL*, 7. 32–7. 33). He apparently did not notice that he thereby allowed that *feelings* may stand in logical relations. The only explanation I can find is that he confounded two quite distinct propositions. One is unexceptionable: that nobody could possess a concept, e.g. *red*, or selectively attend to a red object, unless he could properly apply the word 'red', or some equivalent, when confronted with objects that had qualities logically related to red, e.g. blue and green. The other is the exploded associationist doctrine that if you have in your mind two strings of images, one of red things and the other of things having colours other than red, then you are thereby aware of what being red and being not red are.[1] His final definition of a concept or a number of them as 'a selection together with its context of evocations', which confounded what is selected with the concept by which it is selected, was pure associationism (*NL*, 7. 39).

This lapse explains what otherwise I find unintelligible: why in *The New Leviathan* Collingwood allocated conceptual and propositional thinking to different orders of consciousness. At 'the lower levels of consciousness', he wrote, 'thought is at first merely apprehensive, capable of framing abstractions from what is "given"'; at the 'higher levels' it is 'first "propositional"', capable of discriminating good from evil and truth from error . . .' (*NL*, 10. 51). Although his definition of 'proposition' fluctuated, and although according to one of its fluctuations the most primitive form of conceptual thinking was undoubtedly not 'propositional' (cf. *NL*, 11. 22), it is clear that in the passage quoted, as in others, he used the word 'proposition' in the traditional way, to mean that which is either true or false (e.g. *EM*, 25 et passim; *NL*, 11·32–11·35). Now nobody who conceived conceptual thinking as abstract in the sense of predicative could possibly deny that conceptual thinking is normally true or false.

On an associationist theory of concepts, however, it would be not only possible but reasonable to do so. Objects or feelings selected

---

[1] The theory of universals I have in mind is Berkeley's (in *The Principles of Human Knowledge*) and Hume's (in *A Treatise of Human Nature*), to which F. H. Bradley conclusively objected in his *Principles of Logic*, vol. ii, 2, 1. Cf. Richard Wollheim, *F. H. Bradley* (London: Penguin Books, 1959), pp. 26–27.

for attention are individuals. They are indeed abstract in the sense of being selections, but not in the sense of being universal or predicative. If a concept were indeed a selection together with its context of evocations, and if making that selection involved nothing predicative, then conceptual thinking would not be propositional.

We have already found that Collingwood did not consistently adhere to the second of these conditions. In arguing that you cannot selectively attend to anything without clarifying it, he implied that you must bring it under a universal. He departed from it again when he acknowledged that 'logic [is] the science which studies the structure of concepts' (*NL*, 7. 33); for whatever the subject-matter of logic may be, assuredly it is not the structure of feelings, either with or without contexts of evocations.

§ 4. *Concepts and Propositions in Revolutionary Logic*

Collingwood's forays into logic resemble Caesar's invasions of Britain:[1] their execution was bungled, and his account of them, which unlike Caesar's was given in advance, did not accord with his actions. Although in his *Autobiography*, he proclaimed himself 'in logic . . . a revolutionary' (*A*, 52), his revolutionary manifesto turned out to be an embarrassment, and in what he afterwards wrote about logic he more and more ignored it.

The established system which he hoped to overthrow he designated as 'propositional logic', a comprehensive title intended to embrace not only the traditional logic of the Oxford realists and the symbolic logic of Russell and Whitehead, but even part of the idealistic logic of the school of Green (*A*, 34, 52). We must consider what that logic was, since what Collingwood found to say about it was even more summary than Marx's analysis of 'bourgeois' society in the *Communist Manifesto*. We may take the logic of Russell and Whitehead as a point of departure; for, despite a foolish gibe (*A*, 35 *n.*), Collingwood himself conceded it to be the most advanced form of the 'reactionary' system (*A*, 52).

---

[1] Cf. *A*, 130–1; R. G. Collingwood and J. N. L. Myres, *Roman Britain and the English Settlements* (Oxford, 1937), pp. 31–35, 39–42, 51–53.

The logic of Russell and Whitehead, like traditional logic, is about reasoning, which is taken to consist in inferring certain propositions, namely conclusions, from others, namely premisses. Every proposition is presupposed to be either true or false. The task of logic is not to investigate whether or not a given conclusion is in fact true, but only whether or not it is logically necessary that it be true, given that this or that premiss or set of premisses be true. Since an inference that purports to be valid by logical necessity is called deductive, the logic of Russell and Whitehead is deductive. Both of them knew, of course, that most inferences drawn in daily life are not deductive or at least not wholly so, and recognized that their logic was not a theory of scientific reasoning. But although many of their followers added chapters on scientific reasoning to their textbooks, most of them tacitly distinguished logic from methodology. The solid core of modern propositional logic is the theory of deduction.

That theory is now customarily divided into three parts: the propositional calculus, the predicative calculus, and the calculus of classes. The propositional calculus treats of inferences whose validity in no way depends on the character of the simple propositions they contain. Such an inference is: 'It is not true both that the Opposition is incompetent and that it would make a tolerable government, so either it is false that the Opposition is incompetent or false that it would make a tolerable government.' It would remain valid no matter what simple propositions were substituted for *the Opposition is incompetent* and *the Opposition would make a tolerable government*.

Both the predicative calculus and the calculus of classes treat of inferences whose validity depends partly on the character of the simple propositions they contain. They do not, however, treat of any inference whose validity depends on the character of the concepts employed in its simple propositions, e.g. such inferences as 'Tom is John's brother, so Tom's parents have had at least two children', whose validity depends on the character of the concepts *brother* and *two*. There are so many inferences of this kind that it is neither possible nor desirable that logicians should investigate them all. Fortunately, however, most of them can by definitional substitutions be reduced to inferences whose validity is purely formal, and independent of the concepts employed in them. Given the ordinary definition of *brother* and Russell's definition of *two*, substitutions can be made in 'Tom is John's brother, so Tom's parents have had at least two children', which would convert it into an inference whose validity was purely formal, and independent of the concepts employed in it. The predicative calculus and the calculus of classes treat of such formally valid inferences. For example, 'No horses are quadrupeds, so no quadrupeds are horses' is a valid deduction in the calculus of classes, and remains valid no matter what class-concepts are substituted for *horse* and *quadruped*; likewise 'Everything that is visible is coloured, and everything coloured occupies space, so everything that is visible occupies space' is a valid deduction in the predicative calculus, and remains valid no matter what predicate-concepts are substituted for *being visible*, *being coloured*, and *occupying space*.

Collingwood struck at one of the roots of this system of logic by denying that 'truth or falsehood, which are what logic is chiefly concerned with, belongs to propositions as such' (*A*, 34). While no propositional logician would concede that truth and falsehood are what logic has for subject-matter, they all presuppose that the propositions whose logical relations they study are true or false as such. This Collingwood denied, because the logician's proposition seemed to him 'a kind of ghostly double of the grammarian's sentence' (*A*, 34), and he could not believe that a thing of that kind could be true or false as such.

The crux of the problem lies in the sense in which the logician's proposition is a ghostly double of the grammarian's sentence. That it is so in some sense there is no doubt. The sense in which Collingwood understood it, however, is strained. 'The central doctrine of propositional logic', he wrote, is 'that there is, or ought to be, or in a well-constructed and well-used language would be, a one-one correspondence between propositions and indicative sentences, every indicative sentence expressing a proposition, and a proposition being defined as . . . that which is true or false' (*A*, 35–36). Now the propositional logic of Russell and Whitehead did not contain this doctrine at all, although Russell, when he was a Logical Atomist, had believed that it was true, not of 'well-constructed and well-used' natural languages, but of a logically ideal language.

Propositional logicians may with perfect consistency reject the philosophical theory of an ideal language, and acknowledge that in any well constructed natural language several indicative sentences may express the same proposition, and some no proposition at all. They may also agree that it is sometimes impossible to find what proposition is expressed by this or that well constructed indicative sentence, except by considering who uttered it and in what circumstances. Accordingly, they are not obliged to deny that the sentence, '*L'état, c'est moi*', if King Louis XIV in his prime had ever uttered it, would have expressed a very different proposition from what it does in the ravings of a confined madman. Most propositional logicians, it is true, maintain that *some* indicative sentences of themselves express propositions, e.g. 'Horses are graminivorous'; and to that extent they do conceive propositions as 'doubles' of grammarians' sentences. But that is all.

Even that Collingwood found objectionable. Against it he argued 'not only that you cannot tell whether a proposition is "true" or "false" until you know what question it was intended to answer, but also that a proposition which in fact is "true" can always be thought "false" by anyone who takes the trouble to excogitate a question to which it would have been the wrong answer, and convinces himself that this was the question it was meant to answer' (*A*, 38). Propositional logicians would reject both of these contentions as simply false. Must you find out to what question 'Horses are graminivorous' was intended for an answer before you can decide whether it is true? And is it possible to excogitate a question to which it would be the wrong answer, as distinct from not an answer at all? There are, it is true, *some* indicative sentences which can be interpreted as expressing true or false propositions according as they are taken as answers to different questions; but Collingwood played for higher stakes. It was all or nothing.

His own theory rested on the proposition that 'truth, if that meant the kind of thing which [he] was accustomed to pursue in [his] ordinary work as a philosopher or historian . . . which seemed to [him] the proper sense of the word—was something that belonged not to any single proposition, nor even, as the coherence-theorists maintained, to a complex of propositions taken together; but to a complex consisting of questions and answers' (*A*, 37). In such a complex each answer had to be commensurate with its question: that is, neither more nor less specific than it (*A*, 32). Furthermore, each question and each answer had to 'belong' both to the whole and to the place it occupied in the whole. That implied, on the one hand, that each question had to arise either out of answers to preceding questions in the complex, or out of the presuppositions which gave rise to the complex as a whole (*A*, 37, 66–67); and, on the other hand, that each answer must be 'right', in the sense of being the answer which enables us to get ahead with the process of questioning and answering (*A*, 37).

An answer that is right is not necessarily 'true' in the conventional sense. When a thinker follows a false scent, either inadvertently or in order to construct a *reductio ad absurdum*, his complex of questions and answers will be as a whole false, in what Collingwood held to be the proper sense of that word. In that case, the individual answers in the complex will be false, in the ordinary sense of the word. Collingwood therefore proposed that an answer, as opposed to a complex, be regarded as true in a derivative sense only if it is part of a well-constructed complex which, as a whole, is true in his 'proper' sense (*A*, 37–38).

The received conception of truth was far from being the only victim of Collingwood's logical revolution: from the beginning he claimed to have perceived that it must transform the concepts of meaning, consistency, and contradiction as well. None of them, he declared, belongs to propositions by themselves, but only to propositions as parts of complexes of questions and answers (*A*, 33).

That this extreme position is untenable can be readily shown by considering one of its corollaries, namely, that 'no two propositions . . . can contradict one another unless they are answers to the same question' (*A*, 33). In *The Principles of Art* Collingwood had cited with approval Cook Wilson's assertion that the sentence, 'That building is the Bodleian' indifferently represents two quite different propositions according as it is employed in answering either the question, 'Which of those is the Bodleian?' or the question, 'What is that building?' (*PA*, 265 *n*.). Now suppose that you point to a building when somebody asks you, 'Which of those is the Bodleian?' and say to him, 'That building is the Bodleian'; and suppose further that, on another occasion, when that same person points to that same building, and asks me, 'What is that building?' I reply, 'Not the Bodleian, at any rate': in such a case, Collingwood would be obliged to hold that your answer and mine did not contradict one another, because they were answers to different questions. A consequence so absurd must ruin the doctrine that gives rise to it.

While this example does not show that the position against which Collingwood argued is true, by showing that his own logic of question and answer is false, it reveals that his logical revolution arose from a false disjunction. He imagined that if what he called 'the central doctrine of propositional logic' were false, i.e. the doctrine that in a well constructed language every indicative sentence expresses one and only one proposition, which must be either true or false (*A*, 35–36), then his own alternative would necessarily be true. In fact, neither is true.

A subsidiary consideration may clinch the matter. Plainly the sentence, 'That building is the Bodleian', although well constructed, does not of itself express a proposition; some indication must be given of what building is referred to, e.g. by a gesture. What Collingwood called 'the central doctrine of propositional logic' is therefore false. But his logic of question and answer succumbs to the same objection. If the sentence, 'That building is the Bodleian' is used in answering the question, 'Which of those buildings is the Bodleian?' then the proposition expressed by that answer is not made clear by the question alone; for any of the buildings mentioned in the question may be the one referred to in the answer.

Propositional logicians like Russell and Whitehead did not, as Collingwood imagined, neglect the problem of ambiguity. Nor did they hope that logic might provide a simple and safe way not only to ascertain the proposition expressed by a given indicative sentence and the meanings of the expressions in it, but also to decide whether a given proposition contradicted this or that other one. Collingwood, however, seems to have believed that his logic of question and answer would do so (cf. *A*, 39–42). His hope was visionary; and it led him, as their hopes have led other utopians, to misrepresent and traduce the piecemeal results of the system by which he imagined himself oppressed.

After he had written the *Autobiography* reality began to break in. The first plank of his revolutionary platform to go was the doctrine that truth in the proper sense of the word was a property not of propositions, but of complexes of questions and answers. The *Autobiography* itself contains signs of the change to come. It was there that he first outlined the sceptical doctrine which was to be the core of his *Essay on Metaphysics*, that metaphysics is an historical science; and part of that doctrine was that the beliefs whose history metaphysicians study are neither true nor false. They 'are not answers to questions but only presuppositions of questions, and therefore the distinction between what is true and what is false does not apply to them . . .' (*A*, 66). Here, by regarding the distinction between what is true and what is false as applying primarily to answers rather than to complexes of questions and answers, Collingwood jettisoned the use of the word 'true' in what he had called 'the proper sense of the word' (*A*, 37). He also disregarded a plain implication of his earlier doctrine, namely, that if a whole question and answer complex is true in the 'proper' sense, then its presuppositions have as good a claim to be true, in his derivative sense, as the answers it contains.

In the *Essay on Metaphysics* Collingwood excluded the possibility that a question and answer complex as a whole could be true. Only an answer to a question can be true or false; so that 'proposition' may be defined as both an answer to a question and as that which is either true or false. But an answer is not an answer unless its question 'arises'; and questions only arise if appropriate presuppositions are made. Furthermore, the truth or falsity of an affirmation is not absolute, but contingent on whether it is made in answer to a question or not. In the next chapter we shall return to the foundations and ramifications of this theory of presuppositions; at present it suffices to remark that it assorts ill with Collingwood's original revolutionary manifesto (*EM*, 23–27, 32–33, 193–4).

In *The New Leviathan* he revised it yet further. While he retained his objectionable definition of a proposition as both that which is either true or false, and as that which is an answer to a question (*NL*, 10. 51, 11. 22), he relinquished everything else. He denied that either the meaning of a conceptual expression, or its logical relations (e.g. its compatibility or incompatibility) with other conceptual expressions depends on the question and answer complexes in which those expressions occur (*NL*, 7. 33–7. 34, 10. 51). It is true that an inconsistency remains. Since concepts are predicative, it is self-contradictory to hold, as Collingwood did, both that concepts have logical relations independently of question and answer complexes, and that propositions do not; for predicative and propositional thinking are inseparable. Collingwood's plight is common among old revolutionaries. Although his working principle in *The New Leviathan* was the reactionary or at least reformist one that 'in the first instance logic applies only to concepts', and that it applies to propositions because 'the "predicate" of a proposition . . . is . . . always a concept' (*NL*, 11. 35), he could not bring himself to repudiate the slogan of his revolutionary past: that there can be nothing true or false, i.e. no proposition, except as an answer to a question (*NL*, 10. 51, 11. 22).

§ 5. *Concrete Functions of Second-order Consciousness*

Although he did not perceive it, Collingwood's doctrine in *The New Leviathan* that concepts are predicative and stand in logical relations entails that conceptual and propositional thinking are inseparable; and that conclusion, when conjoined with his doctrine that conceptual thinking is found at the second order of consciousness, entails that propositional thinking is also found at that order. It is, however, a simple matter to prove that neither conceptual nor propositional thinking is confined to the second order. An act of consciousness must belong to the third order if it involves consciousness of some act of the second order. The expression '. . . am conscious that I have seen a red blanket on a green lawn' is abstract and predicative, and so conceptual. Yet, since it expresses consciousness of an act of selective attention, and so of second-order consciousness, nobody can use it truthfully unless he is performing an act of consciousness of at least the third order. Accordingly, that concept and the propositions in which it is exercised express acts of at least third-order consciousness. And, in general, to form the concept of being aware of an act of consciousness which belongs to the order n, and truthfully to exercise that concept in a proposition, generates a concept and a proposition which express an act of consciousness of the order $n+1$.

It was therefore a mistake to identify the second order of consciousness with the conceptual and the third with the propositional. Both conceptual and propositional thinking may be found at the second order of consciousness and at every higher order. Yet although Collingwood was obliged to draw some curious and artificial distinctions because he failed to perceive this, he was not necessarily mistaken in his analysis of the concrete functions of second-order consciousness. To these we must now turn.

He acknowledged only two: appetite and passion. Appetite is awareness of something you feel as unpleasant, combined with a disposition to seek a feeling-state that does not contain the unpleasant element (*NL*, 7. 4–7. 44, 8. 13). So defined, it is blind; not only in the sense that a man in a condition of mere appetite is unaware of it, but also in the sense that his concept of what he wants is purely negative. He wants a feeling-state that is different from the one he has, but his only concept of that state is that it must be unlike his present state in a certain respect (*NL*, 7. 5–7. 54). Appetite has two specific forms, hunger and love. In hunger, you are aware of a feeling of defect or weakness that you crave to annul; in love, what you want to annul is loneliness (*NL*, 8. 11–8. 12, 8. 15–8. 16).

By these definitions, neither hunger nor love is a passion, which Collingwood defined as an activity in which a man reacts to the action on him of something not himself (*NL*, 8. 4): in both you react, not to the action of something not yourself, but to feelings in yourself. Collingwood acknowledged only two passions: fear and anger, in both of which you form a concept of your own state, and a contrasting concept of something not yourself that menaces you. In fear, you cower away from that menace in order to escape it; in anger, you fight against it (*NL*, 10. 26–10. 27, 10. 44).

Many of Collingwood's readers have been surprised to find that, after showing that acts of second-order consciousness were acts of selective attention to feeling, and illustrating his analysis of second-order attention by the example of picking out a red patch from a green background, he should have recognized no functions of second-order consciousness other than appetite and passion. Prima facie, innumerable acts of selective attention to feeling are neither appetitive nor passionate. The act of picking a red patch from a green background, Collingwood's own example, does not appear to express hunger or love, fear or anger.

This apparent inconsistency may be resolved by paying strict attention to the questions Collingwood was trying to answer at each stage of his argument. In his discussion of second-order attention and conceptual thinking he sought clear and familiar examples, in order that his readers might verify his conclusions by their own reflections (cf. NL, 1. 88). The act of selecting a red patch for attention is both clear and easily performed by a reader in his study. It may be an element in an act either of appetite, e.g. rejecting a red blackberry as unpleasant to taste, or of passion, e.g. cowering away from 'a scarlet curtain blazing in the sunlight' (cf. PA, 161); but, for most adults, it will be a primitive survival in the higher-order act of looking for an example of second-order attention. When Collingwood was illustrating the concept of selective attention, it did not matter in the least whether his examples were mere acts of second-order consciousness or primitive survivals of second-order consciousness in acts of a higher order.

The case was altered when he came to take soundings at the second level of consciousness in order to find what functions belong to it but not to any higher level. In answering that question it would have been inadmissible to include anything that belonged to any order of consciousness higher than the second. Presumably, those who have attained no higher order of consciousness than the second are children in infancy; and it is not extravagant to suppose that very young children perform acts of selective attention only in hunger or love, fear or anger. This conclusion is perfectly compatible with the fact that not all acts involving selective attention are acts of hunger or love, fear or anger; for there may be primitive survivals of appetite and passions in acts which are neither appetitive nor passionate.

IV

QUESTION AND ANSWER

§ 1. *Interrogative Thinking and the Theory of Presuppositions*

THE step from second-order to third-order consciousness is taken at the function of anger; for in anger you become conscious of your own fear, and so of your own second-order consciousness. In becoming angry you turn not only against an external menace, but also against your own fear of it. Your renunciation of fear is shame. 'What a man is ashamed of', Collingwood remarked, 'is always at bottom himself; and he is ashamed of himself at bottom always for being afraid' (*NL*, 10. 48–10. 49).

Collingwood held that every step from one order of consciousness to another is brought about by a linguistic act. That from the first order to the second is brought about by conceptual speech; that from the second order to the third by asking questions that offer definite alternatives as answers (*NL*, 11. 12–11. 13). No man becomes angry until he asks himself, 'Do I want to avoid what menaces me, or to overcome both it and my fear of it' and, having become through his question aware of those alternatives, adopts the latter. It is only by asking himself that question that he becomes aware of his fear of what menaces him (*NL*, 10. 49–10. 5, 11. 22–11. 24).

Because he mistook the asking of such questions for propositional thinking (see above, Ch. III, § 5), Collingwood fell into two further errors: he wrongly denied that acts of conceptual thinking can be either true or false; and he wrongly identified second-order consciousness with non-propositional conceptual thinking, and third-order consciousness with propositional thinking (*NL*, 10. 51). However, these errors do not invalidate his distinction between employing concepts and asking questions of the kind he described as 'precise and real', that is, questions that offer definite alternatives.

Not all questions do so. Some are what he called 'bogus', that is, questions of the form, 'Is *p* true or not?' where no definite alternative to *p* is offered (*NL*, 11. 12–11·13). A question is 'precise or real', as opposed to 'bogus', only if it is of the form, 'Which of the propositions, *p* or *q*, or . . . is true?' where none of the propositions mentioned is the logical contradictory of any of the others.

While the distinction between those questions which offer non-contradictory alternatives and those which do not is perfectly legitimate, Collingwood had no justification either for describing the latter as 'bogus', or for asserting that scientific method depends on replacing questions which, because they do not offer non-contradictory alternatives, are 'vague' and so unanswerable, with 'real' questions, i.e. questions which do offer non-contradictory alternatives (*NL*, 11. 12). The distinction between questions which are asked in the course of scientific inquiry and questions asked at hazard is, no doubt, an important one; but it is also important not to confound it with a distinction between two logical varieties of question. In scientific inquiry questions of any logical variety may be asked.

Collingwood's examples of systematic questioning do not corroborate his position in *The New Leviathan*. In his *Autobiography*, when showing that systematic questioning must proceed by 'detailed and particularized' questions rather than by 'vague and generalized' ones, he pointed out that, in trying to find why my car does not start, if 'I take out number one plug, lay it on the engine, turn the starting-handle, and watch for a spark, my observation "number one plug is all right" is an answer not to the question, "Why won't my car go?" but to the question, "Is it because number one plug is not sparking that my car won't go?" ' (*A*, 32). Yet although the question, 'Is it because number one plug is not sparking?' is detailed and particularized, by the definition of *The New Leviathan* it is bogus. Since an equivalent to the example in the *Autobiography* could be found in almost any specimen of scientific thinking, the distinction in *The New Leviathan* between 'precise or real' questions and 'bogus' ones must itself be pronounced bogus.

More than once Collingwood chided his contemporaries for neglecting to study the place of systematic questioning in serious thinking. He was not able to publish in full the results of his own investigations until 1940, in his *Essay on Metaphysics* (chs. 4–5), although he had made a preliminary report of them in his *Autobiography* (pp. 30–42). In *The New Leviathan* he took some of them for granted, and quietly abandoned others.

His point of departure was that questions as well as answers may be impugned. He gave a familiar example. In a divorce action, it would be improper to ask the defendant whether he had stopped beating his wife, unless he had already conceded that he was in the habit of beating her. Until that was conceded, the question would not 'arise' for him (*EM*, 26, 38–40; cf. *A*, 37). It was in view of this example that Collingwood laid down the following definition-in-use of his term 'presupposition': 'To say that a question "does not arise" is the ordinary English way of saying that it involves a presupposition which is not in fact being made' (*EM*, 26). In other words, whenever in ordinary English it would be said that the question Q would not arise unless it were supposed that S, then S is presupposed by asking Q.

In Collingwood's example, unless it is presupposed that you have been in the habit of beating your wife, then the question, 'Have you stopped beating her?' does not arise. But that presupposition does not stand alone. It would itself normally be an answer to the question, 'Are you in the habit of beating her, or do you beat her only on occasion?' which would not arise unless it were conceded that you had at some time beaten her. In turn, that presupposition would be an answer to the further question, 'Have you ever beaten your wife, or are you habitually gentle to her?' And not even that question would arise unless it were presupposed that you were a man and had a wife.

Since these questions and answers are related serially, the presupposition of one question being wholly or in part the answer to another, Collingwood inferred that for any question there is one and only one statement that is 'directly and immediately' related to it in such a way that if that statement be presupposed, the question arises (*EM*, 25–26). This inference is either a truism or false. It would be a truism if the presupposition were regarded as one and only one statement simply as being the whole of what must be presupposed; but it would be false if it were regarded as necessarily being logically simple. Many presuppositions, perhaps 'You are a man' is one, are in fact logically simple: that is, they cannot be resolved by logical analysis into complexes of simpler statements. But many are not. The question, 'Is the average age of the members of the present British government greater than that of the members of the present French government?' presupposes the complex conjunctive statement, 'There is a group of men which governs Britain and there is another group of men which governs France'. Yet neither of the simple statements combined in that complex is more directly and immediately presupposed by the question than the other. If a presupposition is regarded as logically simple, then the question has two presuppositions.

This ambiguity does not compromise the Theory of Presuppositions as a whole; for the proposition that for any question there is one and only one immediate presupposition is not an essential part of it. A much more objectionable feature of the theory is that, although the meaning of the verb 'to presuppose' is laid down by a definition-in-use of what it is for asking a question to involve presupposing something, Collingwood customarily used the verb 'to presuppose' with somebody's name or description as its subject (*EM*, ch. v, *passim*). He thus incorporated into the very fabric of his theory a suggestion that presupposing is an act, and implicitly an act of thought. But, by definition, it cannot possibly be an act of thought.

Since by Collingwood's definition the statement, 'The question Q does not arise for you' is identical in meaning with the statement, 'The question Q involves a presupposition which is not in fact being made by you' (*EM*, 26), it follows that for you to make the presuppositions which Q involves is the same thing as for Q to arise for you. Normally, you show that a question arises for you, not by saying that it does, but by either asking it or not raising objections when it is asked. If you ask whether a man has stopped beating his wife, or raise no objections when that question is asked, you show that you think it arises. It therefore follows, by Collingwood's definition, that you make the presuppositions it involves. This is a sheer matter of logic, just as it is a sheer matter of logic that, when you make a statement, you imply all that it logically entails (cf. *EM*, 27, Def. 3).

You may, of course, withdraw a question when the presuppositions it involves have been pointed out to you, as you may withdraw the question whether a certain man has stopped beating his wife when you perceive that it cannot arise for you unless you presuppose that he has made a habit of beating her (*EM*, 25–26). In the same way, you may withdraw a statement you have made when its implications have been pointed out to you. Until you withdraw your question, however, you have made whatever presuppositions asking it involves. Presupposing something, in short, is the same as being logically committed to accept it by the questions you ask or suffer to be asked. That is why Collingwood asserted that even though Aristotle did not think the world to have been created by God, he nevertheless presupposed it; for, like all Greek scientists, he asked questions which do not arise unless that presupposition is made (*EM*, 214–15).

Ever since the word 'presupposition' was reintroduced into logical theory ten years ago,[1] in the course of discussions of Russell's Theory of Descriptions, it has proved to be an apple of discord. It is therefore necessary to distinguish the sense in which Collingwood used it from that which has been given to it in those discussions. An authoritative definition of the latter has been furnished by Mr. P. F. Strawson, in his *Introduction to Logical Theory*, namely:

S presupposes $S^1 = df.$ the truth of S^1 is a necessary condition of the truth or falsity of S.

This definition manifestly diverges widely from Collingwood's. The radical difference is that while the logical relation in terms of which a presupposition is defined is, for Strawson, a relation between two statements, for Collingwood it is a relation between a statement and a question.

There are, however, other differences. According to Strawson's

---

[1] By P. T. Geach in *Analysis*, x (1950), pp. 84–88, and P. F. Strawson in *Mind*, lix (1950), pp. 320–44, and in *Introduction to Logical Theory* (London, 1952). Geach's and Strawson's positions resemble Frege's in *Über Sinn und Bedeutung*: cf. Max Black in Seize Uyeda (ed.), *A Way to the Philosophy of Science* (Tokyo, 1958), pp. 433–48, and G. E. M. Anscombe, *An Introduction to Wittgenstein's Tractatus* (London, 1959), ch. 2.

definition, if the presupposition of a statement is false, then the question whether that statement is true or false does not arise; according to Collingwood's, the question whether a statement is true or false arises for anybody who is prepared to ask it, although it ceases to arise for him if he is no longer prepared to ask it when the presuppositions it involves have been pointed out to him.

Collingwood and Strawson therefore have entirely different conceptions of what it is for a question to arise. Strawson's approach seems to be: let us disregard whether or not those engaged in a discussion think that a question arises, and consider only whether it really does; for that, at any rate, depends only on the facts of the case. By contrast, Collingwood seems at first sight to have paid too much attention to what those who discuss a topic happen to think. He foresaw this criticism, and met it by a direct criticism of the view Strawson was later to espouse. '[I]n the conduct of scientific thinking', he pointed out, '. . . it is possible and often profitable to argue from suppositions which we know to be false, or which we believe to be false, or concerning which we have neither knowledge nor belief as to whether they are false or true' (*EM*, 28). A *reductio ad absurdum* argument in mathematics would be a case in point. There, you begin by supposing that the proposition to be proved is false; then, by following up the questions to which that false supposition gives rise, you derive a self-contradiction from it; and finally, you go on to infer that the contradictory of your original supposition is true. Taken strictly, Strawson's definition would seem to imply that, since their presupposition is false, none of the questions whose answers constitute the body of a *reductio ad absurdum* arises at all. But if that is so, it is hard to see how such proofs can be valid. Collingwood was on strong ground when he insisted that 'these . . . negations in no way affect the validity of the argument' (*EM*, 28).

In stating his position, however, Collingwood omitted an important qualification. He laid it down that, 'The logical efficacy of a supposition does not depend upon the truth of what is supposed, or even on its being thought true, but only on its being supposed' (*EM*, 28). This suggests, although it does not logically entail, that supposing is a special mental activity, like requesting or entreating, which has nothing to do with truth. However, it is no such thing. While you may suppose something, in Collingwood's sense, without thinking it to be true, you cannot do so without being committed, at least provisionally, to accepting it as true. The difference between thinking something to be true and provisionally accepting it as true may be illustrated by what happens in *reductio ad absurdum* proofs. A mathematician constructing such a proof does not think his supposition to be true, but provisionally accepts it as true in order to prove it to be false.

Collingwood ventured further in his definition of an assumption: 'To assume is to suppose by an act of free choice.' Since all acts of free choice are acts of consciousness (see below, Ch. IV, § 4), it would follow that at least one class of presupposings has acts of consciousness as its members. Again, by omitting to modify the verb 'to assume', Collingwood left the impression that assuming is an activity which has nothing to do with truth or falsity. It is therefore necessary to repeat our earlier finding. As Collingwood defined it, presupposing is not an act of consciousness, but the state of being committed by your questions, at least provisionally, to accepting something. It follows that assuming by an act of free choice is not the same thing as presupposing; for what you choose to assume may not in fact be what your questions commit you to accept. In general, it may be assumed that your presuppositions and your assumptions will not conflict; but it is part of Collingwood's theory that they may and sometimes do (*EM*, 215).

Furthermore, it is impossible that a presupposition, as Collingwood defined it, should be anything but a commitment to accept something *as true*. The ordinary expressions 'I assume p', 'I presuppose p', are abridgements of 'I assume p to be true', 'I presuppose p to be true'. Except as such abridgements they lack definite sense. This is shown by the fact that you can assume or presuppose that p is false. If Collingwood had written that the logical efficacy of a presupposition depends only on its being supposed, but not on its being supposed to be true, it would have been clear at once that he had not made an intelligible statement. How could you possibly obey the instruction to suppose that there is a greatest prime number, but not necessarily to suppose that it is true?

We have now explored both Collingwood's definition of a presupposition, and his proposition that whether or not a question arises does not depend on whether its presuppositions are true, or even on whether they are thought to be true, but only on whether they are presupposed (*EM*, 28). This proposition is one of the two fundamentals of his Theory of Presuppositions. The other is that every piece of interrogative thinking begins with presuppositions that are absolute (*EM*, 25–26, 63). From these two propositions, and his definitions of 'proposition' and 'presupposition', he went on to derive the theorem that absolute presuppositions are neither true nor false (*EM*, 32).

Before advancing his argument for the second of the fundamentals of his theory Collingwood defined the term 'absolute presupposition'. A supposition that 'stands relatively to one question as its presupposition, and relatively to another as its answer', may be called a 'relative presupposition' (*EM*, 29); and one that 'stands, relatively to all questions to which it is related, as a presupposition, never as an answer' may be called 'absolute' (*EM*, 31). Since he laid down the proposition that 'a presupposition is either relative or absolute' (*EM*, 29) on no other evidence than his definitions of 'absolute presupposition' and 'relative presupposition', it is reasonable to infer that he considered it to follow from them. It can only do so if his definition of 'absolute presupposition' be taken as equivalent to 'presupposition that is not relative'.

A presupposition that is not relative, by Collingwood's definition, is simply one which is presupposed by somebody in asking a question, but which is not an answer to any other question he asks. It would thus be possible for the same presupposition to be absolute for you, i.e. not an answer to any question you ask, and yet be an answer to a question that somebody else asks, and thus, for him, a relative one. Unfortunately, Collingwood devoted little attention to this possibility, and seems to have been blind to its implications (see below, Chs. VI, § 2; X, § 3). He did, however, mention that 'persons engaged in some kind of "ordinary" thought may wish to pursue it . . . by treating presuppositions as absolute which the best contemporary thought treats as relative, or which the best metaphysical analysis has pronounced to be relative' (*EM*,

83). Here, I take it, 'treating presuppositions as absolute' means refusing to regard them as answers to questions, and 'the best metaphysical analysis' means 'most complete and accurate analysis available of the questions asked by the most advanced scientists' (cf. *EM*, 94–96). What Collingwood seems to have meant is that at certain periods 'ordinary' thought may make certain presuppositions absolutely which advanced scientific thought will make only relatively.

Curiously enough, the argument with which Collingwood followed his admirably rigorous definitions was not deductive, but historical. He tried to show that, as a matter of historical fact, natural scientists after a certain point refuse to entertain questions about whether their presuppositions are justified. He began by claiming that if you were importunate enough to demand of a natural scientist that he justify, first, a question he has asked, then the question to which the presupposition of his first question was an answer, and so on, you would ultimately reach a presupposition which he would refuse to defend. Probably your victim would 'blow up right in your face', but, if he managed to keep his temper, he would answer you in some such way as this: ' "That is a thing we take for granted in my job. We don't question it. We don't try to verify it. It isn't a thing anybody has discovered, like microbes or the circulation of the blood. It is a thing we just take for granted" ' (*EM*, 31).

Now even if all natural scientists should as a matter of historical fact respond in that way, it would follow only that they do make absolute presuppositions, not that they are logically committed as scientists to do so. They would be so committed only if it were logically impossible that any series of scientific questions and answers should arise except from absolute presuppositions. Not only did Collingwood not attempt to prove this analytically, he could not have done so if he had tried; for it seems to be possible to disprove it.

The disproof rests on two premises which are implicit in Collingwood's Theory of Presuppositions, but are not part of it: namely, (1) that no presupposition can be self-evidently a necessary truth or a contradiction; and (2) that any absolute presupposition can be converted into a relative one.

The proof of (1) rests on the fact that all discourse whatever excludes self-contradictions, and logically necessary truths are simply negations of self-contradictions. A presupposition, however, is something we are committed to accept by the particular questions we consider to arise, not by entering into any discourse whatever. It is a special commitment of special discourse, not a general commitment of all discourse. Yet, although the general principle is clear, difficulties arise in applying it to mathematics. Presumably, all true propositions of pure mathematics are strictly analytic. Yet, in constructing lemmas, pure mathematicians may well ask questions that arise only if certain mathematical propositions are true; and it is natural to say that they presuppose those propositions in Collingwood's sense. An even more instructive case is that of the *reductio ad absurdum* proof, in which questions are asked which would naturally be taken to presuppose mathematical propositions which are ultimately shown to be false, and therefore self-contradictory (*A*, 37).

The solution of the difficulty lies in the fact that in mathematics and even in logic itself, few logically necessary propositions and few self-contradictions are self-evident. A question which rests on a self-evident contradiction, like 'What positive integer must be added to one plus one to yield two?' which rests on 'One plus one is less than two by some positive integer', is as self-evidently absurd a question as its apparent presupposition is absurd a proposition. It would be wrong to say, 'The question would arise if you made that presupposition'; for that presupposition cannot be made. Similarly, a self-evidently necessary truth cannot be presupposed, because you cannot refuse to presuppose it. You cannot reject the question, 'What positive integer must be added to two to yield three?' on the ground that you are not committed to holding that three is greater than two by a positive integer. When a necessary truth is not self-evident, however, nothing debars you from wondering whether or not it is true, or from asking questions which commit you provisionally to accepting either it or its contradictory. Even after you have proved or disproved it, you may go on asking such questions in the course of seeking other proofs or disproofs. What you cannot do is to presuppose necessary truths which, being self-evident, there is no question of proving; or self-contradictions which, being self-evident, there is no question of disproving. You can be said to presuppose something only when you are in a position to allow or to reject a question.

The proof of (2), that any absolute presupposition can be converted into a relative one, is less difficult. A question can be constructed out of any absolute presupposition simply by prefixing the words 'Is it true that . . .?' to it; and doing so will convert the original absolute presupposition into an affirmative answer to the new question, and thereby into a relative presupposition. The fact that it is open to anybody who is 'ticklish in [his] absolute presuppositions' (*EM*, 31) to refuse to ask the question, and so to leave his presupposition intact, is beside the point, which is that he could construct and ask the question if he chose. It is also beside the point that Collingwood would certainly have objected to the method I have proposed for constructing questions about absolute presuppositions as mechanical and unsystematic (cf. *A*, 37–40; *EM*, 38–39). Questions so constructed are perfectly proper questions; furthermore, they are questions which many philosophers ask as soon as an alleged absolute presupposition is exhibited to them.

In the *Essay on Metaphysics* Collingwood gave surprisingly few examples of the conversion of absolute presuppositions into relative ones, possibly because he devoted most of his attention to major changes in the absolute presuppositions of natural science, which for the most part have consisted in abandoning old presuppositions for new, and not in converting them into relative ones. He did, however, although off-handedly, mention an example of such conversion in politics. After observing that Locke had conceived nationality as 'a "natural" basis, an absolute presupposition, of all political activity whatever', he declared that for modern historians 'nationality . . . is a relative presupposition; it cannot be an absolute one' (*EM*, 97–98).[1]

From the convertibility of absolute presuppositions into relative ones it follows that no given proposition is necessarily absolute. I

---

[1] I consider Collingwood's description (*EM*, 41–42) of absolute presuppositions as presuppositions of which 'it would be nonsensical to ask whether [they] are true', i.e. of which it is logically impossible that they should be propositions, to be a slip. He nowhere pretended to prove it, and it contradicts *EM*, 97–98.

must now demonstrate that if the absolute presuppositions in a sequence of questions and presuppositions are elicited and converted into relative ones by suitable questions, and if in turn the absolute presuppositions of the new questions are elicited and converted into relative ones, the process of eliciting and converting absolute presuppositions will terminate in questions which rest wholly on self-evidently necessary truths, and not in absolute presuppositions.

That this is so in mathematics has already been pointed out. The examples most favourable to Collingwood's theory are to be found in natural science and history. Take the supposition made by most lion-hunters that lions are carnivorous. This can be converted into a relative presupposition by asking the question, 'Is it true that lions are carnivorous?' which further presupposes, not the self-evidently necessary truth that lions are either carnivorous or not, but the contingent proposition that lions exist. This in turn can be converted into a relative presupposition by asking, 'Is it true that lions exist?' Prima facie, this question presupposes nothing. It arises provided only that either lions exist or do not, which is self-evidently a necessary truth. Collingwood, however, would have dismissed such reasoning as superficial. By their nature, lions can only sustain life in a certain kind of world. It is absurd, not merely empirically but logically, to suppose that a lion could live without air, water, or food. Such a question as, 'Are there lions in empty space?' is logically as objectionable as 'Does that indulgent husband beat his wife?'

The question 'Is it true that lions exist?' therefore presupposes that there exists an environment in which lions can live. And, the further question, 'Is it true that there exists an environment in which lions can live?' presupposes that the universe is such that this environment could have come into being. In an investigation of what contemporary natural scientists presuppose, these questions would be more specific, because the character of the environment in question, and of the kind of universe in which it could come into being, would be laid down. In no system of scientific theory, however, would this series of conditions go on without end. According to Collingwood, in present scientific theory the question 'Is it true that lions are carnivorous?' ultimately rests on four ultimate principles: that there is a world of nature; that this world of nature is a world of events; that all events in the world of nature happen according to one system of laws; and that the world of nature is divided into two realms, the animate and the inanimate (*EM*, 222–3). These principles, he maintained, modern natural science takes as ultimate: it does not question them, but simply presupposes them (*EM*, 225–7).

If Collingwood was right in holding that no system of natural science postulates an infinite hierarchy of conditions for such facts as that lions are carnivorous, as I think he was, then every such system must terminate in a set of ultimate principles. Such sets of principles as those which he recognized as fundamental to modern science are analysable into two parts: a very general specification of what Leibniz would have called a 'possible world', and an affirmation that the possible world so specified is the actual world —that it exists. By our premiss (1), even if such an affirmation is made as an absolute presupposition, it is possible to convert it into a relative one: you need only ask, 'Is it true that the possible world specified in it is the actual world?' Now, what does asking such a question presuppose? It does not presuppose that any further conditions obtain, without which the possible world in question could not exist; for, *ex hypothesi*, the specification is ultimate. Yet, if there are no further conditions for its existence, the question 'Is it true that it exists?' rests on nothing but the logical truth that it either exists or does not. According to our premiss (2), that, being self-evidently necessary, is not a presupposition; and therefore, *a fortiori*, not an absolute presupposition.

Although this demonstration began with a particular example, it plainly applies to all sequences of questions and presuppositions in natural science and history. It would only fail to apply if there were a scientific or historical theory according to which every question of the form 'Is it true that c_x exists?' presupposed that there was a further condition, c_{x+1}, such that, unless c_{x+1} existed, the question whether c_x existed would not arise. I cannot even conceive what such a theory would be like; and Collingwood himself did not even consider the possibility. Accordingly, I conclude that the second of the two fundamental propositions of his Theory of Presuppositions, namely, that every sequence of questions and presuppositions arises from absolute presuppositions, is not merely unproved, but false.

§ 2. *Are Absolute Presuppositions neither True nor False?*

Neither of the fundamental propositions of Collingwood's Theory of Presuppositions was as daring as its most important theorem, that absolute presuppositions are neither true nor false. He advanced two distinct arguments for it in the *Essay on Metaphysics*. One was a formal deductive proof, which is stated *more mathematico* (*EM*, 32–33); the other was a non-axiomatized philosophical argument, deriving from the logical positivist theory of verification (*EM*, 164–5).

The deductive proof runs as follows. Let a statement, i.e. that which can be either true or false, be called a 'proposition', and let stating it be called 'propounding' it. Now Collingwood held that every statement, and so every proposition, is an answer to a question (*EM*, 23). Absolute presuppositions, however, are by definition not answers to questions (*EM*, 31). It follows that absolute presuppositions are not propositions, i.e. are neither true nor false (*EM*, 32–33). An array of corollaries follows. '[A]ny question involving the presupposition that an absolute presupposition is a proposition, such as the questions "Is it true?" "What evidence is there for it?" "How can it be demonstrated?" "What right have we to presuppose it if it can't?", is a nonsense question' (*EM*, 33).

The premiss on which this argument turns is that every statement is an answer to a question. That it must be false follows immediately from our previous demonstration (see above, Ch. III, § 5) that even conceptual thinking, which is of a lower order than interrogative thinking, must be propositional. It is surprising that Collingwood failed to notice the palpable weakness of his argument for it. That argument consisted of nothing but the bald assertion that, in proportion as you were familiar with science, you would know that all the statements you make in scientific thinking are made in answer to questions of which you are conscious, and all those you make in unscientific thinking are made in answer to questions of which you are not conscious (*EM*, 23–24). This must be false. Since by the Principle of Intentionality it is impossible to ask a question without becoming conscious of the question asked, when you make a statement without being conscious of a question to which it is an answer, you do not make it in answer to any question at all. Now Collingwood has conceded that 'in unscientific thinking' you do make statements without being conscious of a question to which it is an answer. He therefore cannot escape the conclusion that some statements are not answers to questions.

Its cardinal premiss disproved, Collingwood's deductive proof collapses. Perhaps he had a premonition of its downfall; for he tried to buttress it with an argument from the nature of verification. It was equally simple. Its major premiss was that what is not verifiable is not a proposition, and its minor was that no absolute presupposition is verifiable (*EM*, 162–3, 165). Since neither premiss is true by definition, he was obliged to prove both.

That obligation he did not discharge. With respect to his major premiss, he did indeed inform his readers that in *Language, Truth and Logic* A. J. Ayer had derived it from a conception of verifiability, which, he assured them, 'if not quite immune from criticism as it stands', was at least 'capable of being restated in some such way as to render it so immune' (*EM*, 165). Yet, instead of explaining how Ayer had derived the proposition to be proved from his conception of verifiability, Collingwood contented himself with a profession of faith. '[W]hether or not [Ayer] derives his conclusion from true premises', he announced, 'it is a conclusion that I entirely accept and have already stated . . . in my own words' (*EM*, 165). Although it disconcerts our expectations to find Collingwood drawing no distinction between the questions 'Is the statement S true or false?' and 'Is the statement S verifiably true or false?' we must remember that anti-realism makes strange bedfellows.

Perhaps because he sensed that his minor premiss was even feebler than his major, he did not put aside his responsibility to demonstrate it. His method was to examine a number of examples. The absolute presuppositions of the natural lore of certain primitive societies (he seems to have had the Azande in mind),[1] of Aristotelian

[1] Cf. his reference at *PA*, 8 *n.*, to E. E. Evans-Pritchard, *Witchcraft, Oracles and Magic among the Azande* (Oxford, 1937).

physics, of Newtonian physics, and of post-Newtonian modern physics can none of them, he argued, not even the most primitive, be 'undermined by the verdict of "experience", because [each] is the yard-stick by which [in some society] "experience" is judged' (*EM*, 193-4; cf. 211-12, 325-7). No empirical observation can support or subvert the presuppositions which are made in interpreting it; and it is logically possible to interpret it in accordance with any consistent set of presuppositions.

Here Collingwood plainly took it for granted that 'the verdict of experience' cannot condemn any assertion that can be reconciled with the observed facts by some hypothesis or other. His likening of absolute presuppositions to 'yardsticks' or units of measurement must not be taken literally: a presupposition says something; a unit of measurement does not. His point was that if you interpret your experience in the light of some presupposition, even one we now know to be absurd, e.g. that the earth is flat; then, provided that the presupposition is logically possible, you can always invent some hypothesis or other which will square it with what you observe. There is no proposition whatever about the world of nature which cannot be squared with what is observed, provided only that you are not squeamish about inventing hypotheses.

Yet when a natural scientist claims that 'the verdict of experience' favours Newton's physics against Aristotle's, he does not mean that no hypothesis can be imagined which would reconcile Aristotle's physics with the facts on which all competent observers agree. Rather, he means that the only hypotheses that would do so would be *ad hoc*; that is to say, they would have nothing to recommend them except that they bring about that reconciliation. The verdict of experience, as natural scientists think of it, is always given according to a principle of economy or simplicity, by which *ad hoc* hypotheses are required to be as few as possible. A good hypothesis should solve more than one problem. The verdict of experience condemns Aristotle's physics because it can only be brought into conformity with what has been observed by making enormously more *ad hoc* hypotheses than Newton's system requires.

Having overlooked the fact that 'the verdict of experience' to which natural scientists appeal is reached according to the principle of theoretical simplicity, Collingwood was in no position to detect the unsoundness of his premiss that absolute presuppositions are not verifiable. The principle of theoretical simplicity enables us to subject not only answers to questions, but also whole complexes of questions and answers, to the verdict of experience. When one whole complex is rejected in favour of another, its absolute presuppositions are rejected along with it; and, like the answers contained in that complex, they are rejected as false. Aristotle's physics was not only earlier than Newton's, and more remote from present intellectual fashions, it was more remote from the truth; and so, where they differ from Newton's, were his absolute presuppositions. This conclusion, to which we shall return, resolves some of the difficulties in Collingwood's analysis of metaphysics.

§ 3. The Functions of Interrogative Thinking

Although the passion of anger is the function at which third-order consciousness is first achieved, the function that Collingwood considered to be characteristic of third-order consciousness was desire. Desire is the result of converting appetite into an object of consciousness. Anybody who has reached the level of consciousness of a representative modern European can convert at least some of his appetites into desires at will; but it does not follow that the original step from second-order to third-order consciousness is lightly taken. It would not be taken at all except under the spur of practical need: the need to discover which of the alternatives before you will satisfy your appetite (NL, 11. 1–11. 13, 11. 24). You cannot find out by introspection; for even if you could introspectively contemplate your appetites, you would not see what their objects were: appetite is blind (NL, 11. 18, 11. 36). No question would arise at all about which objects would satisfy your appetite unless some function of consciousness other than appetite had given you the idea that there were alternative possibilities; and Collingwood could only identify that function with passion. You come to recognize that you hunger for or love something by first fearing it and then being angry with yourself for doing so (NL, 11. 16–11. 17). Having come to view the same object as standing in two quite different relations to you, you are in a position to inquire which of the various objects of which you have become aware will satisfy your present hunger or love, and which will not.

It is difficult to decide how seriously to take the details of Collingwood's account of passion and desire. Whether it is true that 'desire only comes into existence through the experience of passional relations towards that which appetite renders attractive' (*NL*, 11. 16) I do not know; but I do not think that Collingwood gives any evidence that it is. You certainly cannot verify it for yourself by taking stock of your own acts of love and hunger, fear and anger. The most that could be claimed for Collingwood would be that he was possibly right, and that again and again his perceptions about particular functions of consciousness are corroborated by your own reflections. My own reflections appear to me to corroborate Collingwood's on many points (e.g. in parts of *NL*, 11. 17, and all of *NL*, 11. 19).

When you succeed in transforming appetite into desire by asking the question, 'Which do I want, *a* or *b*?', your desire, like your answer, may be either true or false. The mere fact that you give yourself the answer, 'I want *b*', does not guarantee that you do want it; you can only find out whether you do or not by asking yourself whether, when you have obtained it, the discomfort of your unsatisfied appetite abates or persists (*NL*, 11. 37). Desire, or consciousness of appetite, is true when the appetite of which you are conscious really has the object you think it has, and it is false when it does not (*NL*, 11. 3–11. 31).

At this point, Collingwood believed, the philosophy of mind coincides with ethics. ' "*Good*" ', he declared, '*means "desired"*; or, what is not easily to be distinguished from this, *desirable*, meaning "worthy to be desired" ' (*NL*, 11. 5). The difficult distinction between what is desired and what is worthy to be desired is that desire itself may be either true or false, whereas what is worthy to be desired can only be desired truly. Collingwood drew this distinction explicitly. 'You may very easily be mistaken in thinking what you desire to be good', he remarked, '*that is to say* you may be mistaken in desiring it or thinking you want it' (*NL*, 11. 52, my italics). Now the fact that something is truly desired is a perfectly ordinary empirical or natural fact. Hence in defining 'good' in terms of true desire Collingwood reaffirmed and clarified a naturalistic ethical tradition which he himself traced to Hobbes and Spinoza (*NL*, 11. 4–11. 41), and which may be pursued, through St. Thomas Aquinas and St. Augustine, to Aristotle and Plato.

It is therefore not surprising that he endorsed Aristotle's view that the good for man is happiness (*NL*, 12. 11), or that he held that only those who misconceived what happiness is, as Nietzsche did, could doubt it (*NL*, 12. 12, 12. 45). You only have what you want when you are in a state of complete internal well-being, or virtue, and of external well-being, or power. Virtue is freedom from servitude to passion; and power is mastery of circumstance. While they are not the same, since some men have more power than virtue, and others more virtue than power, neither are they incompatible with one another. Collingwood considered that continued powerlessness was less often a sign of virtue than of lack of it; and he was inclined to believe that any defect in virtue goes with a defect in power, and vice versa (*NL*, 12. 1–12. 24; cf. 12. 37–12. 38, 12. 4).

The pursuit of your own good is not the highest form of ethical activity, just as desire is not the highest form of consciousness. But happiness must be respected, and not lightly forgone, in any higher system of action. Collingwood's retort to Nietzsche's celebrated taunt that 'only Englishmen want to be happy' was that 'we need not blush to confess that, at a rather low level of consciousness, what was good enough for Greek philosophers and Roman emperors is good enough for us' (*NL*, 12. 4, 12. 44).

§ 4. *Choice and Rational Thinking*

Most men at some juncture put aside their own good in favour of some other end: it may be the good of their families. Such a choice is necessarily an act of fourth-order consciousness; for it requires that they be aware of their own desire for happiness, and reject it as their end (*NL*, 13. 1, 13. 25, 13. 31).

The choice to forgo your own happiness in order to bring about some other end presupposes not only awareness of desire but freedom from it. Since by the Law of Contingency nobody is under any necessity to liberate himself from desire, there is no sense in asking, when a man is found to have done so, why he has done it: he has done it for its own sake (*NL*, 13. 4). But it does make sense to ask how he has done it, and the answer is the same as it has been to earlier questions about how a step from one order of consciousness to another is taken: by the use of speech (*NL*, 13. 42). By naming a desire correctly you become aware of it; and, in becoming aware of it, you convert your state with respect to it from what Spinoza called a *passio* into what he called an *actio* (*NL*, 13. 45). No man could choose to act contrary to his desires unless he had liberated himself from them by speaking about them correctly. A man who is free from the domination of his desires will not flout them. More often than not, he will continue to pursue his own happiness; but he will not pursue it under all circumstances (*NL*, 13. 37–13. 38).

'The act of self-liberation', Collingwood argued, 'begins by being preconscious, and a long time may elapse between its being done and its being reflected upon' (*NL*, 13. 6). Those who have performed it have free will, or the power to choose; and they may even exercise their power, without becoming aware of its nature: thus the 'pre-Christian thinkers of Europe . . . knew that there was such a thing as choice, and they described it with care', but because, unlike Confucius and the Buddha, they did not know that choice presupposes liberation from desire, 'their whole system of thought was moribund before Christianity began to correct its errors' (*NL*, 13. 48–13. 5).

Consciousness of free will, which is necessarily of a higher order than the act by which free will is achieved, is self-respect (*NL*, 13. 31). You can achieve this higher-order consciousness, as you can achieve freedom from desire, only by the use of speech: by finding how to talk about your freedom (*NL*, 13. 39–13. 41).[1] Unless your self-respect has been aroused by your own efforts, either unaided or fostered by education, your possession of free will will be precarious. That is why it is a rule for devils, whose end is to

---

[1] *NL*, 13. 39 is confused; for it implies that to neglect or flout your self-interest is to make 'the strange discovery of freedom'. *NL*, 13. 48–13. 52 shows that freedom can only be discovered by an act of a higher order than that by which it is attained.

destroy your power of decision and to enslave you to your desires, to undermine your self-respect (*NL*, 13. 64–13. 67).

You liberate yourself from your desires by naming them: that is, by developing a language with expressions for happiness, and for the various forms of virtue and power. Having done so, you have made it possible for yourself to forgo your own happiness in order to further something else. Before you have become aware of your freedom, it is unlikely that you will forgo your own happiness except for those you love: not, be it observed, for love itself; for you may forgo the fruition of your own love in order that those you love may be happy. Such acts of self-denial, however, will be sporadic until you develop a language capable of expressing your own freedom. This is the language of what Collingwood called 'practical reason' (*NL*, 14. 32).

Although he did not expressly describe the difference between a language expressive of free will and a language expressive of self-respect, his views can be reasonably conjectured. You liberate yourself from desire by asking and answering questions of the form: What shall I do, *a*, which will contribute to my happiness, or *b*, which will jeopardize it? If you can ask and answer such questions, you are free, although you may not be aware of it (*NL*, 13. 27–13. 3, 13. 42). The language of self-respect adds to this question the further element of reasoning. Suppose you answer your question, 'I shall do *a*': you might, of course, have answered, 'I shall do *b*'; I choose the former because freedom from desire does not necessarily imply acting contrary to it, but only the capacity to do so. You may then have qualms. Perhaps, after all, you ought to do *b*. Your intention 'threatens to become unstuck and "lose the name of action" ' (*NL*, 14. 32; cf. 13. 86–13. 9). So you seek for a reason to do what you intend to do: for something from which what you intend to do may follow as a necessary consequence (*NL*, 14. 32). Such a reason can be nothing but a further intention (*NL*, 14. 4). Your question therefore becomes: Shall I for the reason *R* do *a*, which will contribute to my happiness, rather than *b*, which will jeopardize it? Now unless you were aware that you could do either *a* or *b*, according to whatever reasons you accepted as sufficient, it would be futile either to ask or to answer this question. You would, therefore, neither ask nor answer it unless you were not only free from the domination of desire, but also conscious of your freedom (cf. *NL*, 14. 32–14. 33).

Interrogative thinking of all three of the orders we have examined must have the structure described in Collingwood's Theory of Presuppositions, so far as that theory is sound. Adapting his own example in his *Essay on Metaphysics*, we may distinguish three questions which you might ask yourself:

1. Do I want to stop beating my wife, or to go on? (Third Order.)
2. Shall I stop beating my wife, which will jeopardize my happiness, or shall I go on? (Fourth Order.)
3. Shall I, because of my promise to cherish her, stop beating my wife, even though it will jeopardize my happiness, or shall I go on? (Fifth Order.)

All three of these questions presuppose that you have a wife, and are in the habit of beating her. But that is not all: (1) presupposes that you have appetites; (2) that you are conscious of your appetites, i.e. that you have (true or false) desires; and (3) that you are conscious of your desires. By asking and answering each of those questions you attain the order of consciousness next above the one the question presupposes.

These questions and presuppositions differ from the examples in the *Essay on Metaphysics* because they are practical rather than theoretical. Roughly, practical reasoning is making up your mind *to*, and theoretical reasoning making up your mind *that* (*NL*, 14. 3). In practical reasoning, you find a reason for acting in one way rather than another (*NL*, 1. 65, 14. 3, 14. 32); in theoretical reasoning, you find reasons for thinking that one proposition is true as opposed to another (*NL*, 1. 64, 14. 3, 14. 35). The Theory of Presuppositions applies to both.

§ 5. *Theory and Practice*

Collingwood emphatically declared that thought as a whole is 'primarily practical; and only in the second place theoretical, because it is in the first place practical' (*NL*, 1. 66); it is therefore no surprise to find that, of the two forms of reason, theoretical and practical, he considered practical reason to be the prior. '[I]t is', he wrote, 'the original form of reason, theoretical reason being a modification of it . . .' (*NL*, 14. 3).

His reasons for the former and more general of these views are implicit in his inventory of the various functions of consciousness which he found in his successive soundings. The most primitive form of thought that he found was conceptual thinking, the characteristic forms of which were expressed in infants' manifestly practical cries of hunger and love. At that stage of consciousness, he found nothing whatever that could be described as theoretical. The temporal priority of practical thought to theoretical must, therefore, be acknowledged.

The temporal priority of practical reason to theoretical may also be conceded, although it is far more doubtful. Collingwood, however, demanded even more than that. In every single case of theoretical reason, he claimed, there is an element, a 'primitive survival' of practical reason (*NL*, 14. 3). Consequently, there is no such thing as purely theoretical reasoning. He offered two arguments for this doctrine, of which I find neither satisfactory, and one an outright sophism.

The more plausible of his arguments was this. 'Real thinking is always to some extent experimental in its method; it always starts from practice and returns to practice; for it is based on "interest" in the thing thought about; that is, on a practical concern with it' (*NL*, 18. 13). There appear to be three false premisses here: (1) that all real thinking is always to some extent experimental in its method, (2) that all thinking that is experimental in its method starts with practice and ends with practice, and (3) that all thinking that begins and ends with practice is based on practical concern with the thing thought about. While each of these premisses is true in some cases, and may even be true in most, exceptions to every one of them are readily found. Thinking in pure mathematics and logic is not experimental in method; much thinking in astronomy (e.g. that which led to the discovery of the planet Neptune) while experimental in method, neither begins nor ends with practice, i.e. with an intention to *do* something; and a scientist who accomplishes, for an adequate fee, a piece of thinking that begins and ends with practice (e.g. a colour-blind chemist who discovers a cheap way of synthesizing a dye) may have no practical concern whatever with what he thinks about.

Collingwood's less plausible argument was a sophism so transparent that it is hard to believe that he himself took it seriously. It was this.

Theoretical reason . . . is based on the presupposition that a certain kind of propositional thinking, viz. that about which questions beginning 'why' can be legitimately asked, is a matter of free will; is not the mere acceptance of something 'given', but is a voluntary decision to think *this* and not *that*. This is why theoretical reason always contains a primitive survival of practical reason. (*NL*, 14. 37–14. 38.)

In offering this argument, Collingwood appears to have forgotten his own distinction of theoretical reason from practical as 'making up your mind *that*' from 'making up your mind *to*' (*NL*, 14. 3). If making up your mind *that* is to be accounted practical merely because it is voluntary, as every act of consciousness on a higher level than desire is, then there is no distinction whatever between theoretical and practical reason. All reason would be practical, and making up your mind *that* and making up your mind *to* would be two different species of practical reason. Collingwood's argument therefore collapses. According to his original distinction between theoretical and practical reason, it is an *ignoratio elenchi*; for it does not even appear to prove that in every case of making up your mind *that* contains a primitive survival of making up your mind *to*. On the other hand, according to the conception of practical reason implicit in the argument itself, it proves too much; for it shows not merely that theoretical reason contains a practical element, but that all reason is generically practical.

One reason why Collingwood repeatedly depreciated pure theory was that he identified it with 'academic thinking or make-believe thinking', in which 'insignificant' or 'nonsense' questions are discussed by way of training (*NL*, 18. 13; cf. 2. 49–2. 55). Another was that he suspected many academic thinkers of taking refuge from serious problems by devoting themselves to 'academic' ones (cf.

A, 47–51). Both these reasons are muddled. Academic thinkers for the most part occupy themselves with purely theoretical questions; but it may be hoped that many of them eschew those which are trifling or nonsensical. Nor does their devotion to pure theory show their contempt for serious problems: a theoretical problem may be serious as well as a practical one. The Copernican heliocentric theory, the Newtonian theory of gravitation, and Einstein's theory of relativity were all, when first proposed, academic answers to academic questions; and they remain purely theoretical by Collingwood's own definition.

Although theory and practice are not identical, and although some questions are purely theoretical, and contain no practical element, Collingwood was right when he protested in the last chapter of his *Autobiography* that in any thinker theory and practice are intimately connected and mutually dependent, 'thought depending upon what [he] learned by experience in action, action depending upon how he thought of himself and the world' (*A*, 150). Whether or not a man will become a good scientist, a good historian, or a good philosopher depends quite as much on his moral qualities as on his mind; and, on the other hand, moral difficulties cannot be overcome by moral force alone, but only by moral force directed by clear thinking (*A*, 150). What Collingwood did not perceive was that by identifying theory and practice he made nonsense of his doctrine of their mutual dependence.

It is undoubtedly the duty of philosophers to do their work with gloves off: that is, to choose problems for investigation responsibly, with an eye to their importance for civilization; and to try to communicate their results to the public (*A*, 150–3). However, they are most practical as philosophers when they are most intelligently theoretical. Like anybody else, a philosopher ought to speak out on the questions of the day when he has something worth saying about them; but his practical effectiveness as a philosopher does not consist in that. Collingwood altogether misjudged his own practical achievement: it lay in his well directed theoretical work as a philosopher and an historian, which he came to disparage, and not in his vituperative attacks on the foreign policies of Baldwin and Chamberlain. Although in denouncing schemes to appease

Hitler his cause was good, he was neither hard-headed nor even-tempered enough to advocate it effectively. Nowhere did he betray his *naïveté* in practical politics more foolishly than in his description of ' "liberals" such as John Stuart Mill' as 'gloves-on philosophers' (*A*, 152; cf. 157–67).

§ 6. *Survey of the Results of Collingwood's Soundings*

In *The New Leviathan* Collingwood distinguished five distinct orders of consciousness to which the 'modern European mind' has attained. Together with the principal functions he assigned to each, they were as follows:

1. Consciousness of a whole here-and-now of feeling, which is not specified into distinct functions.
2. Conceptual thinking: the functions of which are appetite (hunger and love) and one of the passions (fear).
3. Propositional thinking, or, more correctly, Interrogative thinking: the functions of which are one of the passions (anger) and desire.
4. Free choice, which, like first-order consciousness, is not specified into distinct functions.
5. Rational thinking or Reason: the functions of which are practical reason and theoretical reason.

This inventory naturally suggests the question: Is fifth-order consciousness the highest that the modern European mind has yet attained?

Although Collingwood did not ask this question, in *The New Leviathan* he implied that both practical and theoretical reason range over an indefinite number of orders of consciousness. At its lowest level, rational thinking consists in seeking a reason for a choice to act in one way rather than another; but in principle a reason can be sought for any choice whatever: whether it be to do or to think something, and no matter how high may be the order of consciousness to which that choice belongs. When you confirm your intention to do *a* rather than *b* by giving the reason R_1, you perform an elementary act of practical thinking. But you may not be content with it: Is R_1 a good enough reason? You may now confirm your former piece of practical reasoning by giving the further reason R_2 (*NL*, 14. 4–14. 43). Now by Collingwood's definitions, in relation to the act of consciousness expressed by 'Because R_2, I shall do *a* rather than *b* because R_1', the earlier acts expressed by, 'I shall do *a* rather than *b* because R_1', and by, 'I shall do *a* rather than *b*', are first-order and second-order objects respectively, and so belong to lower orders of consciousness (*NL*, 5. 26). Since the latter acts belong to the fifth and fourth orders respectively, the act expressed by, 'I shall do *a* rather than *b* because R_1, because R_2', must belong to the sixth order. It is clear that, in principle, there is no upper limit to this series.

In the system of *The New Leviathan* the generic character of each of the orders of consciousness is reproduced in every higher order. Thus, not only the second order, but every order above it, is conceptual; and not only the third, but every order above it is interrogative. Above the fifth order, however, no new generic element appears. Interrogative thinking is conceptual, but it enriches conceptual thinking by adding methodical questioning to it. In the same way, rational thinking is an act of free choice, but it adds to free choice the search for reasons. By contrast, acts of consciousness of a higher order than the fifth add no further function to rational thinking; they consist simply in the application of reason to its own operations. It may therefore be said that reason is the highest function of consciousness of the 'modern European mind'.

The lowest order of consciousness at which Collingwood recognized a distinction between truth and falsity was the third (*NL*, 10. 51). There, as we have seen, he was quite certainly mistaken; for the characteristic forms of conceptual thinking are true or false. But he did not stop there. He asserted that knowledge cannot be had at the lower levels of consciousness on which even he recognized a distinction between truth and falsity. He defined knowledge as 'the conviction or assurance with which a man reaffirms a proposition he has already made after reflecting on the process of making it and satisfying himself that it is well and truly made' (*NL*, 14. 22). That such a conviction or assurance would be fallible is a conclusive objection to this definition, but not the most fundamental one. As Collingwood himself pointed out in *The Idea of History*, knowledge is 'thought in relation to its object', not in relation to its thinker (*IH*, 2). Roughly, a man knows something when he has come to think it in the right way, a way that is determined by what he is thinking about. No matter how great his conviction or assurance, and no matter that what he thinks is true, if he does not think it in the right way, he does not have knowledge.

It is curious, too, that Collingwood should have considered that you do not know a truth until you reaffirm it. Although he did not give the linguistic forms such reaffirmations might take, his definition required that they should express 'conviction or assurance'. Presumably then, they would include expressions like, 'I am convinced that . . .', 'I am certain that . . .', and, one must suppose, 'I know that . . .'. I suspect that Collingwood fell into the error of supposing an analysis of knowing to be an analysis of what is expressed in first-person utterances like, 'I know that p'. Yet by the Principle of Order, 'I know that p', and, 'I am certain that p', would express, not knowledge or assurance, but consciousness of knowledge or of assurance. They would therefore express acts of consciousness of a higher order than simple knowledge. If the Principle of Order is true, knowledge must be expressed in affirmations, not in reaffirmations.

V

HOMO NASCITUR POETA

§ 1. *The Problem of Usage: Art and Tradition*

EZRA POUND once claimed that literature 'has to do with the clarity and vigour of "any and every" thought and opinion. It has to do with maintaining the very cleanliness of the tools, the health of the very matter of thought itself.' And he went on to say that when the work of those whom he described as 'the damned and despised *literati*' goes 'rotten . . . i.e. becomes slushy and inexact, or excessive and bloated, the whole machinery of social and of individual thought and order goes to pot'.[1] Most academic philosophers, including most of those who interest themselves in aesthetics, would ascribe these pronouncements to the insanity which in the end overtook their author. Yet Pound's opinions were Collingwood's. Indeed, in *The Principles of Art* Collingwood went even farther than Pound: '. . . the effort to overcome corruption of consciousness, is an effort that has to be made not by specialists only but by everyone who uses language, whenever he uses it . . . Bad art, the corrupt consciousness, is the true *radix malorum*' (*PA*, 285).

Intensity like Collingwood's cannot but embarrass those for whom art is at best a source of enjoyment, if a superior one. Artistic discrimination, they protest, is not as serious a matter as he made out. Sound moral principles, a true religious faith, those we must have; and we must spare no effort to reach them. For such as would corrupt our awareness of them, no condemnation is too severe. To be beguiled by specious moral judgements or sentimental religious beliefs would be intolerable and even damnable. But religious and moral fervour must not be carried into every department of life. In questions of art, puritanical rigour is misplaced. It would wrong

[1] Ezra Pound, *How to Read* (London, 1931), p. 17.

our own deepest convictions to place our artistic judgements on a footing with them, especially if our criticism has a minority or 'highbrow' tendency. A saint may enjoy *Marmion* far more than *Paradise Lost*; and sour critics have no right to deprive him of his innocent pleasure.

Those who find views such as these congenial will only be able to make head or tail of Collingwood's theory of art by a strenuous effort of imagination; for he thought it plain that anybody who could find more enjoyment in *Marmion* than in *Paradise Lost* would so far be spiritually deficient. His reason was not that aesthetic judgement is reducible to moral or religious judgement, and still less that it is more important than they are. Art is what it is, and that is neither morals nor religion. But although all his life Collingwood distinguished art from other activities of the mind, he did not commit the characteristically modern *non sequitur* of inferring that excellence in one of those activities has nothing to do with excellence in the others. Art must be pursued as art; but just as it cannot thrive for long unless religion, morality, and science do also, so they cannot thrive if art does not. Cut off from the other activities of mind, art, science, morality, and even religion itself will each one tend more and more to lead its followers into some desert where the world of human life is lost, and the very motive for going on has disappeared (*SM*, 34; cf. *PA*, 331–6).

The cardinal problem of aesthetics, according to Collingwood, is to define what art is (*PA*, 1). Given that definition, it will become possible to determine what a work of art is and what it is not, and what kinds of criticism are artistically to the point and what are not. It is not the function of aesthetics to show a man how to be either a good artist or a good critic, but to provide those who are already in some measure one or the other with a theory of their work, so that they may know their last and stick to it. The obstacles to a sound definition of art are many. First, it is necessary to settle what the usage of the word 'art' is; for, as Collingwood pointed out, 'no one can define a term in common use until he has satisfied himself that his personal usage of it harmonizes with the common usage' (*PA*, 2). Yet the word 'art' is used equivocally (*PA*, 1). We must therefore decide which one of its various common usages is aesthetic. Nor can the others be disregarded. Unless each of them is identified and discriminated from the genuine aesthetic usage, they will linger in the back of our minds, infecting both our critical theory and our artistic practice (*PA*, 1-2).

The aesthetic usage of the word 'art' is of recent origin. In the classical period it did not exist; for neither the Greek τέχνη nor the Latin *ars* meant anything more than a specialized form of skill (*PA*, 5). Even in the Renaissance, artists did not distinguish their work as art from products which we should now assign to craft. Not until the eighteenth century was it recognized that there is a fundamental distinction between what were called the 'fine arts' (*les beaux arts*) and what were called the 'useful arts'. In the nineteenth century this distinction was consolidated, and the implication that art is useless avoided. What had been described as 'useful arts' were no longer called 'arts' at all, but 'crafts'; and the word 'art' was applied, without an epithet, to the various forms of aesthetic activity. Art and craft were no longer spoken of as though they belonged to the same genus (*PA*, 6). Yet even after it had become generally recognized that art was generically distinct from craft, its nature was imperfectly discerned. Many critics continued to confound art with other activities, recognizing as works of art things which were not, and refusing to recognize as works of art things which were (*PA*, 7-11).

Collingwood had nothing but scorn for the idea that when 'superior people' call something 'art', their usage may be relied upon as aesthetically proper. 'There is no difference in attitude between the people who go to see Gracie Fields and the people who go to see Ruth Draper except that, having been differently brought up, they are amused by different things' (*PA*, 90). But if the usage of superior people is not a criterion, what is? Despite his historical narrative of how the aesthetic usage of the word 'art' emerged, he did not clearly explain how he discriminated that usage from its fellows.

Such an explanation can be given most economically by employing a word which for some reason Collingwood eschewed, namely 'tradition'. As Mr. T. S. Eliot observed, in an essay which Collingwood had evidently studied, 'No poet, no artist of any art, has his complete meaning alone. His significance, his appreciation is the appreciation of his relation to the dead poets and artists. You cannot value him alone; you must set him, for contrast and comparison, among the dead.'[1] The artistic tradition, as Eliot conceived it, is the body of work of artists in the past, inasmuch as it has influenced and has been developed by the work of artists in the present. It is a continuous growth; for while on the one hand it incorporates new work into itself, on the other, except for the few with which the tradition originated, all the works which belong to it were themselves influenced by earlier ones. A traditional poet of our own time, according to Eliot, should have 'a feeling that the whole of the literature of Europe from Homer and within it the whole of the literature of his own country has a simultaneous existence and composes a simultaneous order';[2] and Eliot would be the last to deny that Homer himself was a traditional artist.

A tradition, whether of art or of anything else, is something objective (cf. *PA*, 88–93); its existence does not depend on whether anybody is aware of what it is. One man may engage in the same activity as another, and have been not only aware of the other's work but also influenced by it, while remaining quite unaware of the fact that he has been influenced. There is a tradition of a given productive activity if and only if there is a growing body of original work which effectively influences those who now practise that activity; that body being of such a kind that all the works that compose it serve the same generic purpose, and that each of them, except for those with which the whole body originated, is a development from one or more of the others. If there has never been such a body of work, then the given activity has never had a tradition; if there has once been, but it is no longer effective as influence, then that tradition is dead.

A single work or group of works may embody more than one tradition. A motor-car, for example, may be in both the Italian tradition of 'styling', and the Detroit tradition of engine-building. In the same way, Shakespeare's *Twelfth Night* belongs both to the tradition of art and to a rather brutal Elizabethan tradition of

---

[1] T. S. Eliot, *Selected Essays* (3rd ed., London, 1951), p. 15.
[2] Ibid., p. 14.

entertainment (*PA*, 87). It is to this that the various aesthetically improper usages of the word 'art' can be ascribed (*PA*, 69–77). The various traditions to which a given work may belong can often be discriminated only by extensive comparisons and analyses. Moreover, the same tradition may have several branches. Epic and drama have distinct origins, and may be considered to be specifically distinct traditions; and so may literature, music, and the plastic arts; yet it does not follow that they are generically distinct. Poets commonly recognize that their work may be affected by what is done in music and painting. Thus Eliot found it natural to say that changes in the artistic mind of Europe do not 'superannuate either Shakespeare, or Homer, *or the rock drawing of the Magdalenian draughtsmen*'.[1] When a tradition has branches, as the tradition of art does, it is too often overlooked that they are only branches.

If there is an aesthetically proper usage of the word 'art', as Collingwood believed, then there must be a tradition to which everything belongs that is correctly called a 'work of art'. It is the business of artists to work in that tradition, and of critics to identify it, and to distinguish what works belong to it (*PA*, 88–89). Every critic must therefore discriminate the tradition of art from those with which it might be confounded. It follows that the problem of usage is not a philosophical but a critical one. And since every philosophy of art presupposes some solution of it, every aesthetician must begin as a critic.

Criticism is notoriously a controversial activity. Although in every art some works are established as classics, critics agree neither upon the precise placing of some acknowledged classics, e.g. in literary criticism, of the work of Donne, Milton, or Shelley, nor about the reasons for those placings upon which they are agreed. Every well constructed philosophy of art, as Collingwood was careful to point out, must therefore rest on a controversial foundation. On those aestheticians who try to disguise this fact by avoiding all examples in which the usage of the word 'art' is controversial, i.e. about which critics disagree, he bestowed this sardonic reproof. 'The aesthetician who claims to know what it is that makes Shakespeare a poet is tacitly claiming to know whether Miss Stein

---

[1] Eliot, *Selected Essays*, p. 16, my italics.

is a poet, and if not, why not. The philosopher-aesthetician who sticks to classical artists is pretty sure to locate the essence of art not in what makes them artists but in what makes them classical, that is, acceptable to the academic mind' (*PA*, 4). Collingwood therefore dismissed as simply unqualified for work in aesthetics any philosopher who in 1937 was unequal 'to adjudging the merits of Mr. Joyce, Mr. Eliot, Miss Sitwell, or Miss Stein' (*PA*, 3). Today some of the names would be different, but his point remains good.

The answer to the question, 'How did Collingwood identify the usage of the word "art" that is aesthetically proper?' is 'By the methods of criticism'. It is by those methods that the tradition of art is discriminated from others. Yet although Collingwood's opinions about what good criticism is can be inferred from *The Principles of Art*, he did not begin by expounding them. To have done so would have been out of place in a work on aesthetics. *The Principles of Art* was not intended for readers who were ignorant of criticism. That is why, again and again in it, Collingwood professed to 'remind' his readers of 'facts well known to us all: such facts as this, that on occasions of a certain kind we actually do use the word art or some kindred word to designate certain kinds of thing' (*PA*, 105; cf. 5–10, 125–6). By the pronoun 'we' in such passages he did not refer to everybody into whose hands his book might fall. In a later book he advised his readers to demand of every philosopher who uses the word 'we' that he specify to what group or society he refers by it (*EM*, 340), and he took pains to identify the group or society referred to by the 'we' of *The Principles of Art*. It is composed of all those whose work in art, or whose lively and sympathetic interest in it (cf. *PA*, vi) has led them to draw the fundamental critical distinctions which he considered to be well established. Although those persons are a minority even of the educated public, only they have 'experience of the subject-matter ... sufficient to qualify [them] for reading books of this kind' (*PA*, 125).

§ 2. *Classical Errors in Defining Art*

What is the definition of 'art', when it is used aesthetically? And what are its definitions when it is used in the several ways that may be mistaken for the aesthetic one? Collingwood began by answering the latter question, because he planned to introduce his own definition of art 'properly so called', i.e. properly from the point of view of aesthetics, by exhibiting it as what results when allowance is made for the errors by which the several forms of art 'falsely so called' are mistaken for it (*PA*, 105–9). This strategy, as we shall see, was misconceived.

The classical definitions of art, which were alive in Collingwood's day and remain alive in ours, embody the more seductive of these errors. Although they were not generally accepted until the early eighteenth century, they derive from Plato's and Aristotle's analyses of particular branches of art, especially from Plato's analysis of representative poetry and Aristotle's of tragedy. As we have seen, neither Plato nor Aristotle was in a position to offer a definition of art properly so called; for they lacked a concept of it. Greek had no expression that stood for it. The modern English word 'art', when it is used aesthetically, 'carries with it all the subtle and elaborate implications of the modern European aesthetic consciousness' (*PA*, 6).

Following the Platonic pattern of definition *per genus et differentiam*, the authors of the classical definitions, here departing from Plato and Aristotle (*PA*, 48–51), took the genus of which art was a species to be representation (μίμησις). They knew perfectly well that not all representation is art, e.g. that most scarecrows are not works of art. But while the authors of the various classical definitions were at one upon the genus of art, they differed about its differentia. Although all of them found that differentia in the purpose art serves, each differed from the others in identifying that purpose. According to the most popular of all the classical definitions, it is to amuse. An artist's task is to produce representations, more or less selective, of make-believe situations; and those representations are designed to evoke in those who see or hear them certain specific emotions, which will be discharged in the act of make-believe itself, such discharge having been found to be pleasurable (*PA*, 54–55, 78–80).

Despite the persuasiveness of this definition—no less an artist than Eliot himself once remarked that if you call poetry anything but 'a superior amusement', you are likely to call it something still more false[1]—it has never been entirely respectable. The Greeks considered Homer to be the greatest of poets because they thought his work not merely amusing but beneficial; and they would not have honoured Aeschylus or Sophocles or Pheidias as they did if they had not believed their works to have been of some definite benefit to the community. On this matter Plato sided with common Greek opinion; and it is to his attempt, in the *Republic*, to define the educative value of poetry and music that the second of the two principal classical definitions of art may be traced. According to Plato, such representative art as is educationally valuable will represent types of situation which both artist and audience believe to be real, in such a way as to evoke useful emotions, which will be discharged in practical activity when a situation of the type represented occurs (*PA*, 68–69).

Croce's name for this kind of evocation was 'oratory';[2] but since oratory need not employ representation, Collingwood sought a more exact name, and he believed that one could be found in the modern anthropological theory of magic. Primitive magical rites like war-dances have the same function as the literature and music which Plato prescribed for schoolrooms in his ideal republic: to represent real situations, in the case of a war-dance, a battle, and to arouse in performers and spectators alike the emotions which are desirable in those who must confront those situations in life. Just as war-dances prepare a warrior for real battle, literature and music were to prepare schoolchildren for adult life. According to this conception, the function of art, like that of primitive magic, is 'to develop and conserve morale' (*PA*, 66–67). It may therefore be described as 'the definition of art as magic'.

Magical representations are not the only ones that arouse desirable emotions. In magic only situations which are already believed to occur are represented. But a representation may be designed to evoke emotion by changing opinions. If it does so by changing opinions about a point of fact, it is instruction; if about

---

[1] T. S. Eliot, *The Sacred Wood* (2nd ed., London 1928), pp. viii–ix.
[2] Benedetto Croce, tr. R. G. Collingwood, article 'Aesthetic' in *Encyclopaedia Britannica* (14th ed.). This article has now been displaced.

whether something is expedient, it is advertisement or propaganda; if about whether something is right, it is exhortation
(cf. *PA*, 32). While all of these have at some time been confounded
with art properly so called, the most rooted confusions are those of
art with amusement and with magic; and of these two, the amusement theory has struck deeper roots. Sometimes it is developed, as
in Aristotle's theory of tragedy, by arguing that the kind of amusement provided by art purges or refines the emotions. Sometimes it
is combined with one or more of the others: with magic, as in
Horace's remark *omne tulit punctum qui miscuit utile dulci*; or with
instruction, as in the Johnsonian formula that it is the business of
poetry to instruct while pleasing (cf. *PA*, 82).

The classical definitions of art break down when they are applied
to pure cases of amusement and magic. It is true that many works
of art are amusing representations; but the converse does not hold.
Charley's Aunt and *The Murder of Roger Ackroyd* have amused extra-
ordinarily large numbers of people; but they are not works of art
at all. Again, the ugly public monuments of Britain, of which
Collingwood took the Albert Memorial as the prototype, while
unintelligible as art, make perfect sense as magic (cf. *A*, 29–30;
PA, 73). If art be definable as amusing or magical representation,
then it must be both a necessary and a sufficient condition of something's being a work of art that it be either an amusing or a magical
representation. That neither being an amusing representation, nor
being a magical representation, is a sufficient condition is shown by
the fact that neither *The Murder of Roger Ackroyd* nor the Albert
Memorial is a work of art.

Although he might have refuted by similar arguments the definition of art as a combination of the amusing and magical, and the
less important definitions of it as instruction, propaganda, or
exhortation, or of any of them in combination, Collingwood took
a bolder course. Instead of a series of piecemeal refutations, he
attacked any and every theory of art as representation, on the
ground that, whereas representation in all its forms is a craft
($\tau \acute{\epsilon} \chi \nu \eta$), art is not a craft of any kind whatever. This argument, if
sound, would demolish all the classical definitions at a stroke (*PA*,
19–20, 42).

It rests on the Socratic analysis of a craft, which has proved to be one of the enduring achievements of philosophy (*PA*, 17). A craft is an activity in which something is produced that will discharge a pre-conceived function. If a man cannot tell you what his product is intended to do when it is made, then he is not a craftsman (*PA*, 15–16). Collingwood argued that it is not a necessary condition of a work of art that it be a craft product, or of artistic creation that it be a craft activity.

Both are easily proved by examples. 'Suppose a poet had read his verses to an audience, hoping that they would produce a certain result; and suppose the result were different; would that in itself prove the poem a bad one? It is a difficult question; some would say yes, others no. But if poetry were obviously a craft, the answer would be a prompt and unhesitating yes' (*PA*, 21). A poem is not a craft product, because it is not necessary that a good poem be a good craft product.

Nor is it necessary that a poet be a craftsman.

[S]uppose a poet were making up verses as he walked; suddenly finding a line in his head, and then another, and then dissatisfied with them and altering them until he had got them to his liking? . . . He may, no doubt, have been hoping to compose a sonnet on a particular subject specified by the editor of a review; but the point is that he may not, and that he is none the less a poet for composing without having any definite plan in his head. (*PA*, 21.)

By these and similar arguments Collingwood had no difficulty in disproving not only the classical definitions, but any definition whatever of art as a specific kind of representation or of craft. He then addressed himself to the question, 'What systematic distortion produced the classical definitions?' hoping that, by correcting that distortion, the true definition might be found (*PA*, 107). However, Professor Morris Weitz has shown that this procedure involves a questionable presupposition.[1] Collingwood at no point raised the question whether the usage of the term 'art' that is relevant to aesthetics permits 'art' to be defined at all.

In a well-known passage, Wittgenstein, after pointing out that

[1] Morris Weitz in *Journal of Aesthetics and Art Criticism*, xv (1956), pp. 27–35, reprinted Morris Weitz (ed.), *Problems in Aesthetics* (New York, 1959), pp. 145–56.

many philosophers take it for granted that the word 'game' stands for something definable that is common to all games, proffered this advice. 'Don't say: "There *must* be something common, or they would not be called 'games' "—but *look and see* whether there is anything common to all.'[1] Various activities might be classified as games, not because they share a definable set of common properties, but because they belong as it were to a family: there might be a number of family properties ('family likenesses'), one or more of which was possessed by each member of the family, but none by all. There is therefore no *a priori* reason why art properly so called should be definable. There may be no necessary and sufficient conditions of a thing's being a work of art. Like the word 'game', the word 'art' may be used for a group of things related by family likenesses.

However, Weitz has not been content with that. He has also tried to show that no term which is open in texture, i.e. for which it is impossible to anticipate all the kinds of thing to which it might be correctly applied, can be defined. Since not only the term 'art', but virtually all terms outside logic and mathematics are open in texture, it would follow that, outside the exact sciences, no term of philosophical or scientific interest would be definable. Fortunately this unpalatable conclusion rests on a dubious premiss. It is not at all evident that no term which is open in texture is definable; all that seems to be true is that if what is to be defined is open in texture, the definition must also be open in texture. A term which is open in texture is not necessarily obscure. There is nothing obscure about the medieval definition of 'man' as 'rational animal', even though both 'rational' and 'animal' are open in texture. Weitz's argument shows that open concepts cannot be defined as though they were closed concepts, but not that they cannot be defined at all. As we shall see, when Collingwood came to define art properly so called, he took care that his definition should be as open as what was to be defined.

Whether art properly so called is definable or not cannot be settled *a priori*. You must look at the aesthetic usage of the word 'art', and see. The only acceptable proof that 'art' is definable is to produce a definition of it that withstands all criticism.

[1] Wittgenstein, *Philosophical Investigations*, i, §§ 65-75.

§ 3. *The Problem of Definition: Collingwood's Solution*

Since no critical remark is more commonplace than that works of art express emotion, Collingwood inquired whether that might be the definition that he sought (*PA*, 109). Difficult questions at once confronted him. What is it to express emotion? How does expressing it differ from evoking it? And, although it has been shown that the end of art is not necessarily preconceived, must not expression be preconceived and the means of accomplishing it planned?

Before attempting to answer these questions, Collingwood had first to clarify the concept of emotion. In *The New Leviathan*, it will be remembered, he was to classify the principal functions of consciousness as appetite, passion, desire, self-liberation, choice, and reason, with their subordinate species. The remarkable thing about this list is that it does not include emotion. That was not an oversight. Collingwood did not think that emotion was a separate function of consciousness, but an inseparable element in every act of consciousness and every preconscious feeling. Every feeling and every act of consciousness carries its own emotional charge.[1] The expression 'emotional charge' itself is a figure of speech derived from electricity. Just as an electrical charge is either positive or negative, so an emotional charge is either one of attraction or repulsion (*NL*, 4. 1).

The bearer of an emotional charge is always an object of feeling or consciousness, never the feeling or act of consciousness in which it is an element. This is a straightforward deduction from the Principle of Order. A child before it has reached the stage even of first-order consciousness may be distressed when he feels hungry; his distress, however, will not be a charge which his feeling of hunger bears, but an element within that feeling itself. A feeling, like an act of consciousness, only bears an emotional charge when it is made the object of a higher-order act of consciousness. Furthermore, an emotional charge is not a feeling which accompanies acts of consciousness or other feelings. Thus the emotional charge upon an object of feeling is not a separate feeling, but an inseparable element in the feeling upon the object of which it is a charge (cf.

[1] *NL*., 4. 1–4. 11, 7. 4; cf. 10. 43–10. 44, 11. 16–11. 18, 13. 3–13. 31.

NL, 4. 11). Nor is the emotional charge upon the object of an act of consciousness necessarily a feeling: it must be of the same order as the object which bears it. In shame, for example, a man is aware of himself as afraid, and is repelled by his own fear (*NL*, 10. 49). This repulsion is a charge borne by the passion of fear which is the object of his awareness, and is of the same order as that object. It may indeed be accompanied by organic feelings, e.g. those that go with blushing, or with contractions of the stomach; however, these are not the emotion of shame, but primitive survivals in that emotion. The James–Lange theory, which reduced shame to such manifestations as blushing, was a straightforward blunder (*PA*, 232). An emotion is not a 'distinct experience' accompanying feelings and acts of consciousness, as the smell of food may accompany the note of a bell: it is always a charge upon the object of some activity of feeling or consciousness, and is inconceivable without the object of that activity (cf. *PA*, 161, 231–3, 266).

Although *The Principles of Art* and *The New Leviathan* are in agreement on these matters, Collingwood's classification of emotions in *The Principles of Art* rested on an analysis of certain of the functions of consciousness which he corrected in the later book. According to *The Principles of Art*, emotions are of three kinds: 'psychical emotions', which are charges upon sensations, and so preconscious (*PA*, 230); 'emotions of consciousness', which are charges upon acts involving consciousness of self (*PA*, 231); and intellectual emotions, which are charges upon acts of thought (*PA*, 266–7). The principal defects of this classification are that it neither allows for those acts of consciousness, e.g. appetites, which do not involve self-consciousness; nor discriminates either the various orders of self-consciousness, e.g. desire from choice, or the various orders of thought, e.g. simple conceptual thinking from theoretical reason. These defects, which led Collingwood into such errors as classifying hatred, love, anger, and shame as emotions of the same kind (cf. *PA*, 231), may be corrected by reference to *The New Leviathan*.[1]

We may now turn to the question, What is expression? An

[1] On acts of consciousness which do not involve self-consciousness, *NL*, 7. 5; on the various orders of consciousness and thought see above, Chs. II–IV, the results of which are summarized at Ch. IV, § 6; on hunger, love, fear, shame, and anger, *NL*, 8. 15–8. 19, 10. 18–10. 2, 10. 3, 10. 43–10. 51.

analysis of expression, like an analysis of art itself, must respect actual usage. Collingwood therefore began by succinctly expounding 'what it is that people are saying' when they use the phrase *express* emotion (*PA*, 109):

When a man is said to express emotion, what is being said about him comes to this. At first, he is conscious of having an emotion, but not conscious of what this emotion is. All he is conscious of is a perturbation or excitement, which he feels going on within him, but of whose nature he is ignorant. While in this state, all he can say about his emotion is: 'I feel . . . I don't know what I feel'. From this helpless and oppressed condition he extricates himself by doing something which we call expressing himself. This is an activity which has something to do with the thing we call language: he expresses himself by speaking. It has also something to do with consciousness: the emotion expressed is an emotion of whose nature the person who feels it is no longer unconscious. It has also something to do with the way in which he feels the emotion. As unexpressed, he feels it in what we have called a helpless and oppressed way; as expressed, he feels it in a way from which this sense of oppression has vanished. (*PA*, 109–10.)

This passage is not Collingwood's philosophical analysis of emotion, but only a preliminary to it. Even after a good deal of discussion of it, he warned his readers that 'we do not [yet] know what is the nature of the connexion between [imagination and emotion] described by saying that imagination expresses emotion' (*PA*, 152). To gain that knowledge, the analytical work of either Book II of *The Principles of Art*, or Part I of *The New Leviathan*, must be mastered.

Yet even his preliminary analysis suffices to dispose of one objection. Collingwood is often alleged to have defined a work of art as something produced by means of a particular psychological process. Such a definition would, of course, be eccentric; for it is plainly impossible to ascertain through what psychological processes the vast majority of artists passed when they created their works. Now the passage quoted shows that he did not conceive of expression as a psychological process. It is true that he called it an 'activity'; but not all activities are processes. In the whole passage, expression is described not as a process, but as an achievement; as though it were like, not racking your brains or running a race, but solving a problem or winning a race. An analysis of an achievement must specify the task in the performance of which that achievement consists. Accordingly, Collingwood specified the task performed by a man who expresses an emotion as that of raising his emotion from 'unconsciousness' to consciousness, and, by so doing, extricating himself from an oppressive perturbation. What he did not do was to specify the process by which this task is accomplished, beyond saying that 'it has something to do with . . . language'.

In our examination of Collingwood's philosophy of mind in previous chapters, we have largely anticipated his final philosophical analyses of expression and of the linguistic acts by which it is brought about. Since every emotion is an element in a feeling or an act of consciousness, the acts by which those feelings or acts of consciousness are raised to consciousness will be acts of expression. By the Principle of Order, no feeling or act of consciousness *per se* involves consciousness of itself. Every mental act remains preconscious, although not strictly speaking 'unconscious', until it is made the object of another act (*PA*, 206–12; *NL*, 5. 92). You cannot become conscious of anything by an inner sense, e.g. introspection, because no sensation can raise anything to consciousness (*PA*, 221). All consciousness is linguistic, although not all language is conventional, or even verbal (*PA*, 235–41; *NL*, 6. 17). Linguistic expression, in this wider sense, is what critics and aestheticians in the nineteenth century called 'imagination'; but they did not perceive that imagination has to be linguistic, because they wrongly believed that all language was conventional (*PA*, 226–7).

One sign that an emotion has been expressed is that it is no longer an obscure perturbation but something lucid: 'a person who expresses something thereby . . . enables others to become conscious of it in himself and in them'. Inasmuch as acting is an art, 'it is not her ability to weep real tears that would mark out a good actress; it is her ability to make it clear to herself and her audience what the tears are about' (*PA*, 122). The transition from the oppression of preconscious emotion to the lucidity of consciousness 'is accompanied by a new feeling of alleviation . . ., the sense that this oppression is removed'. If you will, you may call this feeling a specific 'aesthetic emotion', provided that you remember that it is not an emotion 'having the peculiarity that when it comes to be expressed it is expressed artistically', but 'an emotional colouring which attends the expression of any emotion whatever' (*PA*, 117).

An expressive utterance does not necessarily, or perhaps even often, evoke the emotions it expresses. It will do so only if its audience unwittingly shares them. If a man is enraged with you, and expresses his rage in an eloquent curse, he will certainly make you conscious of the rage in him, but he is most unlikely to evoke that same emotion in you. The only effect that an expressive utterance necessarily produces on a hearer who understands it is that of grasping how the man who made it felt; however, to grasp an emotion somebody else feels is not the same as sharing it.

Even less is expressing an emotion the same as deliberately evoking it. A man who sets out to evoke a certain emotion in an audience, e.g. an entertainer who sets out to evoke certain emotions about a make-believe situation, must begin by forming concepts of the emotions he plans to evoke, i.e. must describe them to himself. But he could not describe those emotions unless he were already familiar with expressions of them.

Collingwood himself distinguished description from expression by saying that description generalizes whereas expression individualizes (*PA*, 112). He did not mean by this to deny that expressive utterances may contain universal or conceptual terms. His theory of language implied that, except for the primitive ejaculations of first-order consciousness, all language is conceptual. Rather, he meant that in expressing an emotion you are concerned simply with it; you do not classify it along with other actual or possible emotions. There is therefore a distinction between becoming conscious of an individual emotion, and becoming conscious of what that emotion is, although in his preliminary analysis Collingwood did not draw it (cf. *PA*, 109).

When you express an emotion, and so become conscious of it, you become conscious of it as the emotional charge upon an object of consciousness; but when you describe it, you make your original expressive act into the object of a further act, and you classify it with other acts that contain a similar emotional charge. When

Macbeth expressed his emotions about a terrified servant, none of the words Shakespeare put into his mouth—

> The divell damn thee blacke, thou cream-faced Loone:
> Where got'st thou that goose-looke—

described Macbeth's emotions. Some of them, it is true, were general descriptive terms describing how the servant looked; but Macbeth's emotion, which was a charge upon how his servant appeared to him, was expressed entirely through what Macbeth said to and about that servant. Had Shakespeare wished to represent Macbeth as describing his emotion, he would not have given him those words. He would have shown him speaking, not about his servant, but about himself. His rage with his servant would then have been, not an emotional charge upon an object of consciousness, but itself an object of consciousness; and the emotional charge upon this higher-order object of consciousness could not possibly have been rage at the servant, or indeed any emotion whatever about him. It must have been an emotion about Macbeth himself, and we may hope that it would have been shame.

The distinction between expression and description explains a commonplace of criticism, that if you want to express an emotion, you must not apply epithets to it. If Macbeth had described his rage to his servant, e.g. by saying, self-approvingly or otherwise, 'I am in a towering rage with you', his language would have been frigid, and quite inexpressive of it; for the emotion expressed by such a description would not be his rage itself, but whatever emotion he had on contemplating it, whether self-approval or shame. That is why 'a genuine poet, in his moments of genuine poetry, never mentions by name the emotions he is expressing' (*PA*, 112).

Our example makes necessary a further distinction, which Collingwood did not draw, although he tacitly observed it (e.g. *PA*, 124, 294–5). While the emotion Macbeth expressed was rage, the emotion Shakespeare expressed was not. By presenting Macbeth's rage, Shakespeare exhibited him as in decline, unable to control himself. Most imaginative literature involves a double act of expression: the artist expresses his emotions by presenting an action in which his characters express theirs. Where there is danger of confusion, it is advisable to reserve the unqualified term 'expression' for the expression of the artist's emotions, and to employ the qualified term 'dramatic expression' for his presentation of dramatic characters as expressing theirs. In dramatic expression, the dramatic characters may or may not be lifelike, and their emotions may or may not be shared by the artist. All that is necessary is that they and their emotions be dramatically coherent. However, since an emotion is significant in proportion as is the object on which it is a charge, the emotions dramatically expressed in great art must be of great significance and usually of great power; for the object of the artist's emotion is the interaction of the characters whose emotions he dramatically expresses (*PA*, 293–4, 331–4).

We are now in a position to understand Collingwood's definition of art: 'The aesthetic experience, or artistic activity, is the experience of expressing one's emotions; and that which expresses them is the total imaginative activity called indifferently language or art. This is art proper' (*PA*, 275). By distinguishing expression from both evocation and description, Collingwood was able to use this definition to distinguish the nature of art from the nature of craft. A craftsman preconceives his product. That is why those who set out to evoke emotions, whether for the sake of amusement or of their practical utility, are craftsmen: they specify in advance what emotions they plan to evoke, and apply their skill to evoke them. But a man who sets out to express his emotions cannot specify in advance what they are. When he begins he is conscious that he has *some emotion or other*, but he is not conscious of *it*. His activity as an artist is exploratory. Not until he has expressed what he feels is he fully aware of it. That is why expression is fitly described as creative: it brings into consciousness what was preconscious. It is also why every genuine work of art is new and fresh.

While the nature of art is distinct from the nature of craft, and while some acts of creation may contain no element of craft whatever (cf. *PA*, 21), Collingwood did not deny that the vast majority of works of art are also works of craft. Many of them are amusing or magical as well as aesthetic (*PA*, 77, 87). And, aside altogether from works of art that are amusing or magical, most works of art could only have been created by somebody who had mastered one or more crafts. A painter must know the craft of painting, a sculptor of moulding or carving, a poet of versifying. Mastery of those crafts is not the same thing as being an artist, or every art-school prize-winner would be a painter, and every clever versifier a poet. Yet competence in the relevant crafts is necessary to anybody who would work in a given branch of art.

Collingwood went out of his way to make this clear.

> [A] writer on art . . . does well to insist on what every artist knows, but most amateurs do not: the vast amount of intelligent and purpose-ful labour, the painful and conscientious self-discipline, that has gone to the making of a man who can write a line as Pope writes it, or knock a single chip off a single stone like Michelangelo. It is no less true, and no less important, that the skill here displayed . . . though a necessary condition of the best art, is not by itself sufficient to produce it. (*PA*, 26–27.)

And that is not all. Even though mastery of a craft is necessary to the best art, an artist does not employ it as a craftsman does, to construct 'appropriate means to a preconceived end' (*PA*, 29). Ben Jonson's *Queene and Huntresse, chaste, and faire* is an extra-ordinarily skilful poem, 'and a critic might, not unfruitfully, display this skill by analysing the intricate and ingenious patterns of rhythm and rhyme, alliteration, assonance, and dissonance, which the poem contains' (*PA*, 27). Yet Jonson did not apply his know-ledge of these things, as a joiner applies his knowledge of materials and the use of tools. He did not begin with certain words, and arrange them according to the lore of a craft. 'The words which occur in the poem were never before his mind as a whole in an order different from that of the poem' (*PA*, 23); and arriving at them was the very same thing as creating 'his imaginative vision of the goddess and her attendants' (*PA*, 27).

Collingwood's doctrine that emotions are expressed by finding utterances for the objects of feeling or consciousness on which they are charges is exposed to a simple objection which he overlooked. It is this. The same object of consciousness seems to have quite different emotional charges for different people; and even when the nature of the charge is the same, it may vary in intensity from one person to another. Now while it is certain that Collingwood would have rejected this objection as false, it is less clear what reasons he would have given for doing so. Inasmuch as two men have significantly different emotions towards an object of consciousness, he would have contended that they must be aware of it as different; and inasmuch as they have widely different emotions towards an object of feeling, that they must feel it as different. I think he might have conceded the possibility of minor differences of emotion towards felt objects. Some people might be attracted to sweet-tasting foods, and others repelled by them, even though they tasted them as the same. But he would certainly have denied that sane persons could either be attracted to the feelings that go with hunger or loneliness, or repelled by those that go with eating when you are hungry, or finding a friend when you are lonely.

To the obvious objection that a man who is acquainted with exactly the same women as another man does not necessarily wish to marry the same one, he rejoined that, just as a man probably never feels the same emotion twice, so the same object will appear different to him on any two occasions. 'The anger which I feel here and now, with a certain person, for a certain cause, is no doubt an instance of anger . . .; but it is much more than mere anger: it is a peculiar anger, not quite like any anger that I ever felt before, and probably not quite like any anger I shall ever feel again' (*PA*, 112–13). It is peculiar because I have never before thought of that person or that cause exactly what I now think, and probably I never shall again. A man who hopes to marry a woman not only feels towards her different emotions from those felt by a man who does not, he has a different conception of her.

The difficulty with this rejoinder is that, even if it is true, it does not seem to be necessarily true. A philosophical statement about the relation between consciousness and emotion ought not to be merely an empirical truth, if for no other reason than that empirical generalizations hazarded by a philosopher in his study cannot possibly arise from proper empirical investigation. Collingwood gave only one hint of the way in which he thought his position might be defended *a priori*. It was this. The possibility of one man's understanding another's expressions of emotion depends on whether his experience

has been such as to equip him for it. . . . . [N]o idea can be formed as such in consciousness except by a mind whose sensuous-emotional experience contains the corresponding impression. . . . . If words, however eloquent and well chosen, are addressed to a hearer in whose mind there is no impression corresponding to the idea they are meant to convey, he will either treat them as nonsense, or will attribute to them . . . a meaning derived from his own experience and forced upon them in spite of an obvious misfit. (*PA*, 251.)

If men understand each other well enough to go on talking, i.e. without one having to treat what another says as nonsense, or to attribute to it a meaning that is an evident misfit, then their 'sensuous-emotional experience', and the structure of consciousness erected on it, must be of the same nature, however different in detail. However, Collingwood did not work this idea out.

One mistake in *The Principles of Art* remains to be corrected by reference to *The New Leviathan*. In *The Principles of Art*, having distinguished three kinds of emotion, psychical emotions, emotions of consciousness, and intellectual emotions, Collingwood went on to distinguish two kinds of expression, psychical and imaginative. Psychical expressions are the involuntary cries and gestures which naturally accompany preconscious feeling (*PA*, 229–33). Psychical or preconscious expression is not, strictly speaking, expression at all: it is rather a symptom or betrayal of feeling than an expression of it; for it lacks the lucidity of expression proper (*PA*, 121). Imaginative expression is what Collingwood elsewhere called simply expression (*PA*, 234–8).

In *The Principles of Art* Collingwood argued that, since every act of imaginative expression brings into existence an act of consciousness, imaginative expression must transform feelings into something else, viz. ideas (*PA*, 213); and further, that your acts of imaginative expression, being voluntary, must be acts of which you are conscious as your own (*PA*, 235). He then inferred that 'psychical expression is the only expression of which psychical emotions are capable', and that the only emotions that are capable of imaginative or artistic expression are emotions of consciousness, i.e. emotions involving consciousness of self (*PA*, 231–2). By the Law of Primitive Survivals enunciated in *The New Leviathan*, neither of these conclusions was legitimate (cf. *NL*, 9. 51). While it is true that nobody can imaginatively express his psychical or preconscious emotions except by raising the sensa on which they are charges to objects of consciousness, the nature of a thing is not changed by making it an object of consciousness. Moreover, not all acts of consciousness involve self-consciousness. The appetites of hunger and love do not involve self-consciousness, yet both are functions of consciousness (*NL*, 8. 14; cf. *PA*, 231).

Collingwood failed to perceive this when he wrote *The Principles of Art* because he had not then fully grasped the Principle of Order. An emotion expressed, like the object on which it is a charge, is necessarily of a lower order than the act of consciousness by which it is expressed. Every act of imaginative expression is conscious; but it does not follow that its object is an act of consciousness.

Perhaps Collingwood was led to acknowledge this in *The New Leviathan* by some of his own examples in *The Principles of Art*. There he had described the emotions expressed by Renaissance painters, when looked at as Mr. Berenson has taught us, not as emotions of consciousness, but as emotional charges on feelings, especially the tactile and kinaesthetic feelings that go with bodily exertion (*PA*, 146–7). In his description of Cézanne's work, he had been even more explicit. 'His still-life studies, which enshrine the essence of his genius, are like groups of things that have been groped over with the hands; he uses colour not to reproduce what he sees in looking at them but to express almost in a kind of algebraic notation what in this groping he has felt.' And again: 'A bridge is no longer a pattern of colour, as it is for Cotman; . . . it is a perplexing mixture of projections and recessions, over and round which we find ourselves feeling our way as one can imagine an infant feeling its way, when it has barely begun to crawl, among the nursery furniture' (*PA*, 144).

§ 4. *The Work of Art and its Audience*

Collingwood defined art by defining the artist's act of creation. His very terminology revealed the gulf between his point of departure and that of academic aesthetics today. The phrase 'the aesthetic experience' is now used for the experience of the audience or spectators of a work of art; what Collingwood meant by it was the experience of a creative artist (*PA*, 275). It does not follow, as some critics have contended, that his definition of art must inevitably entail false or inadequate conclusions either about the nature of works of art, or about the relation of their audiences or spectators to them. However, under the influence of Croce,[1] Collingwood did make a mistake about the nature of a work of art which he never retracted, although he provided most of what was needed to correct it. In itself of minor importance, it has brought upon him a good deal of derision, and is much better known than the sounder parts of his theory of art.

The root of his mistake was a simple ambiguity. He used the verb 'to imagine' to mean both the act of forming images and the act of raising something preconscious into consciousness. In the first sense, only an 'image' existing solely in somebody's head can be described as 'imaginary'. 'A bridge which "exists only in the engineer's head" we . . . call an imaginary bridge; one which "exists in the real world" we call a real bridge' (*PA*, 131). *A fortiori*, the act of imagining in this sense is done wholly in the head. In the second sense, however, the act of imagining something is simply the linguistic act of bringing it to consciousness. Neither the object brought to consciousness, nor the linguistic utterance by which it is brought, need be 'in the head'. Utterances made in the head are in no way more privileged than utterances made aloud. A word uttered in your head, no less than a word uttered aloud, acquires its meaning by being used in a certain way: either as a deliberate repetition or imitation of some preconscious expression, or as an artificial symbol used according to a certain training or a certain set of rules.

On the relation of art to imagination Collingwood began by establishing two points: first, that a work of art need not exist anywhere but in its author's head; and, secondly, that all works of art are imaginary creations in the second of the above senses of 'imagin-

---

[1] Benedetto Croce, tr. Douglas Ainslie, *Aesthetic* (London, 1922), pp. 111–14, 118–20.

ary', i.e. that they are, in the wide sense, linguistic utterances. That he was right in his first point is particularly obvious in poetry and music. Both Milton and Mozart are recorded to have composed in their heads, and to have dictated or written down their compositions some time after their creative work was finished. Nor is there any reason of principle why this should not happen in the plastic arts. Michelangelo may have conceived his David down to the last detail before attacking the marble as though he saw his statue within it. The familiar objection that an artist may be able to imagine but not to execute what he imagines was refuted once for all by Croce: if you can imagine as magnificently as Raphael, only blindness or paralysis can prevent you from painting as he did. Genuine imagination is in terms of the medium employed, whether words or sounds, paint or stone; and it is exact to the last detail. Accordingly, nobody who really does accomplish a great feat of imagination will have any difficulty in crossing 'the *Pons Asinorum* of expression'[1] (*PA*, 301–8). The second of Collingwood's points was a straightforward corollary of his definition of art. Since, according to that definition, aesthetic creation is linguistic, in the wide sense, it follows that every work of art is a linguistic, i.e. an imaginative creation.

Collingwood combined these two points in a muddled argument. The business of 'an artist proper', he wrote, is

not to produce an emotional effect in an audience, but, for example, to make a tune. This tune is already complete and perfect when it exists merely as a tune in his head, that is, an imaginary tune. Next, he may arrange for the tune to be played before an audience. Now there comes into existence a real tune, a collection of noises. But which of these two things is the work of art? Which of them is the music? The answer is implied in what we have already said: the music, the work of art, is not the collection of noises, it is the tune in the composer's head. The noises made by the performers, and heard by the audience, are not the music at all; they are only means by which the audience, if they listen intelligently . . ., can reconstruct for themselves the imaginary tune that existed in the composer's head. (*PA*, 139.)

[1] Croce, *Aesthetic*, p. 11.

This argument appears to be that because of 'what we have already said', namely, that the noises made by the performers are only the means by which the audience grasps the composer's imaginary, i.e. expressive or linguistic creation, it therefore follows that the musical composition itself, the work of art, exists only in the heads of the composer and the audience. But the fact that the audience must try to reconstruct what the composer imaginatively expressed entails neither that they must form in their heads an auditory image distinct from the noises made by the performers, nor even that the composer had auditory images as he composed, distinct from those which he struck on his pianoforte. A work of art is necessarily imaginary in the sense of being an imaginary or linguistic creation; but it need not be imaginary in the sense of existing merely in people's heads. A composer may create a sonata at the keyboard, playing every note as he imagines: in such a case there would never be a time when the sonata or any part of it existed 'complete and perfect . . . merely as a tune in the composer's head'.[1]

In Book III of *The Principles of Art* Collingwood quietly relinquished the sense of 'imaginary' in which an imaginary object exists only in the head, and denied that artists form complete images of their works in their heads, which they then 'externalize'. 'There is no question', he wrote, this time having painters rather than composers in mind, 'of "externalizing" an inward experience which is complete in itself and by itself. There are two experiences, an inward or imaginative one called seeing and an outward or bodily one called painting, which in the painter's life are inseparable, and form one single indivisible experience, an experience which may be described as painting imaginatively' (*PA*, 304–5). In this passage Collingwood conceded that a work of art is not imaginary in the sense that it is an image in the artist's head, but only in the sense that it is expressive or linguistic. That Milton or Mozart might have kept in their heads works which they did not communicate to the public has no aesthetic significance whatever. A man who could form an auditory image of a piece of music identical at every

---

[1] Unfortunately, Collingwood did not consistently use 'imaginary' for 'existing only in somebody's head' (cf. *PA*, 131) and 'imaginative' for 'expressive or linguistic' (cf. *PA*, 304–5). If he had, he could not but have perceived that imaginative creations are not necessarily imaginary.

point with what the composer wanted his audience to hear, or an exact visual image of what a painter wanted him to see, would not thereby 'hear' the music or 'see' the painting imaginatively. A work of art is neither a physical object as such, nor an image of that object in the artist's head, but either of these *as a vehicle of imaginative expression.*

Some philosophers and critics would reject this conclusion on the ground that it commits an ill-defined fault often called 'the intentional fallacy'. Professors Wimsatt and Beardsley, for example, have contended that the imaginative experience of an artist is simply not 'available' to his critics, and that it would not help them if it were.[1] Criticism, they protest, ought to be objective. It must be exercised on an 'available' object, and it must refer only to the public and verifiable characteristics of that object. Their protest is not unjustified. Some critics have indeed introduced into their criticism irrelevant references to artists' states of mind. What effects an artist intended to produce are irrelevant both to the question whether he has succeeded in creating a work of art, and to the question whether his work of art, if it be one, is good or bad.

This, however, is a consequence of Collingwood's view as much as of Wimsatt's and Beardsley's. Collingwood insisted that the fact that a medieval religious artist set out simply to edify those who saw his carvings does not entail that his works were not art, or not great art (*PA*, 76–77). When a man creates a work of art, whether or not he consciously intends to, he does not create it by accident. If he makes a truly expressive utterance of any kind, then his utterance means what he meant in making it. When a medieval sculptor gives his figures features that dramatically express elation or anguish, then they express what he meant them to express, even if the only intention of which he was conscious was to illustrate the apocalyptic story of the joys of the blessed and the punishments of the damned. Not all such illustrations are dramatically expressive; and none are so by accident.

It might be objected that a sculptor who carves a figure that expresses elation or anguish need not himself be elated or anguished.

[1] W. K. Wimsatt, Jr., and M. C. Beardsley, *The Verbal Icon* (New York: Noonday Press, 1958), p. 3.

He may be quite cheerful as he imagines the torments of the damned. Wimsatt and Beardsley have made the same point. '[E]ven a short lyric poem is dramatic. . . . We ought to impute the thoughts and attitudes of the poem immediately to the dramatic *speaker*, and if to the author at all, only by an act of biographical inference.'[1] But once again the objection turns out to be a facet of Collingwood's theory itself. As we have seen, he held that what the sculptor expresses in creating a figure that dramatically expresses elation is not elation, but his emotion on contemplating elation. In the simple examples I have employed, it will be an individualized and concrete form of what is vaguely expressed by, 'How glorious to be that soul in bliss!' and 'How horrible to be that soul in hell!' While the emotions dramatically expressed in literature are more varied, and belong to higher orders of consciousness, than those dramatically expressed in either the plastic arts or instrumental music, the same point holds: the emotions expressed by the artist are emotions about what he dramatically presents. Collingwood could consistently maintain that in his *Sonnets* Shakespeare expressed his emotions, while denying that those emotions necessarily, or even often, coincided with those of his various dramatic speakers.

The doctrine that the imaginative experience of the artist is not available to us presupposes a theory of mind wholly opposed to Collingwood's, according to which inference from what a man's utterances express is a less reliable guide to what is in his mind than his own non-inferential convictions. In some cases, no doubt it is. Most people, if put to it, can tell a lie that will deceive most hearers for some time; yet if they did, they would know themselves, without drawing any inferences at all that they were lying. In other cases, however, it is not so. Many unscrupulous people contrive to hide from themselves the point of some of their actions. When they do, inference from their acts themselves would be a more reliable guide to what was in their minds than their own non-inferential convictions.

Collingwood, as we shall see, considered that it was difficult to fake any expression of emotion that would pass muster with a competent critic, and virtually impossible to fake a very complex or

ARTIST'S MIND

---

[1] Wimsatt and Beardsley, op. cit., p. 5.

intense one that would do so. He therefore considered that a major work of art was much more reliable evidence of the artist's emotions than any non-inferential convictions he might have. Blake's celebrated remark that Milton was of the devil's party without knowing it, whether it is true or false, rests on a profound truth about art. The best evidence of what Milton's emotions were towards the Satan of *Paradise Lost* is *Paradise Lost* itself; what Milton may have written in his diary, if he kept one, or in *De Doctrina Christiana*, is far less reliable.

Nobody has absolute assurance that he knows either his own mind or those of others. If his own consciousness is corrupt, he will falsify his own thoughts and emotions even to himself (*PA*, 217–20). And even if he knows his own mind, he may fail to understand the expressive utterances of others. Yet Collingwood held that he has ample means of doing so. Each man may come to understand his neighbours' utterances by taking them exactly as if they were his own, and asking himself, 'If I had done that, what would I have meant?' '[H]e speaks to himself with the words that he hears addressed to him, and thus constructs in himself the idea which those words express' (*PA*, 250). Absolute assurance that one man understands another's expressive acts is unnecessary. There is 'empirical and relative assurance, becoming stronger as conversation proceeds, and based on the fact that neither party seems to the other to be talking nonsense. The question whether they understand each other *solvitur interloquendo*. If they understand each other well enough to go on talking, they understand each other as well as they need . . .' (*PA*, 251).

No critic can know that the imaginative experience he obtains from a work of art is identical with that of its creator. The greater the artist, the greater the difference is likely to be. But just as a better understanding of another man's mind can be reached by continuing the conversation, so can a better understanding of an artist's mind. If, as he continues to study an artist's work, a critic finds it to be more and more intelligible to him, then he has the best of reasons for believing his grasp of that artist's imaginative experience to be becoming more complete and perfect (cf. *PA*, 309).

§ 5. The Verification of Collingwood's Definition: Art and Criticism

We have now surveyed Collingwood's solution of the problem of definition. Since that problem was not to provide a stipulative definition of the word 'art', but to define its actual usage in the modern European critical tradition, any proposed solution must be either true or false. Is Collingwood's solution true? Since it was impossible for him, in *The Principles of Art* itself, to state and defend his own solution of the problem of usage, Collingwood himself presumably conceived his solution of the problem of definition as a proposal submitted to those of his readers who had a sufficient grasp of the critical tradition: *This is so, is it not?* Every reader who considers himself qualified should examine his own critical judgements, and such judgements of others as he considers to be relevant, and ask himself whether Collingwood's definition is a true statement of what is at stake in them. The truth or falsity of this critical judgement or that is beside the point. Critics may very well disagree about the merits of Shakespeare's *Measure for Measure*, while implicitly agreeing about what art is: they agree about what critics should seek, but not about whether it is found in Shakespeare's play. If, after such an examination, a reader should answer that Collingwood's definition is not true of what is at stake in some relevant critical judgement, then he should ask himself whether that judgement has some flaw; and if so, whether, when amended, it would be consistent with Collingwood's definition. If not, then he is obliged to reject that definition. If, on the other hand, all relevant critical judgements are consistent with Collingwood's definition, he is obliged to accept it.

That you or I should be obliged to reject Collingwood's definition would not entail that it is false; for the critical judgements we consider relevant may not in fact belong to the tradition of art. As I have argued, a tradition may exist even though nobody is aware of it; and it may persist, even after people have become aware of it, but misconceived its nature. Art flourished in ancient Athens, even though the ancient Athenians had no concept of art; and the tradition of poetry persisted in eighteenth-century England, in spite of

Augustan misconceptions of what poetry is. If most of those who understood his definition had rejected it, Collingwood could have defended it in two ways: one would have been to try to show that they were mistaken in thinking it to conflict with the critical judgements they considered relevant; and another would have been to dispute the relevancy of the critical judgements on which they relied.

It is, at the present time, much more urgent to establish what sort of thing Collingwood's definition of art is, and what sort of considerations are to the point in deciding whether it is true, than to try to prove or disprove it; but, since I do consider it to be substantially true, I shall outline what I think Collingwood might have replied to some familiar objections. What I offer will be no more than an outline; for a complete defence would occupy many times the space at my disposal.

Beyond cavil, there is a critical tradition in literature of which Collingwood's definition is roughly true. In his early *Outlines of a Philosophy of Art* he had professed his adherence to the conception of art 'already familiar from the works of Coleridge, Croce,[1] and many others' (p. 3), and in his later work he remained true to it.

In *The Principles of Art* he recognized T. S. Eliot's *The Waste Land* as 'the one great English poem of this century' (*PA*, 295). Of modern poets other than Eliot, he saluted only W. B. Yeats as 'great', and that was in view of what he wrote after 'the call of practical life' had forced him from 'the sham world of his youthful Celtic twilight . . . into the clear air of real Celtic life' (*PA*, 120). The Marxist poets then in fashion among advanced critics he contemptuously dismissed, without naming them, as 'little neo-Kiplings who think of poetry as an incitement to political virtue' (*PA*, 335). The critical position from which Collingwood made these judgements plainly owed much to Eliot's critical essays, which he correctly interpreted as falling within the tradition of Coleridge and Croce.[2] Many critics, their attention distracted by Eliot's

---

[1] See Appendix III (iv).

[2] Discerning critics of Eliot, both friendly and hostile, have recognized that his criticism is in the romantic tradition. Cf. Yvor Winters, *In Defense of Reason* (Denver, no date), pp. 460–74; Eliseo Vivas, *Creation and Discovery* (New York, 1955), p. 176; Frank Kermode, *The Romantic Image* (London, 1957), pp. vii, 44–48. Martin Steinmann

avowed classicism, and by his objections to certain of Coleridge's and even more of Matthew Arnold's critical judgements, have overlooked his agreement with them in principle. For Eliot, as for Coleridge, the cardinal question is whether a poem criticized presents an imaginative vision that genuinely expresses emotion. Sometimes critics in the tradition of Coleridge and Croce will speak only of imaginative vision, and sometimes only of the expression of emotion; but close inspection will usually show that they regard the two as inseparable. For Collingwood, their inseparability was a theoretical necessity, since he held that an emotion can only be expressed through imaginative vision, by raising to consciousness the object upon which it is a 'charge'.

It is true that there are doctrines in the critical writings of Yeats and some of his symbolist and romantic predecessors which Collingwood flatly contradicted. One of them is the notion that the expressive, imaginative language of art is in opposition to the theoretical language of science, which is often invoked in support of the absurd doctrine that a work of art must have no reference to the world. The realm of art, it is claimed, is imaginary; and the imaginary world of art is more 'real' than the sensory world of experimental science. Although in several of his finest poems, especially *Sailing to Byzantium* and *Byzantium*, Yeats expressed something of how a man who holds such an aesthetic theory feels, it follows neither that the theory is tenable, nor that it is part of the critical tradition.[1] That it is not to be found in either Eliot's criticism or his poetry may explain Collingwood's evident preference for his work to that of Yeats.

Although in branches of art other than literature the critical works to which Collingwood looked for a solution of the problem of usage are harder to identify, plainly there is abundant grist to his mill. In *The Principles of Art* he said little about music, except for a sharp censure of Beethoven's 'temperamental inclination to rant' (*PA*, 123), and an ironical remark that Brahms's song *Feldeinsamkeit* is identical in principle with 'the erotic music of a modern dance-

Jr., in *Modern Language Notes*, lxxi (1956), pp. 339–40, has shown that Eliot's important criticism of Beaumont and Fletcher derives, directly or indirectly, from Coleridge and von Schlegel.

[1] Cf. Kermode, op. cit., pp. 87–89.

band' (*PA*, 56). Of the nature of musical expression he said nothing explicit. However, it is reasonable to conjecture that he would have endorsed Croce's familiar judgement upon Eduard Hanslick's *Vom Musikalisch-Schönen* (Leipzig, 1854).

Hanslick maintained that the sole aim of music is form, musical beauty . . . [But he] never thought that symmetry, purely acoustical relations and pleasures of the ear constituted musical beauty; mathematics, he held, are utterly useless to musical Aesthetic. Musical beauty is spiritual and significative: it has thoughts, undoubtedly; but those thoughts are musical. . . . 'There are in music both meaning and connexion, but these are of a specifically musical nature; music is a language we understand and speak, but which it is not possible to translate'. . . . The backbone of the book is the denial that form and content can ever be separated in music. . . . Such observations denote acute penetration of the nature of art, though not scientifically formulated or framed into a system.[1]

In the plastic arts the principal debt he acknowledged was to Bernard Berenson (*PA*, 146–7); and although he said nothing of architecture in *The Principles of Art*, his definition of art is implicit in what many contemporary architects have said about their art. Despite his remark that 'the dance is the mother of all languages' (*PA*, 244), he did not refer to any contemporary criticism of the dance. Yet it is plain enough that most such criticism is in accord with his definition of art.

'But that is not enough', an objector might complain. 'It is true that Collingwood's definition of art roughly fits the critical tradition he recognized, and that it is incompatible with other critical traditions such as the Augustan. But a rough fit is not enough. Does the critical tradition in fact condemn a thing as a work of art precisely in a measure as it fails to express emotion? In short, is expressiveness in all cases a necessary condition of art? And, even more important, is expressiveness a sufficient condition? Even if it be granted that a work fails as a work of art to the extent that it is inexpressive, does it follow that everything expressive, e.g. a Frenchman's shrug, is a work of art? Surely that is a hard saying?'

Collingwood would undoubtedly have claimed that in the critical

---

[1] Croce, *Aesthetic*, pp. 413–14.

tradition every lapse in expressiveness was accounted a lapse in art. The difference between bad art and art falsely so called is that in bad art the artist 'tries to express a given emotion, but fails', whereas in art falsely so called, e.g. amusement or magic, 'there is no failure to express, because there is no attempt at expression' (*PA*, 282). This contention has been derided as a logical blunder. The criteria for recognizing a certain kind of thing, it is objected, cannot logically be used to evaluate any individual of that kind; for between description and evaluation a great gulf is fixed. Now it is true that no definition of 'art' by itself entails that any work of art is a good thing; nor does the definition of 'knife' or 'drain' entail that any knife or drain is a good thing. But the definition of 'knife' as 'a cutting instrument consisting of a longitudinally edged blade fixed in a handle' entails that any knife is bad if the edge of its blade fails to cut appropriate things when appropriate pressure is exerted on the handle. It may be that knives, like thieves, are bad as such, so that bad knives, like bad thieves, are better for the world than good ones; nevertheless, if a given kind of thing is correctly defined in terms of its function, then any specimen of that kind of thing is a bad one in a measure as it fails to discharge that function. Now Collingwood defined art, as we have seen, in terms of its function.

That the critical tradition to which Collingwood appealed condemns every work that is in any degree inexpressive as so far bad seems to me so obvious that I hesitate to do more than state it dogmatically. Would-be works of art that entirely fail to express emotion, while betraying, evoking, or describing it, are rare; and like the works of the Scotch poetaster who sang of the 'sweet waters' of Leith, 'where the girls go down to wash their teeth', are often prized by collectors of the ridiculous. Would-be art that is altogether flat is altogether bad. Most bad art, however, is not altogether bad, but bad in part. One of a critic's tasks is to show what parts of a work of art fail, and how serious those failures are. No good critic would hesitate to condemn as faulty any part of a work of art which was expressive neither in itself nor together with other parts.

Collingwood's solution of the problem of definition is not merely consistent with this quite obvious fact about critical practice. With his analysis of expression there goes an analysis of failure in expression, which he called 'corruption of consciousness'; and that analysis explains, as does no other aesthetic theory known to me, Eliot's teaching about critical procedure in his influential essay 'The Function of Criticism'.[1] There Eliot assailed the common critical practice of judging a work of art by personal and private interpretation; and protested that critics must rely on two methods alone: comparison and analysis. Now I think that Collingwood's analysis of expression and the corruption of consciousness explain why Eliot's teaching about criticism is true.

When an artist fails to express himself, he does not merely do nothing: he misdoes something. Instead of expressing his emotion, what he does is 'either to shirk it or dodge it: to disguise it from himself by pretending either that the emotion he feels is not that one but a different one, or that the person who feels it is not himself, but someone else. . . . If we ask whether this pretence is conscious or unconscious, the answer is, neither' (*PA*, 282). It occurs on the threshold that divides preconscious feelings or mental acts from those of which you are conscious. It is 'the malperformance of the act' of converting what is preconscious into something of which you are conscious (*PA*, 283). Such malperformances reveal corruptions in consciousness itself. But those corruptions 'are always partial and temporary lapses in an activity which, on the whole, is successful in doing what it tries to do' (*PA*, 283).

The only way in which anybody can detect any of his own malperformances of the activity of expression is 'through comparison of this occasion with his memory of . . . others' on which he expressed himself successfully (*PA*, 283). And just as one man comes to understand the expressive utterances of another by taking them as though they were his own, and reconstructing in himself what they express, so he may find, by comparison, that they are not expressive, but failures to express.

No attempt to shirk or dodge your emotions, either by expressing others which you do not have, or by counterfeiting horror at other people whom you represent as having them, can succeed. Genuine expression is by its very nature spontaneous, and uniquely

---

[1] Eliot, *Selected Essays*, pp. 23–34.

adapted to the individual emotion expressed. But when you try to express an emotion you do not have, you have nothing to which you can adapt your would-be expression. Your only course is to fake it from your knowledge of what such emotions are like. Now, to anybody who knows what successful expression is, such fakes will not ring true. Well-chosen comparisons will reveal their falsity.

A great critic has questioned the expressiveness of the speech of Beatrice, in Shelley's *The Cenci*, that begins,

> O
> My God! Can it be possible I have
> To die so suddenly? So young to go
> Under the obscure, cold, rotting, wormy ground!
> To be nailed down into a narrow place . . .
>> (Act v, Sc. iv, 47–51)

by setting it alongside Claudio's speech in Shakespeare's *Measure for Measure*:

> Ay, but to die, and go we know not where,
> To lie in cold obstruction, and to rot,
> This sensible warme motion, to become
> A kneaded clod;
>> (Act iii, Sc. i)

Although the comparison alone is enough, the analysis that accompanied it is worth quoting:

Claudio's words spring from a vividly realized particular situation; from the imagined experience of a given mind in a given critical moment that is felt from the inside—that is lived—with sharp concrete particularity.... [T]hough this vivid concreteness of realization lodged the passage in Shelley's mind, to become at the due moment 'inspiration', the passage inspired is nothing but wordy emotional generality. It does not grasp and present anything, but merely makes large gestures towards the kind of effect deemed appropriate.[1]

This analysis is not a proof, and is strictly ancillary to the comparison it accompanies. Its whole purpose is to help the reader to attend to what matters in the passages compared. If a reader does

---

[1] F. R. Leavis, *Revaluation* (London, 1936), pp. 226–7.

not see that one passage is expressive and the other largely a failure, although doubtless effectively evocative in a theatre, then the critic must try either a further analysis or an easier comparison. Critical comparison is not an 'objective' method, if that means a method by which a matter in dispute can be resolved by the use of a bodily sense, as a dispute about how much a bag of apples weighs can be resolved by putting it on a scale, and using one's eyes to take a pointer reading. But neither is it 'subjective', if that means a matter of taste which cannot be rationally questioned. The criticism of Shelley in our example could in principle be disputed, either by a different analysis of the passages compared, or by comparing Shelley's passage with something else. Yet no rational dispute of this kind would be possible unless the disputants had some power of discriminating genuine from faked expression: not an infallible power, but a power nevertheless (cf. *PA*, 281–4, 317). Does any reader seriously doubt that he has such a power?

§ 6. *Good Art and Great Art*

The most serious of the objections to Collingwood's definition has not yet been answered. It is not difficult to show that expressiveness is a necessary condition of art; but is it a sufficient one? There are at least two reasons for thinking that it is not.

Many critics maintain that art is not the expression of any and every emotion, but only of certain emotions. Some, the so-called 'expressionists', hold that artists should express only their more violent and self-centred emotions, and favour the use of bold effects and distorted forms in doing so. On the other side, critics of a classical temper denounce expressionism as the final degradation of romanticism, and demand that artists should express an intellectual love of the beautiful and well ordered. Collingwood was neither an expressionist nor, in this sense, a classicist (*PA*, 115). One advantage of his theory was that it enabled him to do justice to both expressionist and to classical art. The classicist who rejects Matthias Grünewald, and the expressionist who rejects Raphael, equally do violence to the critical tradition. Irrespective of who was the greater, Grünewald and Raphael were both artists. Another advantage was that it explained why neither classical nor expressionist art can be produced to order. If an artist whose opinions were classicist but who lacked the classic vision, and the emotions that go with it, should try to produce a work of classic art, he would fail; and his failure would betray a corruption of consciousness.

A second reason for thinking that expressiveness is not a sufficient condition of art is that many expressive utterances are trivial, and many others abstractly intellectual. Collingwood's definition entails that you must recognize as works of art, on the one hand, every racy and lively contribution to conversation, every significant gesture; and on the other, every scientific and philosophical treatise written with an eye steadily on its subject. Now, is it not nonsense to recognize the gesticulations of Italian peasants as art (cf. *PA*, 242)? And even if it is not, then surely it is nonsense to say that the writings of Newton and Gauss, Descartes and Kant, are art?

Collingwood would have replied that reflection shows that neither is nonsense. Both are at first glance surprising, because for obvious practical reasons critics write little about conversations or scientific treatises. Yet critics do collect and discuss specimens of conversation, as Boswell did of Johnson's; and there are even anthologies like *The Oxford Book of English Talk*. It is now generally recognized that the reason why great literature is not created except in a society that speaks well is that talk and literary art are continuous with one another. That is why the late Professor Raleigh confidently declared that, 'If we are told that educated people at the court of Edward III spoke French, and that English was a despised tongue, we could deny it on the evidence of Chaucer alone'.[1]

As for scientific works, they are not normally reviewed by literary critics, because their predominant interest is not aesthetic. Yet it does not follow that they ought not to be. It is clear, I think, that Descartes was a great artist; and, although it is widely held that Kant was not, that judgement may be a vulgar error. Too many critics, being unfamiliar with the emotions that go with sustained thought upon abstract subjects, are inclined to depreciate the

[1] Walter Raleigh (ed. George Gordon), *On Writing and Writers* (London, 1926), p. 117.

sciences as dry-as-dust pursuits, without significance for living. The opposite is true. A man who has the capacity and adequate opportunity to think scientifically, but refrains from doing so, is degenerate. As Collingwood protested, the 'progressive conversion [of language] . . . into a scientific symbolism . . . represents not a progressive drying-up of emotion, but its progressive articulation and specialization. We are not getting away from an emotional atmosphere into a dry, rational atmosphere; we are acquiring new emotions and new means of expressing them' (*PA*, 269). Or, as Croce put it, in a neat epigram, 'There is poetry without prose, but not prose without poetry'.[1]

Collingwood did not bring himself to accept the doctrine that all discourse is art until after he wrote his *Essay on Philosophical Method*, and Knox has suggested that it was one of his later aberrations.[2] To me, it seems to be an inevitable, although at first sight unwelcome, deduction from the definition of art which, in one form or another, he had held since the early twenties. In aesthetics as in philosophy of history,[3] late in life he saw the force of some of Croce's arguments which he had earlier rejected. Croce had grasped from the beginning that if art is expression, then all living speech is art. *Homo nascitur poeta*.[4]

There is, however, all the difference in the world between a major artist and an ordinary man whose utterances are genuinely expressive. The latter may be equal to the task of expressing his emotions at every juncture of his life: without help from anybody, he may be able to make himself conscious of what he feels about every situation in which he finds himself. But not all of the emotions that stir preconsciously in us are directed towards this or that particular situation. The general condition of man in our age and society oppresses us, and a steady vision of it is hard to achieve. There are several reasons for this. Everybody is reluctant to allow himself to become fully aware of what is significant in his impressions of his own state, because that awareness would destroy many of the comfortable illusions which help him to endure it (cf. *PA*, 331–4). 'After such knowledge, what forgiveness?' Besides, the very

---

[1] Croce, *Aesthetic*, p. 26.
[2] T. M. Knox, *IH*, xiv.
[3] See Appendix III, Letter (i), note.
[4] Croce, *Aesthetic*, p. 14.

achievements of past artists are a temptation to a man striving to express his own condition: a temptation to pass off, as solutions of his problems, their solutions of problems which resemble his but are not the same. Because his artistic problems are different, no solutions he may copy from the past can fit his needs. The treasury of past art is by nature protected from spoliation: when carried away its riches turn to dust, to 'a repertory of *clichés*' (*PA*, 276).

Artists must therefore develop the several branches of language in new ways. 'Every genuine expression must be an original one. However much it resembles others, this resemblance is due not to the fact that the others exist, but to the fact that the emotion now being expressed resembles emotions that have been expressed before. The artistic activity does not "use" a "ready-made language", it "creates" language as it goes along' (*PA*, 275). Eliot has illustrated this doctrine in discussing the decline of English poetry in the middle of the eighteenth century.

What really happened is that after Pope there was no one who thought and felt nearly enough like Pope to be able to use his language quite successfully; but a good many second-rate writers tried to write something like it, unaware of the fact that the change of sensibility demanded a change of idiom. Sensibility alters from generation to generation in everybody, whether we will or no; but expression is only altered by a man of genius.[1]

Because it is of the essence of art to break through *cliché*, Collingwood described all major art as prophetic. 'The artist must prophesy not in the sense that he foretells things to come, but in the sense that he tells his audience, at the risk of their displeasure, the secrets of their own hearts' (*PA*, 336). If art is a universal activity, bad art, the corruption of consciousness, is universal too. The illusions about our condition with which we comfort ourselves are in large measure derived not from theoretical errors but from faked expressions of emotion, that is, bad art. 'Art is not a luxury, and bad art not a thing we can afford to tolerate. To know ourselves is the foundation of all life that develops beyond the merely psychical

---

[1] T. S. Eliot in Phyllis M. Jones (ed.), *English Critical Essays, XX Cent.* (London, 1933), p. 302.

level of experience. . . . A truthful consciousness gives intellect a firm foundation upon which to build; a corrupt consciousness forces intellect to build on a quicksand' (*PA*, 284). Every community needs artists to be its spokesmen because no community altogether knows its own heart. *The Principles of Art*, despite its hopeful Preface, is at bottom the most desperate of all Collingwood's books. For when he wrote that by failing to know its own heart a 'community deceives itself on the one subject concerning which ignorance means death' (*PA*, 336), he feared that the consciousness of his own community, by which I do not mean Britain alone, was corrupt beyond recovery. Artists might speak, but only a dwindling minority would listen (cf. *PA*, 101–4).

PART II

THEORETICAL SCIENCE

VI

NATURAL SCIENCE

§ 1. *Collingwood's Repudiation of Idealist Objections to
Natural Science*

IN the last fifty years the doctrine that there is no genuine knowledge outside logic, mathematics, and the natural sciences has
attracted more and more adherents. Yet although it has gained
ground, its opponents, while diminishing in numbers, have not
become less vociferous. Some, like Collingwood in later life, are
conciliatory: they concede that, over the past 300 years, knowledge
has been won faster in mathematics and the natural sciences than
in any other rational pursuits; but they plead that there are other
rational pursuits which also are rewarded with knowledge. Others,
like Collingwood as a young man, are intransigent: natural science,
they contend, is not knowledge at all, but a practically convenient
system of theoretical fictions. The intransigent position has tempted
many philosophers who believe both that knowledge has degrees
and that metaphysics is knowledge in the highest degree; and both
those beliefs are implicit in the distinction, characteristic of post-
Kantian idealism, between Understanding or scientific thought,
and Reason or philosophical thought.

In his early work, *Speculum Mentis*, Collingwood took his stand
with the post-Kantian idealists. Scientific thought, or Understanding, he described as abstract (*SM*, 195–6); and he contended
that abstract thinking is necessarily false. 'To abstract is to consider separately things that are inseparable: to think of the universal, for instance, without reflecting that it is merely the universal
of its particulars, and to assume that one can isolate it in thought
and study it in this isolation. This assumption is an error. One cannot abstract without falsifying' (*SM*, 160). The keynote of the
abstract 'spirit' of natural science is therefore classification. 'For

a class as such is a collection of individuals without any mutual cohesion or organization except their common membership of the class. They have no reference to each other, but only to the universal; and each one refers to the universal in precisely the same way as every other' (*SM*, 162–3).

As a further consequence of its abstractness, Collingwood maintained, natural science is inevitably mathematical, mechanistic or deterministic, and materialistic (*SM*, 167). It is mathematical, because mathematics is in the end the theory of classes, and natural science is at bottom classificatory (*SM*, 165); it is mechanistic, because the only universal connexions between classes must be such as are imposed by 'an abstract law which determines every case indifferently from the outside' (*SM*, 166); and is materialistic, because it presupposes its subject to be some 'indifferently self-identical substrate' that is subject 'to the formulae of mechanical determination and mathematical calculation' (*SM*, 167–8).

Since it is abstract, Collingwood argued, science 'isolates' this material substrate from its empirical secondary qualities. And inevitably he went on to infer that, since no such isolated substrate exists, science has for its object not the real but the possible. The real, the realm of individual empirical fact, he assigned to history (*SM*, 185). He did not forget that even abstract science frames its hypotheses with reference to empirical facts; but he held that they remained hypotheses nevertheless. A useful hypothesis is still hypothesis.

Holding that the alleged facts of science are historical facts which, having been transformed by abstraction from concrete individuals into abstract particulars, are 'de-individualized' and 'de-factualized', Collingwood inferred that, while some concrete empirical propositions are true, 'the scientific simplification of them into instances of laws, abstract particulars of abstract concepts, is not true but arbitrary, useful no doubt, but useful precisely because it is not asserted as true but merely entertained in the form of a question' (*SM*, 186). Accordingly, he dismissed abstract natural science as not knowledge but 'supposal'.

Perhaps because he had already resolved upon the further inquiry into natural science which he was to carry out in *The Idea of Nature*, in his *Essay on Philosophical Method* Collingwood studiously withheld his opinions about the nature and status of natural science (*EPM*, 9–10). However, in *The Idea of Nature* he repudiated the doctrine of *Speculum Mentis* that 'the scientific simplification of [empirical facts] is not true but arbitrary'. '[M]odern philosophy from the seventeenth century', he acknowledged, 'has been obliged as its first duty to take physics seriously, to confess that the knowledge acquired for mankind by Galileo and Newton and their successors down to Einstein is genuine knowledge, and to ask not whether this quantitative material world can be known but why it can be known' (*IN*, 112). Still later, in the Conclusion to *The Idea of Nature* which he probably wrote in 1941, he added a remark which he echoed in *The New Leviathan*; 'natural science . . . is a search for truth, and a search that does not go unrewarded' (*IN*, 175; cf. *NL*, 2. 62). He had volunteered similar opinions, but less explicitly, in his *Autobiography*, in the *Essay on Metaphysics*, and in *The Idea of History* (e.g. *A*, 77–78, *EM*, 233–4; *IH*, 269).

Although in all these works he disowned the position he had taken in *Speculum Mentis*, in only one, *The New Leviathan*, did he try to explain the fallacy in the argument that had led him to it. That fallacy, he concluded, was to confound abstraction with separation and isolation. When you look at a red carpet and selectively attend to its redness, you abstract its colour, red, for attention (*NL*, 7. 38). But not even in your head do you either separate the redness from the carpet, or isolate it. You cannot attend to the colour red except as the redness of something. This might be directly deduced from the fact that abstract concepts are predicative; for what is predicative cannot be thought of at all except as applying to something. The thought of red is the same as the thought of what it is for something to be red.

In *The New Leviathan* Collingwood pointed these things out with evident exasperation. 'To fancy that when thought begins making abstractions it condemns itself to live in a world of abstractions', he sarcastically observed, '. . . is as foolish as to fancy that an unborn child, when it begins building itself a skeleton, turns its back on flesh and blood and condemns itself to live in Ezekiel's Valley of Dry Bones' (*NL*, 7. 64). And, after denouncing Bradley and

Bergson as 'obsessed with this fancy', he went on to argue that by abstracting a man does not falsify or impoverish his experience, but becomes more fully aware of it: 'a wealth of abstractions indicates not poverty in immediate consciousness but abundance of it, as a wealth of honey in the comb shows, not that the bees have left off visiting flowers, but that they have visited flowers to some purpose' (*NL*, 7. 67). It is curious that he did not mention that when he wrote *Speculum Mentis* he had himself shared the obsession of Bradley and Bergson.

As he studied the history of the concept of nature, Collingwood came to perceive that his facile deductions in *Speculum Mentis* concerning the nature of science were false. He remembered that Greco-Christian science was neither mathematical nor mechanistic; and he discovered not only that modern physics is neither deterministic nor mechanistic in the old sense, but also that it does not conceive matter as a permanent substrate, indifferent to time. It cannot, because it resolves material substance into function, and asserts that 'there is no nature at an instant' (*IN*, 13–24, 145–52). Of his youthful attempt to humble the pretensions of natural science, virtually nothing remained.

§ 2. *The Absolute Presuppositions of Natural Science*

In *The Idea of Nature* Collingwood divided the history of European natural science into three periods: the Greco-Christian, the 'Renaissance', and the Modern (*IN*, 1–3). Yet in *The New Leviathan* he treated the difference between Renaissance and Modern science as less fundamental than that between either of them and Greco-Christian science, on the ground that, whereas Greco-Christian science was teleological, they were 'regularian' (*NL*, 18. 42–18. 45). By contrast, he pointed out that modern science does not differ from developed Renaissance science in the general form of the explanations it seeks, but rather in the individual explanations it gives: the most striking difference between them is in their conceptions of matter (*IN*, 142–3).

Yet beneath these large differences, Collingwood maintained that all natural science, that of the Greeks equally with that of the present, is distinguished from pre-scientific lore by the fact that it is pursued in accordance with certain absolute presuppositions. They are four in number. He did not think that all scientists were aware of them; but he contended that nobody who was not logically committed to them by the questions he asked in his work could be accounted a scientist. Nor did he claim credit for enunciating them correctly. The Fathers of the Church were the first to do so, after the Greek philosophers had failed (*EM*, 222–7).

Collingwood tried to state them, in non-theological terms, in his *Essay on Metaphysics*. They naturally fall into two groups of two. The first two are:

1. *That there is a world of nature*, i.e. that there are things which happen of themselves and cannot be produced or prevented by anybody's art. . . .
2. *That this world of nature is a world of events*, i.e. that the things of which it is composed are things to which events happen or things which move (*EM*, 222).

Many scientists and philosophers today would dismiss both of these presuppositions as largely meaningless; for neither of them is necessarily true, and there does not seem to be any empirical evidence that would count for or against one or the other. No scientist would ever have occasion to say in his laboratory 'So there is a world of nature', or 'Then the world of nature is a world of events'. Collingwood himself acknowledged these points, but denied their relevance. His position was not that practising scientists have occasion to affirm these presuppositions, or that as a matter of historical fact they ever do affirm them, but that in asking the questions they ask they are logically committed to affirm them. And it is fundamental to his whole theory of presuppositions that no absolute presupposition asserts an empirically testable hypothesis.

Whether Collingwood's presuppositions have a meaning, and, if so, what it is, are questions best answered simultaneously, by establishing that they each have a significant contradictory. This can be done by finding a definite position which each denies. It is clear that Collingwood had such positions in mind.

The position which he thought his first presupposition to deny was not, as might be supposed, a philosophical theory like solipsism or immaterialism, both of which usually arise within a scientific tradition, but a conceivable pre-scientific belief. There are primitive peoples who recognize fewer happenings as natural than European scientists do; for example, the Azande have been reported by Professor Evans-Pritchard not to believe that human death is natural;[1] and it is logically possible to believe that every observed event might happen because of sorcery. A people which held such a belief, Collingwood remarked, 'would afford an example of a society in which no possible science of nature could arise until that belief had disappeared' (EM, 193). And he went on to show that that belief could not be directly falsified by experience, because any experience can be interpreted in accordance with it. In failing to perceive this, Aristotle led the Greco-Roman world into a disastrous error (EM, 214–16, 223–5).

At first glance, Collingwood blundered in his second presupposition; for it is simply the classical Greek definition of nature. Not even Parmenides denied that the world of nature was by definition a world of change. Its whole point, however, lies in its conjunction with the first presupposition: together, the two entail that there really is a world of change. Now this was denied, not only by Parmenides and Zeno, but also, in his middle period, by Plato. It is a fundamental maxim of classical metaphysics that whatever is can be known. Platonism, as Collingwood pointed out, rejected the possibility of natural science because it conceived nature as 'the realm of imprecision, no possible object for scientific knowledge' (EM, 252–3). It thereby rejected the very being of change. The position which Collingwood thought that of his second presupposition as denying, in conjunction with his first, was the Platonic-Parmenidean doctrine that change cannot be.

The third and fourth presuppositions of natural science also form a group. Unlike the first two, they treat of the structure of natural science itself, not of the nature and existence of its objects. They are:

3. *That throughout this world [of nature] there is one set of laws*

[1] Cf. EM, 193–200, which is plainly indebted to *Witchcraft, Oracles and Magic among the Azande.*

according to which all movements or events, in spite of all differences, agree in happening; and that consequently there is one science of this world.

4. *That nevertheless there are in this world many different realms,* each composed of a class of things peculiar to itself, to which events of a peculiar kind happen; that the peculiar laws of these several realms are modifications of the universal laws mentioned in 3; and that the special sciences of these several realms are modifications of the universal science there mentioned (*EM*, 223).

The meaning of these presuppositions is far from clear. They undoubtedly affirm three things: that natural events take place according to laws; that of those laws some are universal, in the sense of applying to everything, and others are special, in the sense of applying only to events of a special kind; and that the special laws are modifications of the universal laws. But what is a law? And what is it for one law to be a modification of another?

It must be remembered that Collingwood put these presuppositions forward as applying to all natural science, and not merely to Renaissance or Modern science. In saying that natural scientists presuppose that natural events take place according to laws, he meant that Greek scientists like Aristotle did so as well as Renaissance scientists like Galileo. In *The New Leviathan* he used the word 'law' more narrowly. There he described Greco-Christian science as 'teleological', and contrasted it with post-Renaissance science, which he described as 'regularian', i.e. law-minded (*NL*, 18. 4–18. 45). The 'regularian' laws of post-Renaissance science interpret natural events by analogy with human actions done in obedience to human law, and it is characteristic of an act done in obedience to law that it is not, as such, teleological (*NL*, 18. 43–18. 44). In the *Essay on Metaphysics* the word 'law' carries no such implication. It appears to mean any universally quantified formula. That natural events take place according to laws therefore means that they take place according to universally quantified formulae which it is the business of scientists to discover. And this was presupposed by Aristotle as well as by Galileo.

One objection to this interpretation might be that it makes the presupposition vacuous. Does not every question about the explanation of any event presuppose that it takes place according to universally quantified formulae? What is explaining an event except showing how it is connected with others according to such formulae? Although no complete answer can be given to the second of these questions until we come to analyse historical explanation, it is necessary to show at once that the answer to the first is 'No'.

It is true that questions in natural science, even when they are about individual events, presuppose general laws. Collingwood pointed out that in asking the question, 'Why did that piece of litmus paper turn pink?' a natural scientist is logically committed to presuppose that its turning pink happened according to law, because he would reject any answer in which it was not implied that any piece of blue litmus paper, if put in the situation of that piece, would turn pink (*IH*, 214). But this is not so when a natural scientist asks non-scientific questions about the acts of his acquaintances. When asking a colleague the question, 'Why don't you stop beating your wife?' not even a natural scientist normally demands an answer in which it is implied that any man of the same kind as his colleague, married to any woman of the same kind as his wife, and placed in the situation in which they were placed, will habitually beat her. Indeed, if he presupposed that there was such a law of nature, he would hardly ask the question.

In sum, the presupposition that all natural events take place according to laws is not vacuous. Its contrary would be that they are like what human acts are ordinarily taken to be. In their questions about natural events, however, natural scientists presuppose much more than that. Aristotle presupposed that every natural event has a material, a formal, an efficient, and a final cause; which implies, among other things, that an adequate explanation of it must be teleological. Galileo laid down the anti-Aristotelian principle, which has been adopted by all modern scientists, that the laws of nature are mathematical. Of the truths of science he once wrote, in a passage to which Collingwood repeatedly alluded, that they cannot be read in the book of the universe 'until we have learnt the language and become familiar with the characters in which it is written. It is written in mathematical language, and the letters are triangles, circles and other geometrical figures, without which means it is humanly impossible to comprehend a single word' (quoted *IN*, 102; cf. *EM*, 250–5, *NL*, 31. 24–31. 29). By discovering analytical geometry, Descartes furnished physicists with the key to more of that language; and it is not altogether fanciful to suggest that, had he written a century later, Galileo might have considered the differential calculus to have revealed its syntax.

As a result of the reception of Galileo's principle, causal laws have been less and less employed in natural science. Newtonian physics, Collingwood remarked, while still recognizing causes or 'impressed forces', explained many events entirely in terms of regular *processes*, a process being an event that goes on of its own accord without instigation. A typical example of such an event would be the motion of a body with uniform velocity, which Newton regarded as essentially uncaused[1] (*EM*, 326–7). Russell had argued, in a paper[2] to which Collingwood acknowledged a profound debt (*EM*, 69, 319), that in 'advanced natural sciences' causal laws have been supplanted by mathematical process laws, i.e. by laws according to which the state of an uninterrupted process at a given time can be calculated from its state at any other time. Such a law is that a freely falling terrestrial body will have traversed $490 (2n-1)$ cm. n seconds after it has begun to fall. Collingwood rashly ventured even farther than Russell, and declared that modern natural science has 'eliminated the notion of cause altogether' (*EM*, 327).

Remembering that, in Collingwood's presuppositions, 'law' does not mean a process law, or a law satisfying Galileo's principle, or even a teleological law, but a universally quantified formula according to which some natural event may be explained, we may turn to the two latter points in Collingwood's third and fourth presuppositions: that the laws of nature are either universal or special, and that the special laws are modifications of the universal ones.

The former denies at least two things: first, that all the laws of nature are universal; and secondly, that they are all special. The

---

[1] These two sentences are paraphrased from N. R. Campbell, *Physics: the Elements* (Cambridge, 1920), p. 66. I do not use 'event', as Campbell does, to signify discontinuous and brief happenings.

[2] Bertrand Russell, *Mysticism and Logic* (London, 1917), pp. 180 et seq.; originally published *Proc. Aris. Soc.* xiii (1912–13).

first may be dismissed as patently false; for in every period of European natural science laws have been employed, e.g. Galileo's laws of projectiles, or Kepler's of planetary motion, which apply only to special kinds of event, and not to every natural event whatever. The second is more difficult to judge. Prima facie, it also is patently false. At all periods natural scientists have affirmed general principles and laws which apply to all events whatever. Greek science depended on Conservation Laws, whether of Matter or of Motion, as much as modern science depends on the Conservation of Energy. In Aristotle's physics, every natural event has a final cause; in Newton's all matter gravitates. Since natural science could not possibly be carried on without such laws or principles, it is tempting simply to endorse Collingwood's point and pass on. But there is a difficulty.

Presumably Collingwood wished to distinguish between universal laws and absolute presuppositions. It must be remembered that although many scientific questions will presuppose universal laws, just as 'Have you stopped beating your wife?' presupposes that you have a wife, not all presuppositions are absolute. Universal laws may be presumed to be highly general relative presuppositions. The difficulty in understanding Collingwood's position in the *Essay on Metaphysics* is that he elevated so many of the most promising candidates for the title of universal law to the higher rank of absolute presupposition, that it may be doubted whether any remaining law can fairly be called universal. Thus he expressly classified as absolute presuppositions not only such things as Galileo's principle, and the Leibniz–Newton principle that a science of nature must consist of differential equations (*EM*, 255-7, 259), but also all Conservation Laws, and at least one of Newton's Laws of Motion, namely, the third (*EM*, 264-5, 270). Even his opinion about the Law of Gravitation is obscure. While he did not expressly describe it as an absolute presupposition, in a curious footnote he attacked Newton for denying it to be an hypothesis and asserting it to be a statement of fact (*EM*, 272 *n.*); and he undoubtedly held that all statements of fact function as relative presuppositions (*EM*, 29-30).

This obscurity is symptomatic of a deep disorder in the theory of presuppositions itself, to which I have drawn attention in

Chapter IV. Collingwood classified Conservation Laws and Galileo's Principle as absolute presuppositions because they are not immediately verifiable or falsifiable by observation or experiment (*EM*, 255–7). Evidently he derived these criteria from the non-formal part of his exposition of the Theory of Presuppositions, in which he argued that the unverifiability of metaphysical affirmations shows that they are not propositions but absolute presuppositions (*EM*, 165).

As criteria of whether an affirmation is an absolute presupposition, unverifiability and unfalsifiability not only are intrinsically unsatisfactory, they also are incompatible with his own express definition. They are unsatisfactory because no abstract law of nature, whether it be universal or special, is immediately falsifiable in Collingwood's sense. By suitable *ad hoc* hypotheses the results of any observation or experiment may be reconciled with the truth of any such supposed law; and if recourse to *ad hoc* hypotheses be excluded by a principle of simplicity, then it is no longer evident that absolute presuppositions themselves are unfalsifiable. The considerations which go to show that absolute presuppositions are unfalsifiable hold for all abstract laws of nature. A theory of scientific verification which permitted only the immediate verification of empirical statements about particulars, and the immediate falsification of generalizations, and which excluded altogether any indirect or mediate falsification in which a principle of simplicity is employed, would be scientifically useless. Reasoning from observation and experiment can prove little unless a principle of simplicity is presupposed; for there can be no connexion between observed facts and scientific hypotheses if *ad hoc* hypotheses may be introduced at will.[1]

Worse is to follow. The criteria of unverifiability and unfalsifiability are incompatible with Collingwood's original definition of

---

[1] When I wrote this paragraph, I knew that my conception of simplicity as the exclusion of *ad hoc* hypotheses was not original, but I could not remember from whom I had learned it. It was first put forward by Karl R. Popper in *Logik der Forschung* (Vienna, 1934), tr. as *The Logic of Scientific Discovery* (London, 1959): see the latter, pp. 82–83, 140–2; but I had not read Popper's analysis when I wrote. Popper's note, op. cit., p. 140, reminded me of my source, which must have been William Kneale's *Probability and Induction* (Oxford, 1949), pp. 229–30, 246–8. Popper's priority is acknowledged on p. 230. [Note added in 1962.]

an absolute presupposition as something which is presupposed by a question, but which is not itself the answer to any other question (*EM*, 31). By this definition a man's absolute presuppositions are what he is logically committed to by the ultimate questions he asks. It is clear that what one man presupposes absolutely another may presuppose relatively (see above, Ch. IV, § 1). The affirmations which are logically presupposed by one man's ultimate questions may be answers to another man's derivative questions; and what one man as a matter of historical fact affirms as an ultimate principle may to another be an answer to a question. Accordingly, Collingwood's definition of an absolute presupposition plainly implies that no presupposition as such is absolute; whether a presupposition is absolute or not depends on what the person who makes it either asks or affirms. Yet if all presuppositions which are not immediately verifiable or falsifiable were *eo ipso* absolute, their absoluteness could not depend on what those who make them ask or affirm. It follows that to take immediate unverifiability or falsifiability as criteria of absoluteness is incompatible with Collingwood's own definition of an absolute presupposition.

Since the system of the *Essay on Metaphysics* cannot stand unless this contradiction is eliminated, the less fundamental of the two incompatible views which give rise to it must be abandoned. Of the two, Collingwood's original definition and his employment of immediate unverifiability or falsifiability as criteria of absolute presuppositions, the latter is plainly less fundamental: it can be excised without affecting the bulk of the book, whereas the former underlies its whole structure. If immediate verifiability and falsifiability are abandoned as criteria of absolute presuppositions, a place can readily be found for universal laws: they will be those laws which apply to all natural events, but which are affirmed in answer to questions. An affirmation which is merely a universal law in one scientific system may be an absolute presupposition in another.

It remains now to elucidate what Collingwood meant by the third point in his second group of presuppositions, that the special laws of nature are 'modifications' of the universal ones. He cannot have meant that they are deductively derivable from universal laws, because such deductive derivations are characteristic of post-

Galilean science, not of Greco-Christian. Nothing like Newton's mathematical proof that if his Laws of Motion and Gravitation are true, then the motions of the planets must accord with Kepler's Laws, is to be found in Greek science, yet Collingwood intended his presupposition to hold good of it as well as of post-Galilean. It is probable, therefore, that he would have recognized as a modification of a generic law any law that gave it specific content in a specific case. Thus I think he would have accounted Aristotle's law that animals reproduce their kind as a modification of his universal law that all natural events have final causes. Nor do I apologize for my examples of Aristotelian 'laws', even though they are immediately deducible from Aristotle's definitions of nature, the soul, and the vegetative soul; for Aristotle proposed those definitions as substantive propositions.

In *The Idea of Nature* and *The New Leviathan* Collingwood discussed two of the realms of nature affirmed by modern science in accordance with his fourth presupposition: namely, the biological and the non-biological; or as he preferred to say in *The New Leviathan*, the physiological and the physical. In *The Idea of Nature* he boldly predicted, 'on the ground of philosophy', that 'the conception of vital process as distinct from mechanical or chemical change has come to stay, and has revolutionized our conception of nature' (*IN*, 136). It would follow that no attempt to explain physiological function wholly in terms of physico-chemical structure can succeed. Neither this prediction, nor Collingwood's few remarks about biology itself, inspire confidence. Few biologists today would countenance either his praise of Bergson as an interpreter of the biology even of his own time (*IN*, 138–41), or his strange view that Darwinian evolution 'implied the philosophical conception of a life-force' (*IN*, 135).

It is therefore agreeable to record that in *The New Leviathan* he renounced any right as a philosopher to adjudicate the future boundaries of the realms of nature. Not only did he forbear to speculate whether physiology is ultimately the same as physics and chemistry, or different from either or both of them; by asserting that as investigation proceeds each of those sciences constantly revises the definition of its subject-matter, he also implied that whether there shall ultimately be boundaries between them, and if so what they shall be, must be determined by the progress of those sciences themselves (cf. *NL*, 1. 36, 1. 46–1. 52). To pronounce, 'on the ground of philosophy', that a division between two special sciences has or has not come to stay is to pretend to settle a scientific question on a non-scientific ground. Such pretensions, Collingwood warned, evoke what he called 'scientific persecution', that is, the persecution of scientists for daring to be scientists (*NL*, 1. 57).

§ 3. *Discovery and Verification*

Paradoxically, it was in his writings on history that Collingwood most emphatically avowed his admiration for the methods of discovery and verification in natural science, which *honoris causa* he described as Baconian. However vehemently he protested that historical reconstructions differ in their very nature from hypotheses in natural science, he consistently proclaimed that the method of scientific history is as Baconian as that of natural science (cf. *A*, 78–81; *IH*, 269). His most concise exposition of that method was as follows.

Francis Bacon, lawyer and philosopher, laid it down in one of his memorable phrases that the natural scientist must 'put Nature to the question. . . .' What he was asserting was two things at once: first, that the scientist must take the initiative, deciding for himself what he wants to know and formulating this in his own mind in the shape of a question; and secondly, that he must find means of compelling nature to answer, devising tortures under which she can no longer hold her tongue. Here, in a single brief epigram, Bacon laid down once for all the true theory of experimental science. (*IH*, 269.)

Of course Collingwood did not think that Nature literally answers scientists' questions. Rather, he held that those questions are so constructed that observable happenings, occurring under either natural or laboratory conditions, may be construed as answers to them. Were it not for such observable happenings, scientific thinking would be mere uncontrolled speculation. On the other hand, but for scientists' questions, no observation would be scientifically significant. Nobody ignorant of physiology will learn anything about a cell by peering at it through a microscope. Bacon made both these points in a simile which Collingwood cited in *The New*

Leviathan. Scientific thinking is unlike the activity either of a spider, which spins its web out of its own bowels, or of an ant, which collects and stores every bit of food it comes across. Scientists are neither mere theorists nor mere fact collectors. Rather, they are like the bee, which gathers food from flowers, but transforms it in its belly: they seek facts, but only in order to answer questions; and by their questions they transmute them into scientific knowledge (*NL*, 31. 27; cf. *IN*, 101).

The questions asked by scientists are of a special kind, which unfortunately Collingwood did not describe at length. What he took them to be must be inferred from several scattered passages. In *The New Leviathan* he asserted that the honey of scientific knowledge consists of laws: of laws not merely as abstract formulae, but applied abstractions (*NL*, 31. 28, 31. 3). A law is applied in interpreting or explaining either an event or another law. An event is explained by showing deductively that, given that some other event occurred, it follows according to a certain law or laws that, under the circumstances, it must have occurred. A law is explained by showing deductively that it must hold if certain more abstract laws hold. Since Collingwood did not explore this distinction, I shall confine myself to the former case.

In his *Autobiography* Collingwood discussed an example which has counterparts in natural science: a motorist's exasperated question, 'Why won't my car start?' No motorist would set out to answer that question unless he believed he knew how his car worked, and such knowledge, of course, would include all the relevant low-level laws, such as 'If the carburettor is flooded, cars like this won't start', 'If one of the sparking-plugs is not sparking, cars like this won't start'. Possessed of this knowledge, he is in a position to establish why his car will not start by systematic elimination. 'Is it because a sparking-plug is out of action that the car will not start?' For the cars of 1938, you could answer this question by taking out each plug in turn, laying it on the engine, turning the starting-handle, and watching for a spark. If you saw a spark, you inferred that the plug was sound and that the answer to your question was 'No'; if not, you had the answer to your original question, unless there were several things wrong with your car. Collingwood's point was that by such detailed questions you could extort from the car an answer to your original question. What you had to do was to get clear what the possible answers were, deduce from each what would be the case if it were true, and then, taking one answer at a time, see whether or not the observed facts would falsify it (*A*, 31–32; *EM*, 123–5).

Although Collingwood did not show how this method could be used to discover a law, how he might have done it can be inferred from *The New Leviathan*. A scientist seeking the process laws by which a given event may be explained, e.g. a lead ball dropped from a tower taking a certain time to reach the ground would have a number of suggestions ready to hand. Feathers and snowflakes fall more slowly than horseshoes, so the laws required may have to do with the ball's weight. No, a half-brick falls as fast as a whole brick. The specific gravity then? But does a brick with an iron plate attached fall any faster than one with a wooden plate of the same size attached? No. Then perhaps it has nothing to do with weight, specific gravity, or any such thing, but with something else. Could it be the time of the fall? But then how explain the slow fall of feathers and snowflakes? Possibly in such cases two processes are involved, the resistance of a fluid medium, the air, as well as free fall. This hypothesis can be tested: if the resistance of the air is of no importance, a feather will not fall more rapidly in a vessel evacuated of air by a pump than in the air. And so forth.

I have not described how Galileo did establish the law of falling bodies, but rather how it is introduced to children by schoolmasters. Yet such caricatures of a scientist's procedure may be useful as illustrations. Unlike a mechanic trying to find why a car won't start, a scientist cannot begin by surveying all the logically possible explanations of an event, because he does not know in advance what they are. Instead, he must follow what Collingwood called the Principle of the Limited Objective: he must try to interpret not anything and everything, as the Greeks did, but only those things which he thinks need be interpreted or can be interpreted (*NL*, 31. 68); and he will not think that an event can be interpreted unless he has some idea of how to interpret it.

He can then begin. Since he has some idea of how to interpret whatever event he has chosen to investigate, then let him formulate his interpretation in such a way that some consequence can be deduced from it. Does the speed of falling bodies depend on their weight? If so, then a half-brick will fall only half as fast as a whole one. Does it? This question will extort from nature, in the shape of a brick and a half-brick dropped together from the same height, the unmistakable answer that the speed of falling bodies does not depend on their weight.

This question, once answered, naturally leads to others. Thus, the observed fact that a feather falls more slowly than a brick can be reconciled with the observed fact that a half-brick does not by supposing that the speed of a thing's fall depends on its specific gravity rather than its weight. A successful but negative answer to the question to which that supposition gives rise leads to a further suggestion. Collingwood drew attention to two things about this process. The first was that scientists do not strike out hypotheses or questions at random. Each question they ask is suggested by answers to previous questions (*A*, 37–38). The second was that scientific thinking joins abstractions created by the mind with facts ascertained either by observation or by experiment. These are the two legs on which natural science stands: and it progresses by using both together; not by hopping, now on one, and now on the other (*NL*, 31. 24–31. 26).

The fact that scientists do not know in advance all the possible hypotheses by which a given event or law can be explained entails that their conclusions that this or that hypothesis is in fact a law of nature are corrigible. Their proofs of laws are proofs that their hypotheses fit all the facts to which they have been ingenious enough to apply them. Advances in knowledge show us how to apply our hypotheses in new ways, and often force us to revise them. Yet this fact does not imply a sceptical conclusion. It is perfectly reasonable to accept a proposition as a law if it has withstood the test of systematic scientific questioning. Even if later investigation shows that it must be revised, it will not usually be simply discarded. As Collingwood wrote in *The Idea of History*: 'If Einstein makes an advance on Newton, he does it by knowing Newton's thought and retaining it within his own, in the sense that he knows what

Newton's problems were, and how he solved them, and, disentang-
ling the truth in those solutions from whatever errors prevented
Newton from going further, embodying these solutions as thus
disentangled in his own theory' (*IH*, 333).

§ 4. *A Contradiction in Collingwood's Philosophy of Natural Science*

Collingwood could not develop a consistent philosophy of natural
science because he was himself in two minds about the nature of
scientific verification. It is impossible to doubt the genuineness of
his protestations that natural science pursues truth and is rewarded,
and that the secret of its discoveries is its combination of abstraction with observation. Yet they are incompatible with other opinions
which he espoused with equal fervour. He also maintained that
natural science rests on absolute presuppositions, which are neither
true nor false; and, if that is so, then the answer which a scientist
gives to his question, 'Why does the sun rise every twenty-four
hours?' would be no more true than the answer a witch-doctor might
give to it, provided that each proceeds rationally within his presuppositions. Unless what natural science has achieved from Thales
to Bohr can be said to be nearer the truth than the pre-scientific
superstitions that preceded it, then it would be irony indeed to
say of it that it pursues truth and is rewarded.

The Idea of Nature is a history, not of natural science, but of the
concept of nature presupposed by it. Yet a reader who studies it,
keeping in mind what is said in the *Autobiography*, *The Idea of History*, and *The New Leviathan* about the Baconian method of natural
science, will be struck by Collingwood's neglect to examine how
scientists have come to change their opinions. In part, this is because
he preferred to examine changes in scientific thought as they are
reflected in philosophy. But that is not a complete explanation. *The
Idea of Nature* conveys an unmistakable impression that pure philosophical speculation itself often did and always could have led to
scientific advances.

Two examples must suffice. Pointing out that Newton did not
solve the problems of light and electricity, Collingwood did not
scruple to describe Newton's work in his *Opticks* as a 'defeat'; and

he even had the audacity to attribute what he called Newton's 'undoing' to 'careless and second-hand thinking on fundamental questions of cosmology' (*IN*, 109–10). When he commended Newton, it was for 'the patient thoroughness with which he worked out the details of what he called, on the title-page of his immortal work, the "Mathematical Principles of Natural Philosophy"'; and he took care to add that the main idea even of that work was Descartes's, and that its more important lesser ideas were taken from Bacon, Galileo, Kepler, Gilbert, and the neo-Epicureans (*IN*, 107).

Hegel, by contrast, he praised without stint for anticipating Whitehead's rejection of simple location and material substance.

[T]he physical science of today [he wrote] has arrived at a view of matter and energy which so far agrees with the implications of Hegel's theory of nature, that a philosopher-scientist like Whitehead can restate Hegel's theory . . . and allow that theory to take him wherever it likes. . . . What is possible for Whitehead, however, was not possible for Hegel, because the physics of Hegel's day was still the physics of Galileo and Newton, a physics conceived in terms of things 'simply located' . . . in space. (*IN*, 127–8.)

Even without questioning Collingwood's highly favourable interpretation of Hegel, it is hard to make sense of his praise. If he was right, Hegel startlingly anticipated some of the results of science a hundred years after his time, but by unscientific methods. Were Hegel's methods, then, valid? Collingwood was careful not to say so. His verdict was that Hegel 'tried to anticipate by philosophy something which in fact could only be a future development of natural science. His anticipation . . . was in many ways startlingly accurate; but scientific thought has no place for anticipation; it only values results scientifically achieved' (*IN*, 132). Such a judgement is sophistical. If Hegel's methods were not valid, why praise him? Collingwood cannot have intended to imply that a true conclusion unscientifically reached is an addition to scientific knowledge; nor did he conceal the fact that, while Hegel's unscientific anticipations of later scientific results were in some ways startlingly accurate, in others they were unsurprisingly inaccurate (cf. *IN*, 131).

In his *Essay on Metaphysics*, Collingwood asked, 'How far was the habitual and monotonous execration of Hegel by nineteenth-century natural scientists due to the fact that he violently disliked the physics of his own day, and demanded the substitution for it of a physics which, it turns out, was to be in effect the physics that we have now?' (*EM*, 271 *n.*; cf. 95). His own concessions in *The Idea of Nature* suggest another question: May not that execration have been due to the fact that Hegel's attempt to do away with a physics which, on non-Baconian grounds he 'violently disliked', and to replace it by another which, also on non-Baconian grounds, he liked, was in effect an attack on the Baconian method itself?

In glorifying Hegel and disparaging Newton, Collingwood betrayed a scepticism about the methods of natural science which, after he had put *Speculum Mentis* behind him, he steadily refused to avow. His doctrine in the *Essay on Metaphysics* that natural science rests on absolute presuppositions which are neither true nor false was another symptom of it. If the change from Newtonian to Einsteinian physics had been a change in unverifiable absolute presuppositions, then Hegel's methods of anticipating it would have done as well as anybody's; for it could not have been brought about by Baconian methods. Yet in his Baconian moments, Collingwood saw through these errors. Both Newton's and Einstein's hypotheses were tested and confirmed by Baconian methods, and every enduring scientific result has been established in the same way. The Theory of Presuppositions, inasmuch as it implies that this is not so, is false.

VII

PSYCHOLOGY AS THE SCIENCE OF FEELING

§ 1. *Collingwood's Conception of Psychology*

EVERY psychologist to whose notice it has been brought has been justly angered by what Collingwood wrote of psychology in his *Essay on Metaphysics*. However true what he wrote may be, and I shall argue that it is by no means wholly false, on his own principles Collingwood ought not to have written about psychology at all. 'When you read the works of an anti-metaphysician', he advised his readers, 'you can and must demand of him . . . an accurate knowledge of what metaphysicians have in fact been doing, based not on hearsay but on a critical study of their works conducted according to the well-known methods of historical inquiry' (*EM*, 235–6). What Collingwood as a metaphysician may demand of anti-metaphysicians, psychologists may demand of him as an anti-psychologist.

It is true that his *Essay on Metaphysics* contains a short history of psychology, according to which psychology originated in the sixteenth century, when feeling, or emotionally charged sensation, was first clearly distinguished from thinking, as being neither true nor false. Before that time, Collingwood held, the philosophical sciences of mind had presupposed that the essential function of mind was to think, and had considered feeling to be true or false as though it were a primitive and confused mode of thinking. Although those philosophical sciences, which Collingwood rather eccentrically identified with metaphysics, logic, and ethics,[1] had until then been

---

[1] *EM*, 104–5, 108–9, 114. In defending logic and metaphysics against psychology Collingwood partly recanted such remarks as the following. 'The moral of this is not that we ought to abandon psychology and return to the old logic and metaphysics. Those sciences have been once for all criticized by and absorbed into psychology, which has made a real advance upon them' (*SM*, 276).

regarded as a complete science of man as mind, the distinction of feeling from thought made a further science of mind necessary; for if feeling is not thought, neither is it a purely bodily phenomenon. The science of feeling had 'to fill a gap between the existing science of bodily function and the existing sciences of mind, in no way competing with any of them' (*EM*, 110; cf. 104–5, 108–9).

In *The New Leviathan* Collingwood defined feeling in a different but related way, by distinguishing it not from thinking, but from consciousness. Mind, he asserted, is constituted not by thinking but by consciousness, the most primitive form of which has feeling for its object. 'Man as mind *is* consciousness, practical and theoretical . . .; he *has* feeling' (*NL*, 4. 2). Feeling can only be studied by becoming conscious of it (*NL*, 5. 82). And, although feelings are raised to consciousness by linguistic acts, the consciousness so attained is not a matter for argument. If you want to answer the question whether you have a headache, it would be misplaced argument to consider pros and cons: you should simply consider how you feel (*NL*, 4. 72).

Nobody is conscious of every feeling he has. Until you perform the linguistic act that raises a feeling to consciousness, it remains preconscious. And when you perform an act of selective attention, you necessarily direct your attention towards some elements in a complex of feeling and away from others. Collingwood identified such withdrawals of attention with what Freud called 'repression'. Yet he argued that it would be misleading to describe either preconscious or repressed feelings as 'unconscious', because that would imply that they necessarily were below the threshold of consciousness. Anybody who has reached the level of second-order consciousness can raise his preconscious feelings to consciousness at will; and nobody could possibly repress a feeling unless he had an undifferentiated first-order consciousness of the complex in which it was an element. You can only withdraw attention from what you are already, in some sense, conscious of; and your first-order consciousness of it is a primitive survival in the act of second-order consciousness in which you withdraw attention from it. 'The Freudian patient in post-hypnotic suggestion does not even, by repressing [part of what he feels], obliterate all the consciousness of it which he began by having. He is conscious of his repressed feelings as something, he knows not what, that urges him to do something' (*NL*, 5. 88; cf. 5. 8–5. 93).

Collingwood professed to respect psychology, understood as the science of feeling. 'As the science of feeling', he declared, 'psychology is not only a science of respectable antiquity; it is a science with great triumphs to its credit, some of long standing, others lately achieved, others even yet incomplete, and (one may hope) others to come in the future' (*EM*, 141). Although he did not specify what those triumphs were, his admission that psychological research is most important, 'whether in the laboratory or in the consulting-room' (*EM*, 141–2), affords a clue. The laboratory research he had in mind was presumably that on sensation by such men as Wundt and William James; or, nearer to his own time, by Ward and Stout, and perhaps by the Gestalt psychologists. However, I recollect no reference in his writings to any particular psychological investigation of sensation, or to any psychologist who has made such investigations, except a passing acknowledgement in his *Autobiography* that, in *The Varieties of Religious Experience*, William James did his work as a psychologist well (*A*, 93).

About research in the consulting-room he was more explicit. In *The Principles of Art*, in which he drew heavily on the psychoanalytic concepts of repression, projection, dissociation, and fantasy-building in his own analysis of corruption of consciousness (*PA*, 218–19), he saluted Freud as 'the greatest psychologist of our age' (*PA*, 64). He also expressed a high opinion of psycho-analytic therapy: 'Whether or no the psycho-analysts have found the means to rescue [those whose consciousness is corrupt] or to save those in whom this evil has advanced less far, their attempt to do so is an enterprise that has already won a great place in the history of man's warfare with the powers of darkness' (*PA*, 220–1).

Both psycho-analysts and the classical psychologists employed what historians of psychology usually call 'introspection': that is, they regarded as data both the feelings of which they themselves were conscious, and those which their 'subjects' or patients reported to them. As we have seen, Collingwood repudiated the term 'introspection' and its implications, because he denied that feelings are raised to consciousness by any form of inner sense (*EM*, 43). Yet he did not deny either that psychologists, their patients, and their 'subjects' can become conscious of what they feel, or that their consciousness of it is direct, in the sense that it is not inferential, i.e. that argument about it is misplaced. He endorsed the method of 'introspectionist' psychology, but contended that 'introspection' was a misnomer for it. Moreover, he appears not to have countenanced any other method for his science of feeling. In that science, as conceived in the *Essay on Metaphysics* and *The New Leviathan*, the methods of behaviourist psychology have no place.[1]

Since by 1939, when the *Essay on Metaphysics* was written, behaviourism dominated American psychology, and had already secured a footing in Europe, Collingwood's neglect of it disqualified him as a critic of psychology in general, because it precluded him from gaining an accurate knowledge of what a large number of psychologists had in fact been doing, based not on hearsay but on a critical study of their works (cf. *EM*, 235–6). He had, therefore, no right to denounce psychologists as a class, as he did when he accused them of making propaganda for irrationalism by applying methods proper in the science of feeling to the study of thought (*EM*, 115–16). Whatever charges may lie against the behaviourists, that one does not; for their methods are not those of 'the science of feeling'.

§ 2. *The Psychological Treatment of Religion*

Although Collingwood did not know enough to discuss psychology in general, he was not disabled from exposing philosophical errors made by individual psychologists whose work he had studied. At the very beginning of his philosophical life he had read William James's *Varieties of Religious Experience*, and he believed that he had detected in it errors of method which had deceived not only other

---

[1] His remark in *Speculum Mentis* that 'we ought . . . to be grateful to the behaviourists for revealing the true nature of psychology and pushing it to its logical conclusion' (*SM*, 275) does not contradict this: he was praising behaviourism for showing that in psychology as such, even in introspectionist psychology, mental events must be investigated in abstraction from their truth or falsity (*SM*, 274–6).

psychologists but the educated public as well. In his first book *Religion and Philosophy*, he had set himself to expose these errors, and much of what he has to say about psychology in his *Autobiography* and *Essay on Metaphysics* is but a generalization of his youthful criticism of James.

James was careful to disarm those who objected to the application of psychology to religion by distinguishing questions about the truth and value of religious 'manifestations' from questions about their psychological nature and origin. 'In the natural sciences and industrial arts', he pointed out, 'it never occurs to anyone to try to refute opinions by showing up their author's neurotic constitution. Opinions here are invariably tested by logic and by experiment, no matter what may be their author's neurological type. It should be no otherwise with religious opinions.'[1] Psychologists investigate the 'psychological conditions' of religious experience, not in order to determine whether such experience is true or not, but to gratify their curiosity. Besides, James argued, 'it always leads to a better understanding of a thing's significance to consider its exaggerations and perversions, its equivalents and substitutes'.[2] The prospects of such a study he thought to be fair:

the moment we renounce the absurd notion that a thing is exploded away as soon as it is classed with others, or its origin is shown; the moment we agree to stand by experimental results and inner quality, in judging of values—who does not see, [he asked] that we are likely to ascertain the distinctive significance of religious melancholy and happiness, or of religious trances, far better by comparing them . . . with other varieties of melancholy, happiness, and trance, than by refusing to consider their place in any more general series. . .?[3]

This collocation of happiness and melancholy with trances is a specimen of what Collingwood rejected in James's work. That the distinctive significance of 'religious' trances is likely to appear when they are compared with other kinds of trance few will question. But what is religious about a trance? That some people fall into

[1] William James, *The Varieties of Religious Experience* (New York: Modern Library Ed.), p. 19.
[2] Ibid., p. 23.   [3] Ibid., p. 25.

trances when strongly excited by religious rituals is no good reason for considering those trances religious. The trances into which some Pentecostalists fall are no more elements of Christianity than the frenzies of some Latin American devotees of Association football are of devotion to football. Frenzies and trances may be partly caused by acts of awareness or thought, but they do not by their very nature involve such acts.

Happiness and melancholy are another matter altogether. The distinctive significance of a mathematician's melancholy when he discovers a contradiction in a proof he has given, or of his happiness when he discovers a new non-contradictory proof, cannot be exhibited by comparing them with other varieties of melancholy and happiness. What is most distinctive about any given case of happiness is what it is happiness *in*. Happiness, therefore, is not a mere feeling, externally related to certain acts and thoughts. Yet James's method of studying it was to compare its varieties while ignoring the nature of the acts of consciousness in which it is found. Such a method must be wrong; for it can only be justified on the presupposition that happiness is a mere feeling. James's work accordingly exemplifies what Collingwood denounced as the besetting sin of psychology: the attempt to study processes of thought by methods which are appropriate only to feeling (*EM*, 114).

James and his followers would not deny Collingwood's accusation, but they would demur to it. Happiness and melancholy, they would protest, are feelings; and they would repeat their assurances that they do not pretend that psychologists can settle questions about the truth or value of the experiences they investigate. This demurrer, however, misses the point. Collingwood's position was not that happiness and melancholy do not involve feelings, but that to treat the feelings involved in religious or moral happiness and melancholy in isolation from what they are about deprives them of their religious character.

The point can be put in another way. James took it for granted that the religious 'experiences' he studied were either true or false, and either beneficial or harmful. While he professed, as a psychologist, to ignore their truth or falsity, and the good or harm they did, he did not doubt what he ignored. Yet he does not seem to have noticed that if religious 'experiences' are true or false, or beneficial or harmful in a high degree, they cannot be feelings. No feeling as such is true or false; and, while pleasurable feelings are good to have and painful ones bad, no feeling taken by itself, except those which are extremely painful, is either a great good or a great evil. James was therefore in a dilemma. If he denied that the 'experiences' he studied were true or false, beneficial or harmful, he could not maintain that they were religious; and if he affirmed it, he could not maintain that they could be treated in isolation as feelings.

Collingwood's argument against James was straightforward. Religious activity is conscious and reflective, and any feelings involved in it are primitive survivals which cannot be studied in isolation without destroying their character as religious. To study *religious* experience as mere feeling is a contradiction *in adiecto*. No inquirer can succeed in investigating experiences which involve systematic thought, as all religious experiences do, unless he masters that thought. Collingwood did not deny that the varieties of religious experience can be impartially studied, nor did he quarrel with James for putting aside the question of their validity while investigating their origin; for he knew that it is sometimes possible to establish the nature of a past belief without incidentally determining its validity. What he denounced in James's work was the doctrine that the origin and nature of religious experiences can be investigated without mastering their intellectual content.

This objection may be clarified by a comparison which James himself effectively employed. If James had inquired into the varieties of scientific experience, for example into Archimedes' exhilaration on discovering specific gravity, his procedure would have been to investigate how Archimedes felt and behaved, and to compare his feelings and behaviour with those of other scientists and with similar feelings and behaviour in non-scientific pursuits. To echo James: Are we not likely to ascertain the distinctive significance of scientific exhilaration far better by comparing it with other varieties of exhilaration, than by refusing to consider its place in some more general series? James would have taken no more interest in what Archimedes thought than he did in the thoughts of Stephen H. Hadley, whose feelings during conversion to Methodism he contrived to describe without saying anything at all about what Methodism was.[1]

The absurdity of such a procedure in the case of Archimedes is obvious. The sudden exhilaration that prompted Archimedes to leap from his bath and run naked through the street crying 'I've found it!' may doubtless find a place in a more general series containing many amusing examples of absent-mindedness, nudism, and enthusiasm. Yet not even James would maintain that the origin and nature of Archimedes' exhilaration could be ascertained without taking account of what his discovery of specific gravity was, and of how the buoyancy of his body in the bath suggested it to him. Why, then, should he have thought that the origin and nature of the feelings of Stephen H. Hadley during his conversion to Methodism could be ascertained without taking account of his thoughts about God and salvation?

Collingwood accordingly declared that James's book was fraudulent: not because the anecdotes in it were false, but because it professed to throw light on religious experience and threw no light on it whatever (*A*, 93). Just as cutting off Archimedes' exhilaration from his scientific thought divests it of its character as a scientific experience, so cutting off religious feelings from the religious thoughts in which they occur divests them of their character as religious experiences. This verdict rests on a general principle: an investigation of an experience which involves thought is fraudulent if it neglects to take full account of that thought. Given Collingwood's definition of psychology as the science of feeling, no psychological investigation of thought can take full account of it as thought; for such investigations treat thought as though it were feeling. In his *Autobiography*, therefore, Collingwood repeated the attack he had made in *Religion and Philosophy* on any and every psychological treatment of religion or of any other activity of thought, which he had concluded by saying, 'The mind, regarded in this way, ceases to be a mind at all' (*A*, 93).

By this principle Freud's work in ethics, politics, the psychology of religion, and primitive anthropology is beneath contempt, although his psychological discoveries are of value to all students

[1] James, op. cit., pp. 198–201, 232–4.

of those subjects (*A*, 95). In *The Future of an Illusion* Freud indeed conceded that before classifying religious beliefs as illusions it is necessary to show that there is no reason to believe that they are true. He even set out to examine what reasons those who teach religion give for their beliefs. Unfortunately, the reasons he found were of the kind one hears from second-rate divines, and did not even resemble those developed by competent theologians, much less those of an Augustine, a Maimonides, or an Aquinas.[1] Having demolished those mock reasons, Freud proceeded to explain religious beliefs as he would any other non-rational belief, like the belief of a foundling that he is of noble blood.

In *Totem and Taboo* he committed the same fallacy. Instead of treating primitive magic and ritual as products of the human mind, he took it for granted that they had no rational basis. Having noticed that the rituals of primitive societies exhibited certain external similarities to the behaviour of some of his neurotic patients, he tried to explain them as neurotic symptoms. That his attempt failed is now a commonplace in anthropology. To Collingwood, however, it was more than a failure. It was a manifestation of a radical intellectual vulgarity, a vulgarity which assorted ill with the depth and sagacity of Freud's purely psychological work.

Forms of social and political organization, systems of morals, religious and magical beliefs, and mythologies are all as much creations of mind as art and theoretical science; and to classify them as non-rational merely because you cannot understand their *rationale* is provincial.

A person [Collingwood declared] who can attempt to equate the difference between civilizations with the difference between mental disease and mental health, in other words to reduce the historical problem of the nature of civilization to a medical problem, is a person whose views on all problems connected with the nature of civilization will be false in proportion as he sticks honestly to his attempt, and dangerously false in proportion as his prestige in his own field stands high. (*PA*, 77 *n*.)

[1] Sigmund Freud (tr. W. D. Robson-Scott), *The Future of an Illusion* (London, 1928), pp. 45–51.

§ 3. *Psychology as 'The Pseudo-Science of Mind'*

Collingwood's demonstration that psychological investigations of religion are fraudulent applies to all psychological investigations of mental activities, provided that psychology be understood as he understood it, as the science of feeling. Mind is constituted, not by feelings, but by acts of consciousness, and the difference between feeling and consciousness is fundamental. Every act of consciousness involves consciousness of an object. Even at a very low level of consciousness, viz. selective attention, acts of consciousness, being conceptual, may be true or false.[1] At the same level, as appetitive, they may be successful or unsuccessful. Higher-order practical acts may be expedient or inexpedient, right or wrong, in accordance with or in violation of duty; higher-order theoretical acts, from simple questioning to advanced scientific thinking, may be ingenious or stupid, fruitful or sterile. On the other hand, no act of feeling involves consciousness of anything; nor can any feeling be true or false, right or wrong, well or ill done. To investigate mind, which is constituted by the various functions of consciousness, as though it were nothing but feeling, is therefore a manifest error. As a science of mind as opposed to feeling, psychology is a pseudo-science.

In his *Essay on Metaphysics* Collingwood alleged that psychologists have tried to substitute psychology for the traditional philosophical sciences of logic, ethics, and metaphysics (*EM*, 104–5, 108–9). This charge is implausible, and he did not bring evidence for it. It is quite clear, for example, that neither James nor Freud wished to substitute psychology for logic; and that both would have distinguished psychology from ethics and from the methodology of science. Few or no psychologists have failed to distinguish psychology from the 'normative', or, as Collingwood preferred to call them, the 'criteriological' sciences, whose object is to determine the nature of the criteria according to which the various kinds of mental act are judged, e.g. truth and falsity, validity and invalidity, right and wrong.

---

[1] See above, Ch. III, § 5. Collingwood did not hold this opinion, but his principles implied it.

Most psychologists put their arguments forward as logically valid, and denounce any fellow-psychologist's logical fallacies. The claim of psychology that they advance is not to supplant the criteriological sciences, but to complement them. Logic enables us to show that a given argument is valid or invalid; but it does not enable us to explain the fact that a man reasons now validly and now invalidly, or to predict how he will reason on any future occasion. The criteriological sciences of mind do not provide for mental acts explanations of the same kind as those which the natural sciences provide for natural events. Although many psychologists have claimed that psychology will one day provide such explanations, the preceding argument holds against this claim also. Psychology as Collingwood conceived it, the science of feeling, cannot treat of mental acts at all, but only of the feelings involved in them. At best it might explain and predict those feelings. Yet it is unlikely that feelings involved in acts of consciousness should be explicable in isolation from those acts of consciousness (see below, Ch. XI, § 2).

Unwisely, Collingwood was not content to rest his case there. Pursuing further his mistaken notion that psychologists are trying to undermine the criteriological sciences, he attempted to show that no activity of which there is a criteriological science is properly an object of psychological investigation. His argument, which he propounded in his *Essay on Metaphysics*, was as follows. 'Any piece of thinking, theoretical or practical, includes as an integral part of itself the thought of a standard or criterion by reference to which it is judged a successful or unsuccessful piece of thinking' (*EM*, 107). Psychology, however, 'has always approached the study of thought with a perfectly clear and conscious determination to ignore one whole department of the truth, namely to ignore the self-critical function of thought and the criteria which that function implied' (*EM*, 115–16). Inasmuch as it pretends to investigate thought, psychology is therefore a pseudo-science.

This argument rests on a premiss which in *The New Leviathan* Collingwood himself exposed as false. No act of consciousness includes as part of itself the thought of a criterion by which it is judged, because the thought of such a criterion presupposes awareness of the act of consciousness under judgement, and, by the Principle of Order, no act of consciousness *per se* involves awareness of itself (*NL*, 5. 91). Nor can it be maintained that any piece of thinking necessarily gives rise to the thought of such a criterion. Acts of consciousness form a series in which the lower are necessary conditions of the higher; but, by what Collingwood called the Law of Contingency, no act of consciousness is a sufficient condition of an act of a higher order (*NL*, 9. 48). It follows that no piece of thinking necessarily involves the higher-order thought of a criterion by reference to which it is judged. It is true that everybody who thinks is potentially a critic of his own thoughts; but he does not necessarily or invariably criticize them.

The special argument in the *Essay on Metaphysics* therefore proves nothing, and has only academic interest. All that is of value in what Collingwood had to say against psychology as a science of thought is implicit in his criticism of psychological investigations of religion, and is no more than a generalization of that criticism.

§ 4. *Psychology, the Social Sciences, and History*

If psychology is not the non-criteriological science of mind, what is? A hint may be found in Collingwood's depreciation of the claims of psychology to be such a science: the claim of psychology

to have thrown light on the processes of thinking [he remarked] is incapable of surviving any critical inspection of the work done by psychologists when they deal with such matters as the nature and function in human life of religion or art; the aims and prospects, hopes and fears, of what is called civilization; or the intellectual structure of institutions which, because they are found in civilizations other than that to which the writer belongs, are called savage. (*EM*, 117.)

It is matters like these with which a genuine science of mind must deal, and not with mere feeling.

If, as Collingwood maintained, it is fair 'to judge the soundness of modern psychology regarded as a science of thought by its success in propounding, for the problems [matters like these] present, convincing and helpful and agreed solutions' (*EM*, 118), then we are obliged to recognize as genuine sciences of mind any which do propound such solutions. Are there such sciences? The intellectual structure of the institutions of civilizations other than our own is being successfully studied by anthropology; the nature and function in human life of religion and art by anthropologists, historians, and sociologists; and the aims and prospects, hopes and fears, of contemporary civilization by historians, sociologists, economists, human geographers, and political scientists. To at least some of the problems raised by these matters there is no doubt that the sciences mentioned have propounded convincing and helpful and agreed solutions.

This answer, however, does not resolve the philosophical problem. Anthropology, sociology, history, geography, and the study of political institutions are names which signify the division of labour in academies and research institutions rather than divisions of principle. It is notorious that students of each of those sciences quarrel bitterly about the nature of their work. In a lecture to the British Academy in 1936 Collingwood pointed out that the fundamental question about which they dispute is whether or not anthropology, geography, history, and the study of political institutions are applied forms of a general science of human behaviour modelled upon the theoretical natural sciences.

Sociology, as its projector, Auguste Comte, first conceived it, was to be such a science: it would discover the regularities or patterns exhibited in human activity, and would formulate them as laws; sciences like anthropology, history, geography, and the study of political institutions would be related to sociology as observational astronomy is to the physics of gravitation, or palaeontology to the biological theory of evolution (IH, 128). Others look to a future social psychology, or to a future combination of individual and social psychology, as the required general science. No less a man than Professor C. D. Broad once declared that the future of mankind hangs on the result of a race between 'physics and death' on one side, and on the other 'psychology and life'.[1]

Collingwood's rejection of psychology as the future science of mind rested, as we have seen, on an inadequate foundation. He did not know enough about behaviourist psychology to forecast that,

---

[1] C. D. Broad, *The Mind and its Place in Nature* (London, 1925), p. 666.

twenty years after he wrote his *Essay on Metaphysics*, it would have achieved much, especially in what is called 'learning theory'. Yet, impressive as its achievements are, not even its most sanguine advocates would claim that it can yet discharge the function of a complete science of mind. It neither has propounded nor promises to propound convincing solutions of any of the principal problems which Collingwood held that a genuine science of mind must investigate.

Nor have the scientists who have propounded such solutions—anthropologists, sociologists, economists, historians, geographers, and political scientists—by any means unanimously agreed that their work presupposes a general science of human behaviour modelled on natural science, whether that science be behaviourist psychology or Comtist sociology. Many of them express their disbelief in such a view by affirming that their sciences are autonomous, and refusing to look to any theoretical natural science either for data or for principles of explanation (cf. *IH*, 318). Sometimes they defend their repudiation of dependency on natural science by contending that their sciences—sociology, anthropology, geography, and the rest—are forms of history, and that history is not merely applied natural science. That was Collingwood's position.

When an historian like Collingwood claims the whole of human action as the province of history, social scientists are apt to dismiss his claim as a manœuvre in academic politics: either an attack on the academic position of their own sciences, or an attempt to bring their work under the academic hegemony of Departments of History. Collingwood's claim was neither. His sole intention was to show that all the social sciences, so far as they have been fruitful, have employed the same methods as history, and that those methods are neither applications nor anticipations of a putative natural science of human behaviour.

Why then did Collingwood single out history? Why not say that all the sciences of human action are forms of anthropology? Economics, sociology, political science, and even human geography are by definition limited either to kinds or aspects of human action; but anthropology, like history, is not. It is important to recognize that while doubtless many reasons for preferring history weighed with him, none was compelling. He would have had no objection to the name 'anthropology', provided that it were stipulated that the methods of anthropology are the same as those of history. If 'history' be taken to mean what is done in academic Departments of History, or 'anthropology' what is done in Departments of Anthropology, then neither could be called a complete science of human action. But if each is defined by the methods it characteristically employs, without regard to its conventional subject-matter, it is clear not only that both employ the same methods, but also that both can in principle be extended to all human action. Thus, although historians conventionally do not investigate surviving pre-literate societies, or anthropologists past literate societies, these conventional demarcations, as Professor A. L. Kroeber has pointed out,[1] do not imply limitations in principle.

Collingwood's chief reasons for preferring the name 'history' were, I think, two. First, he arrived at his analysis of what a genuine science of human action would be by reflecting on his studies of Roman Britain, which he was accustomed to describe as 'history'. A second, and perhaps a more important, reason was that anthropology, like sociology, for the most part investigates societies and cultures rather than individuals. History not only treats of both, but it gives priority to the latter. Virtually all historians are, in practice, what it is now fashionable to call 'methodological individualists'.[2] Collingwood too, as we shall see, was a methodological individualist. By saying that the various sciences of human action must be historical he implied that they presuppose methodological individualism (see below, pp. 206–9).

Whether human action may be fruitfully studied by one or more of the natural sciences, or only by sciences of a different kind, is perhaps the most important question in the intellectual life of our time. A wrong answer could be disastrous; for it is imperative, as Collingwood pointed out, to 'construct a science of human affairs,

[1] A. L. Kroeber in *The American Anthropologist*, xxxvii (1935), pp. 539–64; E. E. Evans-Pritchard, *Social Anthropology* (London, 1951), pp. 60–63.

[2] K. R. Popper, *The Open Society and its Enemies* (3rd ed., London, 1957), vol. ii, pp. 91–92; 324; and *The Poverty of Historicism* (London, 1957), pp. 136, 142. For controversies about 'methodological individualism' consult the essays by J. W. N. Watkins and E. A. Gellner in Patrick Gardiner (ed.), *Theories of History* (Glencoe, Ill., 1959), pp. 488–515, and May Brodbeck in *Philosophy of Science*, xxv (1958), pp. 1–22.

. . . from which men could learn to deal with human situations as skilfully as natural science had taught them to deal with situations in the world of Nature' (*A*, 115). As we have seen, he believed that science to be history; and his analysis of historical method, to which we must now turn, is beyond doubt his greatest philosophical achievement.

VIII

SCIENTIFIC HISTORY

§ 1. *Natural History and History Proper*

COLLINGWOOD arrived at his conception of history after protracted reflection on his own work as an historian. When he had written *Speculum Mentis* he had made no clear distinction between history and the natural sciences as they are practised, and had urged that natural science itself is becoming more and more historical. For example, astronomy is transforming itself into the history of the stellar universe, geology and physical geography into the history of the earth, and biology into the history of the origin of species (*SM*, 186–8, 211–15). Not until nine years after he had decided to make philosophical reflection on history his chief work did he take the step of sharply distinguishing history proper from the study of the past by the methods of natural science. This step he considered so important in his intellectual life, that in his *Autobiography* he recorded when and under what circumstances he first consciously 'registered' it: it was during the summer of 1928, which he spent at Le Martouret, 'that pleasant country-house near Die, sitting under the plane-trees on the terrace and writing down . . . the lessons of . . . nine years' work in historical research' (*A*, 107).

It is natural to suppose that all past happenings, whether natural events, or feelings, or acts of consciousness, ought to be investigated by exactly the same scientific methods; for they are all objects of memory, and the methods of historians of human affairs at least bear a resemblance to those of natural scientists investigating past states of the world of nature. Collingwood did not deny that 'archaeologists had often called attention to the likeness between their own stratigraphical methods and those of geology', and he conceded that 'a likeness there certainly was'; yet the cardinal point in his own conception of archaeology was that 'there was a difference as well' (*A*, 107–8). Archaeology is but a branch of history proper, and he held that a thorough analysis of historical method would show that, despite significant likenesses, in certain fundamental respects it differs from that by which geologists, palaeontologists, and astronomers investigate past natural events. A methodology of history proper must allow full weight to the differences as well as to the likenesses.

One way in which a natural scientist may ascertain that a certain natural event took place at a certain time in the past is by consulting records of past observations, another is by calculating back from his own present observations; and he may verify the results he obtains by one method by comparing them with those he obtains by the other. The former method in no way differs from that of consulting administrative or legal records, and the same problems of determining authenticity, veracity, and accuracy arise in it (*IN*, 176). When a natural scientist employs it, therefore, he is doing exactly what any historian of human action does.

By contrast, the method of calculating back from his own present observations appears to be independent of human records. To take a simple case: it is recorded in various chronicles that a large comet was visible in the year before the Battle of Hastings. Are the chronicles right? To answer this question, an astronomer would first have to identify the comet: but let it be supposed that the descriptions of the comet in the chronicles fit Halley's Comet and no other. He would then need to know the laws governing the orbit of that comet, which Newton showed to be the same as Kepler's Laws of Planetary Motion, the laws governing the orbit of the earth, and the position of the comet relative to the earth and sun at two different times. From his information about the relative positions of the comet and the earth, he could then calculate, in accordance with the orbital laws, what their relative positions were during the year before the Battle of Hastings. This result, together with information about how near the comet must be to be visible, would entail either that it was visible during that year, or that it was not.

At the present time (1961) most astronomers have not seen Halley's Comet at all, and must rely on historical records for their information about the positions which it has been observed to occupy in the past. However, when it next appears, that will not be necessary. They may then make their own observations and computations of its positions relative to the earth and sun, and, to avoid any recourse to records, may simply commit them to memory. They will then need only the general Newtonian laws of the orbits of comets in order to make their calculations.

Although it is something of a dogma among philosophers of natural science that the foundation of natural science is simply observation, whether in natural conditions or in the laboratory, Collingwood rightly protested that it is not the whole truth. Even if a scientist makes his calculations with no other information than what he remembers from personal observation, he has certainly not established in this way all the laws he employs in them. Although it is theoretically possible that an isolated intelligent being might be capable of discovering the whole of natural science for himself, carrying out all the required observations and remembering them without records, it is evident that no human being could do so or has done so. All natural science as developed by the human race depends upon the use of records. Therefore, since 'consultation and interpretation of records is the characteristic feature of historical work', Collingwood argued that 'natural science as a form of thought exists and always has existed in a context of history, and depends on historical thought for its existence' (*IN*, 176–7).

At first glance, this argument will no doubt be dismissed as another of Collingwood's ingenious sophisms at the expense of natural science. Certainly, if he had meant to insinuate that natural scientists need help in their own work from professional historians, it would have been ridiculous. However, he was at pains to obviate that interpretation. By insisting that historical thinking is an element in scientific thinking, he implied that natural scientists already do their own historical work perfectly well (*A*, 87). When he maintained in *The Idea of Nature* that natural science and human history were distinct forms of thought, he did not mean that they did not overlap: his view was that natural science not only has its own characteristic method, which is different from that of human history, but also that it is more complex than human history, in that it employs historical method in conjunction with its own.

The method that is characteristic of natural science is plainly exhibited in our example. It is to investigate a past event by subsuming it, along with all others of the same kind, under 'a general formula or law of nature' (*IH*, 214). That Halley's Comet was at a certain place at a certain time must be subsumed under whatever general laws govern the orbits of comets. Now, if Collingwood was right in thinking that in natural science as we have it all demonstrations of laws of nature involve the authentication and interpretation of records, then, on pain of a vicious infinite regress, it follows that not all authentication and interpretation of records can involve the use of laws of nature. This is the sting in Collingwood's conclusion in *The Idea of Nature* that natural science depends on history for its existence. In the order of knowledge history is logically prior to natural science (*IN*, 176–7).

What then is the characteristic method of history? Its negative characteristic has already been established: it does not presuppose that the acts it investigates can be subsumed under universal formulae or laws of nature. Its positive characteristic is implicit in Collingwood's description of it as concerned with consulting and interpreting records. It is occupied entirely with evidence which, like documentary records, can be interpreted as a trace or survival of a conscious or purposive act. Historical narratives are narratives of conscious or purposive activity, and so of human activity; and historical evidence consists of the relics of that activity, whether written or unwritten. That is why 'the ordinary historian' will maintain that 'all history properly so called is the history of human affairs' (*IH*, 212). By contrast, a natural scientist does not presuppose that either the observed events from which he makes his calculations, or the unobserved past events which he concludes to have occurred, are in any sense purposive or relics of purposive activity. Even if conscious acts can be subsumed under laws of nature, historians do not presuppose it; and even if natural events are expressions of purposes, presumably God's, natural scientists do not presuppose it (*A*, 108–9; *IH*, 214–15).

The study of past natural events by the methods of natural science is therefore sharply distinct from the study of past actions by the methods of human history. In 1928 Collingwood marked this distinction with an abusive label: only the latter was 'history proper', the former was 'pseudo-history' (*A*, 107). By parity of reasoning, he ought to have been willing to call history proper 'pseudo-natural science'; for it must not be forgotten that he held that there is a likeness between them (*A*, 108; *IH*, 269). Such uses of the prefix 'pseudo' ought to be eschewed; for one activity can resemble another without counterfeiting it. 'Natural history' is a less tendentious name for the study of the past by the methods of natural science.

§ 2. *Scissors-and-paste versus Interpretation of Evidence*

Despite Collingwood's argument that history proper must be distinct from and logically prior to natural science, his distinction cannot be accepted on sight as valid. Are laws discovered only by the Baconian methods of natural science? Might not certain fundamental laws be verified without recourse to historical records? Many philosophers would contend that no historian could validly infer a conclusion about an individual act in the past from a premiss about an individual trace or relic in the present, except by invoking a putative law of nature; and should any historian dare to protest the contrary, they would set him down as methodologically incompetent. Collingwood could only vindicate his distinction by a thorough analysis of the nature of historical thinking.

In the Epilegomenon to *The Idea of History* entitled 'Historical Evidence', which he wrote in 1939, he distinguished three forms of historical thinking which have been practised since the Renaissance. On the least scientific of these he bestowed the name 'scissors-and-paste'; the other two he described as 'critical history' and 'scientific history' respectively. Scissors-and-paste history is the attempt to recover the truth about the past by excerpting it from the writings of authorities. An authority is strictly a contemporary or near-contemporary of certain happenings, who has written about them either from his own observations or from what he has gathered from others about theirs. One who has compiled a narrative from lost narratives by genuine authorities will be treated as an authority, but strictly he is not one. Livy is not an authority in the sense in which Herodotus and Thucydides are (*IH*, 33). The conception of history as drawn from authorities does not apply to the authorities themselves, but only to those who construct patchwork narratives out of materials excerpted from their works. Herodotus and Thucydides were not scissors-and-paste historians.

A scissors-and-paste historian must walk by faith; for he has no other light to guide him. Where the authorities he follows contradict each other he must choose between them; but he will display his principles by choosing either capriciously, giving no reasons at all; or consistently, but on some arbitrary principle, such as always to prefer the most ancient authority, or the most 'patriotic' version of the facts. Having wrongly identified history with scissors-and-paste, Descartes and his followers rightly refused to describe it as a form of knowledge (*IH*, 59).

Under the spur of Descartes's criticism, more and more historians began to adopt a critical attitude towards historical narratives (*IH*, 62). Gradually the word 'authority' was supplanted in their diction by the word 'source', by which they meant simply a document containing a statement, without any implication as to its credibility. They had now to establish principles according to which the relative credibility of their sources could be determined; for they could not, in consistency, accept any statement from a source until it had been examined and found trustworthy. The technique of sifting true statements in sources from false Collingwood described as 'critical history'; the principles of which, as he remarked, were 'worked out from the seventeenth century onwards, and officially acclaimed in the nineteenth as the apotheosis of the historical consciousness' (*IH*, 259).

Critical history, however, is not the same thing as modern scientific history: Collingwood held it to be rather 'the final form taken by scissors-and-paste history on the eve of its dissolution' (*IH*, 260). Its defect as scientific history was first discerned by Vico, when he pointed out that false statements are by no means worthless as historical evidence. A critical historian is concerned only to establish whether a given statement in a source is true or not; in the first case it is passed as 'fit for the scrap-book'; in the second, 'it is consigned to the waste-paper basket' (*IH*, 259). Where his sources do not contain statements he can accept as true, he must be silent; for he is tied by the leg to them, and can discover nothing they do not tell him (*A*, 79–80).

To show that historians have now broken through the confinement of critical history, Collingwood proposed a remarkable experiment. Even today, the writings of Herodotus and Thucydides remain of outstanding importance for Greek history down to the end of the Peloponnesian War. With reference to that period, then, take a distinguished work of the middle of the nineteenth century, Grote's *History of Greece*, and a representative work of modern scientific history, the *Cambridge Ancient History*, and mark in each every sentence for which there is an original in Herodotus and Thucydides (*IH*, 260). In the former, Collingwood predicted, you will find that for the most part Grote is tied to the questions Herodotus and Thucydides asked, and to the answers they gave to them. He can select, but he cannot reconsider the whole subject on principles of his own. By contrast, the questions asked by a contributor to the *Cambridge Ancient History* are not those of Herodotus and Thucydides, but his own; and when he extracts from Herodotus or Thucydides an answer to one of his own questions, it is not by excerpting it, but by systematic questioning, 'twisting a passage ostensibly about something quite different into an answer to the question he has decided to ask' (*IH*, 269–70).

Modern historians therefore resemble natural scientists in this at least: their method is 'Baconian'. Just as a natural scientist must 'put Nature to the question', so a scientific historian must put to the question not only everything that critical historians would account a 'source', but anything whatever from which he may extract what he wants to know. It may not be anything in writing, but a coin, a ruined building, a tool, or a utensil (*IH*, 278–80). Anything that is a survival, trace, or relic of a past conscious act is potentially historical evidence (*A*, 96–99; *IH*, 203). Nor does a scientific historian ask questions in order to ascertain the truth or falsity of the evidence at his disposal, a task which in the case of archaeological survivals is logically impossible; his aim is rather to discover what that evidence means (*IH*, 259). Scientific history is the fruit of the marriage of the scientific principle that history must be 'Baconian' in method, with Vico's principle that historians must seek the meaning of their evidence rather than its truth.

Truth, however, is their goal. As soon as an historian knows the meaning or purpose of a relic or trace of the past, he is in a position to infer a truth about a past act. A document was written by some-body for some purpose. As a series of marks on parchment or paper, it is not to an historian evidence of anything. But if he knows the language in which it is written, he can read it, and on reading it he will usually discover part of the purpose for which it was written: to set down certain statements, promises, prayers, commands, or the like. He will know more of that purpose if he knows who was intended to read it, and more still if he knows what the writer intended his reader's response to be, and why. He will only have extracted the full value of the document as evidence when he understands in detail why its writer wrote it as he did, and not in some other way. Now knowledge that a man wrote a document in a certain way for certain reasons is knowledge of a past conscious act.

The same point holds for unwritten survivals. A Roman utensil is of no use to an historian as evidence while it remains an implement of uncertain use (A, 109); but as soon as he knows what it was for, say a hand flour-mill, he can infer that those who left it ground wheat by hand. And this knowledge would suggest other questions: How widespread was the production of flour? What was it used for? How was wheat obtained?

By suggesting such questions, a survival of the past may be part of the evidence for acts other than those of which it is a direct trace. A tax-receipt is a direct trace of the act of an official placing on record that a certain person paid a certain tax. It is also a more remote trace of other acts: if the official was honest and accurate, of an actual payment of tax; if he was corrupt, of his concealment of a failure to pay. The act of which the receipt is a direct trace is itself a trace of an actual payment or a concealed evasion of payment; and quite obviously an historian would not break off his inquiry at this point. By skilfully marshalling his questions, he may discover acts of which he has only the most remote evidence: traces of traces of traces.

It is instructive to compare Collingwood's impression of the history of modern historiography with the conclusions reached by another historian who has investigated the subject in detail, namely those of Professor Butterfield,[1] who does not hesitate to liken the revolution in historical studies in the nineteenth century to the scientific revolution of the seventeenth, as Collingwood had likened it to the Copernican revolution.[2] Moreover, Butterfield's analysis of the work of the Göttingen school in the late eighteenth century, especially of that of Schlözer, whom he describes as 'perpetually' asking 'Where does our knowledge come from and how has it reached us?' strikingly confirms Collingwood's description of the 'critical', as opposed to the 'scientific' historian.[3] Yet in another respect Butterfield's work corrects Collingwood's. Butterfield presents Niebuhr and Ranke, the Galileo and the Newton of the historical revolution, as following in the footsteps of Göttingen. Whereas Collingwood assimilated critical history to scissors-and-paste, Butterfield shows it to have resolutely broken with fabulous and propagandist history. It was scientific history (or, as Butterfield calls it, 'technical history') in embryo.

In another respect Collingwood and Butterfield are at one. To both, scientific history is systematic and sceptical inquiry. Historians must not take documents or narratives at their face value, but must apply Vico's principle, and ask, 'What do they mean?' Butterfield's studies in the historiography of the origins of the Seven Years War, and of the Massacre of St. Bartholomew, are brilliant illustrations of how to apply it.[4] Yet here what Butterfield and Collingwood have to say is liable to be misunderstood. When the general authenticity and reliability of whole classes of documents can be established, the probity of individual documents of those classes is not called in question without special reason. Many professional historians who work largely with such documents, e.g. with certain types of administrative record, see themselves not as torturing answers out of recalcitrant witnesses, but as making known what truthful witnesses have volunteered without leading. A good historian is not only one who can extract the truth from evidence which would deceive an untrained inquirer, he is also one

---

[1] Herbert Butterfield, *Man on His Past* (Cambridge, 1955).
[2] Ibid., pp. 32, 97.   [3] Ibid., p. 58.   [4] Ibid., chs. 5–6.

who collects and assembles information which amateurs or partisans neglect. Carlyle made Dryasdust a figure of fun; but those who have read Sir Lewis Namier's demolition of several recent Nazi memoirs[1] will know how formidable to false propagandists is even the lowly activity of exactly recording and comparing the dates on published documents.

§ 3. *Question and Evidence*

Collingwood's exposition of the method of scientific history does not solve the philosophical problem with which he began. If the Baconian method is to be followed in history, it must be possible to deduce from a proposed answer to an historian's question that certain traces which survive from the past either are or are not of a certain kind. Unless such inferences were legitimate, no historian could connect an answer he has proposed with the evidence upon which he must decide either to reject or to persevere with it. Now in natural history, answers about the past are connected with evidence in the present by calculations according to laws of nature. Yet, Collingwood contended that an historian employs no laws: he 'need not and cannot (without ceasing to be an historian) emulate the [natural] scientist in searching for the . . . laws of events' (*IH*, 214). How can he, then, connect his hypotheses with his evidence?

Let us consider an example. In his *Autobiography* Collingwood described a specimen of the Baconian method in history which may be found in his own contribution to the *Oxford History of England*, vol. i, pp. 31–53. It is well known that Julius Caesar twice invaded Britain, and, after short campaigns, withdrew. What was the nature of these acts? This vague question must be replaced by a precise one. The fact that he did each time withdraw suggests the question: Was his withdrawal planned from the beginning? If it was, then his invasions would have been either punitive expeditions or demonstrations of force. Were they? The only evidence upon which these questions may be answered is contained in Caesar's *Commentaries*. If his invasions had been punitive expeditions, then it is a fair inference, first, that he would have said so in his *Commentaries*, and

---

[1] Sir Lewis Namier, *In the Nazi Era* (London, 1952).

secondly, that the force he took would not have been greatly larger than he believed sufficient for that purpose. However, we find not only that he never did say in the *Commentaries* what he meant to effect by his invasions, but also that the force he took with him was comparable in size with the army later sent by Claudius, which sufficed to conquer the whole south of Britain. Both the answer that Caesar's invasions were merely punitive expeditions, and the answer that his early withdrawals were planned from the beginning, are therefore in conflict with the evidence.

Having disproved that Caesar's withdrawals were planned beforehand, Collingwood's next step was to ask what Caesar's intention had been if he had planned to remain. Presumably, it would have been completely to subdue at least a large part of the country. This answer is consistent with the evidence so far presented. Nor is there any evidence against it, except for those who think either that Caesar was too good a commander to fail in such an undertaking, or that, if he had failed, he was too candid an historian not to record it. However, there is ample evidence that Caesar was not invincible; and that he was scrupulous in avowing failure is not the impression left by his *Commentaries* as a whole: they plainly were designed to show him in as favourable a light as possible. Is there any other hypothesis that might be true? Collingwood at least could think of none. He therefore concluded that Caesar's invasion was a frustrated attempt completely to conquer at least part of Britain; and he claimed for this conclusion exactly what a natural scientist would claim for an hypothesis that satisfied all the experimental tests he could devise: '[F]uture historians will have to reckon with the question I have raised, and either accept my answer or produce a better one' (*A*, 131).[1] A better answer would be one that fits all the evidence which his fits, and also further evidence which his does not fit.

Do Collingwood's inferences, in this elaborate specimen of Baconian reasoning, rest on general laws? Although it is impossible here to examine each of its steps in detail, let us consider the first of them. Beginning with the question, 'Did Caesar intend only a punitive

---

[1] I. A. Richmond, in *Roman Britain* (London: Penguin Books, 1955), p. 10, leaves the question open whether Caesar was trying to annex Britain or only to forestall British intervention in Gaul.

expedition or demonstration of force or did he intend something more?' Collingwood examined the first alternative, that Caesar intended no more than a punitive expedition, and reasoned that, if it were true, then Caesar would have stated that intention in his *Commentaries*, and that, since he did not state that intention, the first alternative must be false. Fundamentally, this argument is of a common logical form, the *modus tollendo tollens*, namely,

It is true that if p then q, but false that q, so it is false that p.

It has, however, one complication. The protasis of the hypothetical premiss turns out, on analysis, to be a conjunction of three statements, only one of which is to be disproved. In full, therefore, the form of Collingwood's argument is:

It is true that if p_1 and p_2 and p_3 then q, but false that q, so, since p_2 and p_3 are certainly true, it is false that p_1.

The argument itself, enunciated in full, runs:

If Caesar's invasion had been a successful punitive expedition (p_1), and if he had written his *Commentaries* to advertise his successes (p_2) and had known that in order to advertise the success of his invasion (if it had been a success) it would have been necessary to make plain in his *Commentaries* what he had intended (p_3), then he would have made plain in his *Commentaries* what he had intended (q);
But he did not make plain in his *Commentaries* what he had intended (q is false);
So, since Caesar did write his *Commentaries* to advertise his successes (p_2), and did know that in order to advertise the success of his invasion it would have been necessary to make his intention plain (p_3), his invasion was not a successful punitive expedition (p_1 is false).

Collingwood contended that neither this argument, nor any of the others that compose his elaborate demonstration of what Caesar's intention was, presupposes any general law.

Only one part of Collingwood's argument can plausibly be supposed to be or to presuppose a general law, namely, its hypothetical premiss. Its categorical premiss, that Caesar did not make plain in his *Commentaries* what he had intended, is evidently not a general law. But it is equally evident that neither is the hypothetical premiss, as it stands, a general law; for it is about a single individual, Caesar. However, it may presuppose a general law. Does it? It is true that there could be no justification for asserting that if Caesar had succeeded in a certain enterprise, and had been writing a book to advertise his successes, and had known that to advertise his success in that enterprise he must make certain things plain in that book, then he would have made those things plain, unless the same assertion could be made of everybody. The hypothetical premiss about Caesar does presuppose a general hypothetical about anybody and everybody. Now, is that general hypothetical a law? A moment's reflection will show that it is not. A general law must admit of possible empirical falsification, but the general hypothetical presupposed by Collingwood's premiss does not. No conceivable empirical evidence would count against the proposition that if you hold to your intention to bring something about, and believe that you must take certain steps to do so, then you will take those steps if you can. Any evidence which goes to show that you held that belief but did not take those steps, although you could have, also goes to show that you did not stick to your intention. Collingwood's hypothetical premiss therefore rests, not on a general law, but on an analytic truth which derives from the very concept of an intention. It follows that his argument neither contains nor presupposes any general law.

This analysis is at least a partial answer to the question with which we began, namely, How can an historian connect his conclusions with his evidence if he employs no general laws? One way in which he might do so would be by hypothetical premisses about what this or that individual would do in such and such circumstances. Our analysis also disposes of the common objection that all such hypothetical premisses about individuals rest on general laws. At least one such hypothetical does not, and it is quite plain that many others like it can be constructed.

Is all Baconian reasoning in history of this kind? Off-hand, many of the hypothetical premisses by which historians connect their conclusions with their evidence appear to be special cases neither of analytic truths nor of general laws. For example, in his *Structure of Politics at the Accession of George III*, Sir Lewis Namier has argued that 'even where a territorial magnate or a combination "of the great men of the county" were able to exert a dominant influence in elections, they had to be extremely careful not to excite the jealousy of the country gentlemen', giving as part of his evidence that 'hardly ever was an attempt made in a county to fill both seats with members of the same family': between 1761 and 1784 there were only two such cases.[1] His argument might be thrown into a *tollendo tollens* as follows:

> If territorial magnates had been able to ignore the jealousy of the country gentlemen, then a fair number of attempts would have been made to fill both county seats with members of the same family;
>
> But only two such attempts were in fact made,
>
> Therefore, territorial magnates were not able to ignore the jealousy of the country gentlemen.

Many arguments like that may be found in the work of any scientific historian.

The hypothetical premiss by which Namier connected the conclusion of his argument with his evidence is certainly not an analytic truth. Neither, however, does it appear to be a general law; for it refers to the territorial magnates and country gentlemen of a certain region during a certain period of time. It is true that the application of some general laws appears to be confined to certain regions of space, e.g. the law that on the earth's surface at sea-level the boiling-point of water is 100° C.; but such laws are covertly general. The law of the boiling-point of water is equivalent to the law that at any time and place, under atmospheric conditions which are the same as those on the earth's surface at sea-level, the boiling-point of water is 100°C.: it refers, therefore, not to a certain place, but to specifiable atmospheric conditions. Namier, however, does not even hint at any specifiable conditions of character and circumstance by the mention of which his hypothetical premiss about

[1] Sir Lewis Namier, *The Structure of Politics at the Accession of George III* (2nd ed., London, 1957), pp. 70–71.

magnates and county gentlemen could be transformed into a general law.

Since it would be unprofitable here to examine any conjectures about what such conditions might be, I can only beg any reader who may choose to amuse himself by doing so to take care that his conjectural conditions are really general. It will not do, for example, to specify 'all territorial magnates who act as the English territorial magnates acted between 1750 and 1780', for that specifies no character in virtue of which the English magnates acted as they did. Provided that the conjectured law is really general, I am confident that any student of history will be able to cite evidence that it is false.

Collingwood's problem can now be formulated. It was this. Since it has been shown that the hypothetical premisses on which many historical inferences turn can be derived neither from analytic truths nor from general laws, how then are they established?

Before turning to the answer Collingwood gave, it may clarify the question itself to state it in a useful terminology which Ryle has introduced, and which derives from, but is not identical with, the logical distinction between open and closed variables.[1] A hypothetical proposition which contains no reference to any individual or group which is only named or pointed out, or to any particular place or time, may be described as 'open'. Every general law admits of being stated as an open hypothetical. If rendered into logical symbolism, it would contain no names, but only name-variables. Such a proposition would be,

1. If a crystal is of sugar, it will dissolve in water,

which, in symbolism, would be,

1a. For all values of 'x' and of 'y', if x is a crystal and of sugar, and y is water, then x will dissolve in y.

This proposition is open because it contains no reference to any individual crystal or to this water rather than that; which is why, in symbolism, it contains no names, but only the name-variables 'x' and 'y'. Any hypothetical that refers to a named or indicated

---

[1] Ryle, op. cit., pp. 88–89, 123–5.

individual, or to a particular place or time, may be described as to that extent 'closed'. Thus the hypothetical proposition,

2. If *that* crystal is of sugar it will dissolve in water,

is partly closed; and its counterpart,

3. If *that* crystal is of sugar, then it will dissolve in *this* water, i.e. the water now in this cup,

is closed altogether. This is revealed by rendering each into symbolism. Whereas (2) becomes

2*a*. For all values of 'y', if a is a crystal and of sugar, and if y is water, then a will dissolve in y,

in which the variable 'y' survives, even though 'x' has been replaced by the name 'a', in (3) even the variable 'y' disappears:

3*a*. If a is a crystal and of sugar, and b is the water now in this cup, then a will dissolve in b.

It should be noticed that hypotheticals about classes which are defined by reference to an individual are also partly closed. Thus,

4. If all the crystals on that plate are of sugar then they will dissolve in water,

contains a reference to that plate, and is therefore partly closed. In symbolism, it would be

4*a*. For all values of 'x' and 'y', if x is a crystal on a, and is of sugar, and if y is water, then x will dissolve in y.

Although most of the hypotheticals employed by historians are only partly closed, for brevity I shall henceforth refer to them simply as 'closed', except where it is important to distinguish them from those which are closed altogether.

In terms of this analysis, Collingwood's problem may be reformulated as: How are the closed hypotheticals employed by historians verified or falsified? When they are special cases of analytic truths, the answer is plain: by logical analysis. But when they are not? The question is complicated by a peculiar feature of many of the arguments in which historians employ closed hypotheticals: being arguments in *tollendo tollens*, their hypothetical premisses are counter-factual, that is, their protases are false.

It is not difficult to verify a closed hypothetical the protasis of which is true. If the hypothetical to be verified is

> If that crystal is of sugar, it will dissolve in the water now in this cup,

and if chemical tests on a portion of the crystal show that it is of sugar, then the hypothetical will be verified if another portion of it does dissolve when dropped into the cup, and falsified if it does not. In a measure as historians employ closed hypothetical premisses with true protases, i.e. which are not counter-factual, they can verify or falsify them in these ways. If, on the other hand, the hypothetical premiss to be tested is counter-factual, and if its protasis can be directly disproved, there is no need to investigate further. In our example, if chemical tests show that the crystal in question is not of sugar, then the hypothetical itself is verified; for, since it is equivalent to,

> It is not true both that that crystal is of sugar and that it will not dissolve in the water now in this cup,[1]

it must be true if its protasis is false.

Unhappily this method of verification is not open to an historian who employs a closed hypothetical in an argument *tollendo tollens*. Since what he is trying to prove by his argument is that the protasis of his premiss is false, he cannot already possess a direct proof of its falsity. Collingwood must show, not how closed counter-factual hypotheticals may be verified in general, but how they may be verified without directly disproving their protases.

In natural science, this problem presents no difficulty. A chemist who had no equipment at hand for directly testing whether a certain crystal is of sugar, and who proposed to show that it is not, would confidently assert the closed hypothetical,

> If this crystal is of sugar, then it will dissolve in the water now in this cup,

---

[1] This analysis of counter-factual partly closed hypotheticals will not do for those hypotheticals which are assumed to be derivable from laws; but that assumption need not be made.

on the ground that it follows from the well confirmed general law that sugar dissolves in water. Accordingly, he would not hesitate, when he had observed that the crystal did not dissolve in water, to infer that it was not of sugar. Yet Collingwood asserted that historians cannot, without ceasing to be historians, 'emulate the [natural] scientist in searching for the . . . laws of events' (*IH*, 214). How, then, can they establish such closed counter-factual hypotheticals?

It must not be forgotten that Collingwood himself insisted upon the difference between history proper and natural science in this respect. He had not the slightest doubt that every true closed hypothetical about natural events can be subsumed under a true open hypothetical, i.e. under a law of nature. Every closed hypothetical, if independently verified, is evidence for any open hypothetical under which it can be subsumed; and, if falsified, is conclusive evidence that that open hypothetical is false. Moreover, a well established open hypothetical or law of nature is the reason why the several closed hypotheticals that can be subsumed under it are true. That Collingwood's opinions on these questions were perfectly conventional is shown by his declaration that 'the [natural] scientist goes beyond the event, observes its relation to others, and thus brings it under a general formula or law of nature' (*IH*, 214).

Nor did he deny that there was some resemblance between history and natural science on this point. He held that just as natural scientists must deduce each of their closed counter-factual hypothetical premisses from other propositions which are independently confirmed, so must historians. Historians differ from natural scientists, not because they have no need to derive their closed hypotheticals from other propositions which are independently confirmed, but because the propositions from which they derive their closed hypotheticals are not general formulas or laws of nature. Collingwood's position was that the part played in natural science by laws of nature is played in history by propositions about the thoughts of historical agents, and that such propositions can be scientifically corroborated.

Namier himself derived his closed hypothetical premiss from two

independently verifiable propositions: (1) that the territorial magnates in question strove to procure as many seats in Parliament as
they could for members of their own families, and (2) that, since in
county elections the voters on the whole decided to obey their
landlords, the only electoral power with which a territorial magnate
had to reckon was that of the lesser landlords, i.e. the country
gentlemen.[1] Both these propositions are about the thoughts of
historical agents: the former, about the thoughts of politically active
English territorial magnates; the latter, about the thoughts of the
electors.

Collingwood's position, then, was this. Historians follow the
Baconian method of systematic questioning, sifting true from false
answers to their questions by means of survivals or traces of the
past. They connect their conclusions with their evidence as natural
scientists do, by means of hypothetical propositions. However, unlike natural scientists, they do not presuppose that every closed
hypothetical premiss they employ must be subsumable under a
general law, i.e. an open hypothetical. Sometimes their closed hypotheticals are analytic truths, sometimes they are not. When they are,
they are about what historical agents will do in certain situations in
virtue of what they think, i.e. of their plans, intentions, and so forth;
and when they are not, they are derived from independently verifiable propositions about what historical agents think (cf. *IH*, 214–15).

Historical knowledge, or knowledge of past conscious acts, cannot be obtained except by a systematic Baconian inquiry into what
historical agents have thought; and hypotheses about past thoughts
do not presuppose any general laws. Nevertheless, when Collingwood wrote that an historian 'cannot (without ceasing to be an historian) emulate the scientist in searching for the . . . laws of events'
(*IH*, 214), he did not mean to deny historians the right to employ
the laws of natural science in their reasoning. Many historical discoveries could not have been made except by techniques developed
in natural science, e.g. radio-carbon dating.[2] His point was that while
historians ought to use the techniques of natural science when they
can, their use of them must be ancillary. An historian who tried to

---

[1] Namier, *The Structure of Politics at the Accession of George III*, pp. 2–4, 69–70.
[2] Professor Ryle pointed this out to me after reading an early draft of this chapter.

investigate the past solely by means of evidence and general laws would have ceased to be an historian (cf. *A*, 108–9).

§ 4. *History and Human Action*

Collingwood's analysis of how the inferences by which historians connect their conclusions with their evidence turn on propositions about what historical agents have thought, although incomplete, was his most original contribution to the methodology of scientific history. It rests on an analysis of conscious action. According to Collingwood, every conscious act, for example, Caesar's act in invading Britain, has two sides: first, a physical side, which in our example would be the passage of Caesar and some 30,000 other men across the English Channel; and secondly, a side consisting of thought, which in our example, if Collingwood was right, would be Caesar's plan to conquer Britain (*IH*, 213). In *The New Leviathan* he showed that it is impossible to define *a priori* the term 'physical': the physical side of Caesar's act is that in it which can be investigated by physics and physiology. Clearly enough this includes such things as the capacity of his ships and the physique of himself and his men, and equally clearly it does not include his thoughts (cf. *NL*, 1. 3–1. 46). Since Collingwood described the physical side of an act metaphorically as its 'outside', and its cogitative side as its 'inside', his conception of an act is summed up by saying that it is 'the unity of the outside and inside of an event', where an event is taken to be a physical event (*IH*, 213).

The inner side of an act is itself complex. In his *Essay on Metaphysics* Collingwood distinguished two elements in it, which he described as the *causa quod* and the *causa ut* of the act as a whole (*EM*, 292). The *causa quod* of an act is the agent's estimate of his situation as he acts. If Collingwood's interpretation of Caesar's invasion of Britain is sound, part of its *causa quod* was Caesar's estimate that five legions and 2,000 cavalry would suffice to conquer the island. Collingwood did not make clear precisely what he meant by '*causa ut*'. He appears to have meant something that comprised both the agent's plan in doing what he did, if he had a plan, and the policy which he was following in doing it. His policy would include not only the purpose he proposed to accomplish, but also the conditions which he set himself for accomplishing it. It is not enough to say of a man that his policy in business is to enrich himself; you must also state the conditions which he is resolved to observe in pursuing that policy, for example, from what forms of business activity he will refrain as wrong (*EM*, 292–3). Since the term '*causa*' suggests a cause in the ordinary sense, and causes are commonly taken to be physical, it must be emphatically stated that *causa quod* and *causa ut* are terms of art, and signify thoughts in the mind of agents. It was a fundamental principle for Collingwood that no physical fact can *per se* be the cause of any act. As he pointed out in a striking passage, a poor man cannot be led to action 'by the fact of his children's unsatisfied hunger, the fact, the physiological fact, of empty bellies and wizened limbs, but [only] by his thought of that fact' (*IH*, 315–16).

Collingwood's application of this analysis of historical action may be illustrated by his own account of Caesar's reasons for deciding to say nothing in his *Commentaries* about his intentions in invading Britain. According to that account, Caesar's *causa quod* was his estimate that, if he told the truth, then his readers would perceive that his invasion was a failure; and that, if he told a lie, their attention would have been drawn to the question, and they would remark the discrepancy between the means he employed and his professed intention. If he held his tongue, on the other hand, there was a chance that the question what his intention was might not occur to them. His *causa ut* was simply to present his exploits in as favourable a light as he credibly could, displaying his successes and concealing his failures.

Collingwood pointed out that in no case could either the *causa ut* nor the *causa quod* be a cause 'if the other were absent' (*EM*, 292). He did not, however, add that their co-presence is not enough. Caesar did not act simply because a certain *causa quod* and a certain *causa ut* were both in his mind, but because he put them together in an act of practical reasoning. Collingwood briefly discussed practical reasoning in *The New Leviathan*, without mentioning the distinction between *causa quod* and *causa ut* which he had drawn in his *Essay on Metaphysics* (*NL*, 14. 3–14. 34). However, since his later analysis in no way traverses his earlier one, his omission may fairly be ascribed to his desire for brevity. Caesar's act of practical reasoning, reconstructed in the terms of the *Essay on Metaphysics* and *The New Leviathan*, may be dramatically represented as follows:

Caesar: (1) In my *Commentaries*, I intend to present my exploits favourably, and to conceal my failures when I can. (*Causa ut.*)

(2) My attempted conquest of Britain was a failure; and the only way in which I can hope to conceal it is to hold my tongue about what I intended. (*Causa quod.*)

(3) Therefore, I shall say nothing in my *Commentaries* about what I intended.

Adapting a remark in *The New Leviathan*, we may say that Caesar's thought is a specimen of practical reasoning in which his intention to conceal his failure, in conjunction with his plan for concealing it, acted as the ground of a further intention to say nothing in his *Commentaries* about the nature of his invasion (cf. *NL*, 14. 34).

There is no doubt that Collingwood believed that all such pieces of practical reasoning occur as linguistic acts, and that a linguistic act cannot be performed except by an actual external or internal utterance. These doctrines follow from his theory of the nature of consciousness in *The New Leviathan*, and his doctrine in *The Idea of History* that historians, when they discover what somebody in the past thought, literally re-enact it. Of course he did not think that Caesar uttered the above internal monologue in full, in his own Latin version; but he did think that Caesar must in some fashion have uttered his thought. Thinking cannot take place except in language, in the extended sense of 'language' explained in *The New Leviathan*. Not all thoughts need be in words. A boxer or a swordsman who thinks as he fights may not think much in words at all, although even the least reflective of athletes is bound to do so a little. The pervasiveness of our linguistic activity is commonly overlooked because we seldom attend to our acts of thinking as we think, and so often remain unaware that we have in any way uttered anything (*NL*, 6. 4–6. 42; cf. *IH*, 300–2).[1]

---

[1] For recent statements of similar views see W. S. Sellars, *Minnesota Studies in the Philosophy of Science* (Minneapolis, 1956), vol. i, pp. 253–329, and P. T. Geach, *Mental Acts* (London, 1957), pp. 75–87.

Each part of an historical agent's acts of practical reasoning entails a number of closed hypothetical propositions about his behaviour. Thus, the statement of Caesar's *causa ut* in keeping silent about his intention in invading Britain entails such hypotheticals as: 'If Caesar had considered an operation to be a success, he would have presented it clearly in his *Commentaries*'; and, 'If Caesar had considered an operation to be a failure, he would have concealed it in his *Commentaries* if that were possible'. The statement of his *causa quod* entails a further set: 'If Caesar had decided to make a clean breast of his failures, then he would have given a clear account of his intentions in invading Britain'; and, 'If Caesar had intended to conceal the failure of his invasion, he would have held his tongue about it'. On one hand, to infer anything from the hypotheticals entailed by the *causa quod*, a premiss about the agent's intentions is required; on the other, the hypotheticals entailed by the *causa ut* require a premiss about his estimate of the facts.

Where the facts must have been obvious to the agent, an historian will often omit to mention his *causa quod*, and will draw conclusions directly from closed hypotheticals entailed by his *causa ut*, and from premisses about the outer side of his acts or about the facts of his situation. Thus he may argue:

> If Caesar had considered his invasion of Britain a success, he would have clearly stated in his *Commentaries* what he had intended to accomplish;
> But Caesar did not clearly state in his *Commentaries* what he had intended to accomplish;
> Therefore, his invasion was a failure.

Prima facie, this inference is to a conclusion about the success or failure of a military operation from a hypothetical entailed by Caesar's *causa ut*, and a categorical premiss about his behaviour. Stated rigorously, however, there should have been a further step, namely, that Caesar therefore thought that his invasion had been a failure (*causa quod*), and that, since he was in a position to know whether it was a failure or not, it was a failure.

The closed hypothetical premisses about action which historians often employ all presuppose verifiable propositions about acts of practical reasoning. Even when historians appear to speak solely of what somebody would have done in certain circumstances, Collingwood contended that they are inescapably committed to assertions about what that person in fact thought. Accordingly, he laid it down that, whatever the appearances to the contrary, 'all history is the history of thought' (*A*, 110). That does not mean that history is the history of theory. Not all thought is theoretical. But even so earthy a subject as military history 'is not a description of weary marches in heat or cold, or the thrills and chills of battle or the long agony of wounded men. It is a description of plans and counterplans: of thinking about strategy and thinking about tactics, and in the last resort of what the men in the ranks thought about the battle' (*A*, 110).

The question, 'How can an historian possibly find out what a long-dead commander, let alone the obscure dead men in the ranks, thought about the various things to which they responded in a battle?' has been implicitly answered already. Every purposive act has an outside, a physical expression; and by Baconian questioning, it can often be shown that only one of the answers proposed to the question, 'What thought constituted the inner side of that act?', will fit the facts about its outer side. No historian, of course, perceives the outer side of any of the acts he investigates; for they all were done in the past. He must work back from their physical traces and relics: first he must reconstruct the acts of which the surviving traces are direct evidence; and then, inferring from his reconstruction of those acts that certain others must have been performed, he must reconstruct the acts of which the surviving traces are more remote evidence. What he can find out is a function both of the evidence he has and of how sharp his wits are in using it.

§ 5. *Collingwood's Practice as an Archaeologist*

Since, if Collingwood's philosophy of mind is sound, you may make mistakes in describing your thoughts, his own methodology of history may not be an accurate account of his practice as an historian. It is therefore hazardous to draw from his practice inferences about what his methodological theories were; and especially hazardous to draw such inferences from his mistakes or blunders in practice, unless those mistakes were habitual, or unless he put them forward as virtues. Theories of method, like sermons, more often reflect their authors' best practice than their worst.

One of Collingwood's oldest friends and admirers, Professor I. A. Richmond, in pointing out that Collingwood's practice as an archaeologist was in certain respects unsound, has suggested that his errors in practice had roots in some of his theories. In an obituary appreciation of Collingwood's work as an archaeologist, he wrote this:

. . . Collingwood's powers of analysis and appreciation outshone his ability in field-work. His attitude to excavation was profoundly influenced by the selective method of excavation, introduced and perfected by F. G. Simpson on Hadrian's Wall: and the first lesson which he drew from these methods, that excavations should be conducted with specific problems in mind upon sites likely to provide an answer, was salutary and useful. But Collingwood's corollary, that to pose a problem permitted its answer to be predicted, was a product of the study rather than the field. For there are problems thus soluble, particularly those purely philosophical problems which it was Collingwood's daily task to consider. But to the field-worker excavation, no matter how carefully planned in advance, is always a plunge in the dark: and, while problems under consideration form a more regular pattern on Hadrian's Wall than on most Roman monuments, even there no excavation has ever followed a preconceived course: the expected is always accompanied, and often overshadowed, by the unexpected: and while Collingwood's favourite *dictum*, that 'what you are not looking for, you do not see', is of wide application, an excavator's first duty is to see everything without the blinkers imposed by prearranged concentration of vision. Collingwood's own excavations, however, illustrate that he was by no means alive to these and other pitfalls. . . . [H]is planning of the excavations at Bainbridge left much to be desired. To examine the headquarters building in isolation, relating it neither to stratification within the fort nor in turn to the history of the rampart, was in fact to miss the opportunity of even a preliminary survey of the fort's history. Still less fortunate was his excursion into pre-history at King Arthur's Round Table, near Penrith. There he had made up his mind in advance what he was to find and found it with fatal precision. (*Proc. Brit. Acad.* xxix (1943), pp. 478–9.)

Although it would be folly, in 'a product of the study' such as this, to question so careful and informed an appraisal of Collingwood's field-work, it is perfectly in order to compare Richmond's recollection of Collingwood's *dicta* about methodology with what Collingwood himself wrote in his *Autobiography* and *Idea of History*. Nor must it be forgotten that in 1943, when Richmond wrote, *The Idea of History* had not been published.

Richmond's principal criticisms of Collingwood's methodology are two: first, that while Collingwood's doctrine that historians should proceed by systematic questioning is salutary and useful, he inferred from it a false corollary, that to pose a problem permitted its answer to be predicted; and secondly, that in following his *dictum* that what you are not looking for you do not see, Collingwood at times failed to see what stared him in the face, simply because he was not looking for it. As for the first of these criticisms, I think it can be shown that, despite his deficiencies in archaeological practice, Collingwood held that historians' questions must be answered by appeal to evidence; and that their answers cannot be deduced from their questions themselves. As for the second, in his *Autobiography*, far from advancing the dictum, 'What you are not looking for, you do not see', as justifying blinkered vision, Collingwood himself theoretically condemned the kind of oversight that marred some of his own field-work. I shall adduce evidence on each point.

That Collingwood in his *Autobiography* clearly distinguished asking a question from being able to answer it, or even to predict its answer, is quite clear from the many passages in which he asserted that historical thinking is Baconian (e.g. *A*, 81, 124–7). If he thought that an archaeologist could predict the answers to his questions before he dug, why describe excavation as 'looking for' information (*A*, 124)? Such remarks as the following, I think, are decisive: 'The historian has to decide exactly what it is that he wants to know; and if there is no authority to tell him, as in fact . . . there never is, he has to find a piece of land or something that has got the answer hidden in it, and get the answer out by fair means or foul' (*A*, 81). If the answer is 'hidden' from him, then he is in no position to predict it.

In *The Idea of History* Collingwood was even more explicit: 'every time the historian asks a question, he asks it because he . . . has already in his mind a preliminary and tentative idea of the evidence he will be able to use. Not a definite idea about potential evidence, but an indefinite idea about actual evidence' (*IH*, 281). If he had thought that an historian could predict what the 'actual evidence' of which he has an idea, whether a piece of land or a document, will reveal, he could not possibly have written that he has only an 'indefinite' idea of it. His point was that it is idle to ask a question unless there is reason to believe that evidence is available which contains the answer. An historian cannot predict what that answer will be, because his idea of that evidence remains 'preliminary and tentative' until he has inspected it.

It is ironical that Collingwood's mistakes in his excavations at Bainbridge resemble those made by the Society of Antiquaries in their excavations at Silchester, which he himself exposed. Collingwood did not relate the stratification in the headquarters building to that within the fort, or to the history of the rampart; but he had himself complained that, although long before their Silchester excavations were completed, the dating of strata on Roman sites by coins and pottery was a well established practice, the Society of Antiquaries had 'fixed the date neither of the town's beginning nor of its end, nor of the walls nor of the street-plan, nor of a single house or public building . . .' (*A*, 125). What Collingwood at Bainbridge and the Society of Antiquaries at Silchester were not looking for they did not see. The lesson is that both ought to have looked for more than they did.

However, Richmond has rightly drawn attention to a distinction from which Collingwood's dictum distracts it. It is true that a man who does not know what a stratum or a temple is cannot 'see' a stratum or the remains of a temple even when he looks at them: that is, he cannot see what is before his eyes *as* a stratum or *as* the remains of a temple. Yet he can see something. For example, he can see that, at a certain spot, masonry or pottery fragments of a certain kind are found at a certain depth. Neither the depth at which those fragments are discovered, nor the fact that similar fragments are found at a different depth at another spot on the same site, may strike him as significant. Ought he then to record them? The essence of Richmond's criticism is that although a good archaeologist ought to describe the sites he excavates as minutely as possible, whether or not he can grasp the significance of the details he records, Collingwood's *dictum* suggests that archaeologists may disregard whatever does not help to solve the problems they have set themselves. An archaeologist excavating a site is more than an historian, he is the custodian of that site for future historians; and he must not forget his duty as a custodian to leave a record which other historians may use to solve their problems.

Both in his *Autobiography* and in his *Idea of History*, however, Collingwood conceded Richmond's point, even if he did not always act according to it. In *The Idea of History* he wrote: '[T]he past leaves relics of itself.... We preserve these relics, hoping that in the future they may become what now they are not, namely historical evidence' (*IH*, 203). And in his *Autobiography* he recognized that archaeologists must record not only what they are not looking for, but even what they do not understand at all. 'If in the case of one object', he wrote, '[an archaeologist] does not understand [what it was for], he has, as an archaeologist, no use for the object; he would throw it away, but that he hopes some one more learned or more resourceful than himself may solve the riddle' (*A*, 108). This clearly implies that it is an archaeologist's duty to record what he is not looking for, in the hope that somebody else might make something of it. His duty is the more urgent, Collingwood pointed out, because excavation destroys a site; after it, nothing remains except the excavators' reports (*A*, 127).

§ 6. *Historical Explanation*

One of Collingwood's best-known sayings about history, and perhaps his boldest, was that 'when [an historian] knows what happened, he already knows why it happened' (*IH*, 214). A natural historian who has established that a certain event must have taken place at a certain time has not thereby explained it; to do that, he must calculate back to a yet earlier time. Moreover, from the mere statement that a certain natural event occurred, it is by no means possible to infer its explanation, because all explanations in natural history involve general laws. Collingwood maintained that neither of these propositions is true of history proper: an historian explains a fact in the very process of establishing it, and the mere statement of an historical fact is also its explanation (*IH*, 214–15).

To this there is an obvious and apparently decisive objection. While every schoolboy knows that Julius Caesar invaded Britain for the second time in 54 B.C., on Collingwood's own showing that fact was not correctly explained until he himself took up the problem. Moreover, even a cursory acquaintance with historical controversy suffices to show that while some of the bitterest debates among historians are about such questions as why a war broke out (e.g. the British or the American Civil Wars, the Seven Years War, the First World War); there is no question whatever about the fact that the war in question did break out. Again, nobody doubts that in 1929 the New York stock market crashed; yet no explanation of that fact has yet received universal informed assent.

However, Collingwood had a comprehensive rejoinder to such objections. The happenings which it is an historian's business to know are not 'mere events', but conscious acts: for history proper, 'the object to be discovered is not the mere event, but the thought expressed in it' (*IH*, 214). Only when he has discovered the thought contained in an event has an historian ascertained a fact; for every historical fact is about an action, and 'an action is the unity of the outside and inside of an event'. That is why Collingwood remarked that although an historian's work 'may begin by discovering the outside of an event . . . it can never end there' (*IH*, 213).

The schoolboy who knows that in 54 B.C. Caesar invaded Britain for a second time knows little more than the outside of that event. He knows indeed that Caesar's army crossed the Channel on a hostile expedition, and not on a pleasure cruise; but that is only a tiny part of the thoughts in the minds of Caesar and his army which constituted the inner side of that event. Until that is established the historical fact, 'what happened', is unkown. Collingwood would therefore maintain that the nature of the invasion, of what happened, is unknown to those who are neither acquainted with his discovery nor have made it for themselves.

An historian's reconstruction of the inner side of an event must be complete if he is to know why it happened; and the sign that it is complete is that it is a sufficient condition of the event explained. In history proper, as in natural history, while it is not often necessary that an explanation be fully stated, it ought always to be possible for a fellow-historian to supply what is omitted. A proposed explanation of why a deed was done, which was consistent with some other deed having been done instead, would simply not explain what it is supposed to explain. Only if the agent's *causa ut*, his *causa quod*, and his process of inference from them to his decision to act, are either explicitly or implicitly reconstructed, has his act been explained.

Some philosophers would deny that even that would suffice, on the ground that such an explanation would explain the agent's intention rather than his deed. Collingwood dissented, because he considered the vacillations in which weakness of will is expressed to be themselves acts (*NL*, 13. 86–13. 9). An historical explanation of an act, whether it be a deed or a short-lived resolve, is a reconstruction of an act of practical reasoning: the agent's *causa ut* and *causa quod* and his inference from them. In order to find out whether somebody's will has been strong or weak, either in general or in a particular situation, an historian must first explain that man's deeds and his resolutions beforehand, and then compare the explanations. The strength of a man's will cannot be ascertained until after his deeds have been explained.

There is, nevertheless, a lacuna even in Collingwood's analysis of the explanation of the acts of individuals. As Ryle has shown, many expressions which signify acts are unlike 'walk', 'point', 'nod', or 'go to sleep', when used of persons in good health, because they signify either the achievement of a success or the failure to achieve one. 'Win', 'surpass', 'persuade', and 'overcome' invariably signify achievements; 'take the bait' (of a trap), 'betray' (oneself), 'fallaciously infer', and 'lose' invariably signify failures. Besides, many verbs of action other than these may be modified by adverbs either of achievement or of failure. You may fight, flee, seek, reason, and negotiate either successfully or unsuccessfully.

The success or failure of some activities, e.g. of reasoning,

depends solely on what the agent does. Whether or not a conclusion he draws is valid depends on what he does with his
premisses, and nothing else. His success in other activities, however, may depend on what his situation is. A man fights successfully only if he subdues his adversary; and that depends in part on
how well his adversary fights—i.e. on his situation.

Historians, Collingwood acknowledged, are concerned with
whether the actions they investigate were successful or not (*IH*,
309–10). Yet it is only plausible to say that to know what happened,
in the sense of knowing both the inside and the outside of a given
action, is to know why it happened, if the success or failure of the
action is excluded from investigation. It is not at all plausible if that
success or failure must itself be explained. To explain Brutus' killing Caesar as contrasted with his stabbing him, or Napoleon's
defeat at Waterloo as opposed to his battle-commands there, it
would be necessary to ascertain not only the inside and the outside
of what Brutus or Napoleon did, but also their situation.

By Collingwood's own principles, the explanation of the physical
fact that Brutus' stab was mortal, like that of any other physiological fact, falls into the domain of natural science. However, the
knowledge of natural science that is required in order to explain it
is too elementary and familiar to be mentioned. An historian does
not need to inform us why certain stab wounds in the body are
mortal. But it is not so in all cases. The explanation of why a particular method of farming slowly exhausts the soil farmed is seldom
both familiar and elementary; nor is the explanation of the capabilities of even simple weapons like the long-bow or the needle-gun.
To explain actions the success or failure of which depends upon such
facts as that a particular method of farming exhausts the soil, or that
the Prussian needle-gun was superior in fire-power to the muzzle-
loader, an historian must explain to his readers the performance
of certain obsolete weapons, or certain advanced theories about the
fertility of soils. A nodding acquaintance with the commonplaces
of popular science and historical methodology is not enough.

So reluctant was Collingwood to concede that historical explanations might incorporate some of the results of natural science,
that in his unrevised manuscript, *The Principles of History*, after

acknowledging that the situation in which a man proposes to act 'is what it is, and neither he nor any one else can ever change that', he inconsistently added that it 'consists altogether of thoughts, his own and other people's' (*IH*, 316). This is flagrantly opposed to the facts. Plainly, the success or failure of the design of an implement, a utensil, or a machine depends in large measure on the physical situation, and not on what anybody thinks. Even one of Collingwood's chosen examples, the situation which Caesar confronted when his murderers closed in upon him, did not consist only in the fact that Caesar and his murderers had certain thoughts, but also in the physical fact that his murderers had weapons which, if used as they proposed to use them, would kill him.

Historians consider the acts which they investigate as what Professor Toynbee has called 'responses' to 'challenges'.[1] In acting, a man responds to the challenge to adapt his situation to his ends, according to his principles. His ends and principles are his *causa ut*, and his conception of his situation his *causa quod*. Whether his response succeeds or fails depends first on whether his *causa quod* corresponds to his situation as it really is, and then on whether if it does, he solves the problem of accomplishing his purpose without violating his principles. Despite his eccentric doctrine that an historical situation 'consists entirely of thoughts', Collingwood held fast to the common-sense conviction that whether a man's action 'is to prove successful or not depends on whether he grasps the situation rightly or not.... If he neglects the situation, the situation will not neglect him. It is not one of those gods that leave an insult unpunished' (*IH*, 316).

The principle that actions are responses to challenges also entails that a man's actions can be affected only by changing his thoughts: his *causa quod*, or his *causa ut*, or his reasoning from them. Pure physical force, e.g. a push, can produce only a pure physical effect, e.g. a fall, but not an action, e.g. a walk or a run. Of course, changing a man's situation will, if he becomes aware of it, change his *causa quod*; and may, in certain cases, lead him to revise his *causa ut*. Under great inducements or threats many of us will revise the principles on which we act. Yet no man changes either his *causa ut*, or his

---

[1] A. J. Toynbee, *A Study of History* (London, 1934), vols. i–ii.

causa quod, or his reasoning from them, willy-nilly; for all such changes are acts of will. To change a man's mind, you must do it on his terms, though some men are more pliable than others in setting their terms (*EM*, 293).

That is why the biological, geographical, and economic theories of historical explanations which recur in popular quasi-historical thinking are one and all fallacious. It is true that biological facts (a man's resistance to organic disease, strength, intelligence, fertility, and so on), geographical facts (the soil and minerals accessible to him, the climate of the region where he lives, the terrain over which he must transport his goods, his access to rivers or to the sea), and economic facts (his productivity, the capital he controls or can borrow, the mode of exchange) are all elements in the situation to which a man responds. Yet the effect of a man's conception of nature on his actions is not the same thing as an effect of nature itself (*IH*, 200). Neither a man's situation as a whole nor any element in it determines his acts, although it is true that his situation may, and often does, present him with a problem he cannot solve. If he fails to solve it, his failure results from his inability and his situation together, not from his situation alone. Even if some problems are in fact insoluble, it is generally rash to pronounce that a given problem is: too many problems thought insoluble for centuries (e.g. periodic famine) have been solved (*IH*, 200).

It is therefore a gross error to imagine that any historical act, or any large pattern of historical acts, can be explained by geographical or economic or biological factors in the situation of those who do them (*IH*, 200). The decline of the Roman empire has sometimes been attributed to a fall in agricultural production owing to the exhaustion of the soil in some regions. Neither the act of a single farmer in abandoning an 'exhausted' farm, nor the complex pattern of acts of which the decline of the Roman empire consists, could possibly be 'caused' by any such thing.[1] At most, the exhaustion

[1] C. N. Cochrane, *Christianity and Classical Culture* (2nd ed. New York, 1944), pp. 155-7. '[W]hat here confronts us is, in the last analysis, a moral and intellectual failure, a failure of the Graeco-Roman mind . . . [W]e . . . may freely admit that . . . all [the various theories proposed] have a place within the complex tissue of material fact. If, however, the Romans themselves proved unable to come to grips with that fact, the reason must surely be supposed to lie in some radical defect of their thinking' (ibid., p. 157). Cf. *EM*, 227 *n*.

of the soil presented a problem: How could it be replenished? Failure to solve this problem would lead to others: How can one continue to live on a farm the soil of which is exhausted? How can another source of agricultural produce be opened? Analysing the process afterwards an historian may decide that certain problems were crucial: that while it was far from impossible to solve them when they arose, failure to solve them gave rise to others which were far more difficult.

The fundamentals of Collingwood's analysis of historical explanation are now complete. He was a methodological individualist, in the strongest sense of that disputable term. In his view, the most elementary historical explanations are of acts of individuals, and consist in a full statement of what those acts are, both outside and inside. The outside of an act is its physical side, i.e. certain bodily movements, for example, those involved in speaking or writing; its inside is an act of practical reason, in which a *causa quod* and a *causa ut* are conjoined. Of course, not all historical explanations are elementary. Historians interest themselves in processes which take place in groups: the expansion and contraction of populations, the rise and fall of empires, wars, religious movements, economic booms and depressions, struggles between parties and factions, constitutional changes, and so forth. Collingwood maintained not only that all such processes are in principle analysable in terms of the acts of individuals and the relations between them, but also that all historical explanations of such processes are in terms of acts of individuals or of classes of such acts[1] (cf. *IH*, 310).

One problem, which is acute for those who consider that the social sciences are at bottom identical in structure with the natural sciences, cannot even arise if Collingwood's analysis be accepted. If there were historical laws of nature, it is quite conceivable that there might be several sets of laws, one set by which acts of individuals might be explained, and other sets by which the various processes in groups might be explained. If there were, the question would arise whether, by means of composition laws, the latter sets of laws might be reduced to the laws of individual action. On Collingwood's

[1] See May Brodbeck, in *Philosophy of Science*, xxv (1958), pp. 1–22. Here and in the remainder of this chapter my debt to Professor Brodbeck is great.

analysis, this question cannot be asked. Since historical explanations presuppose no laws whatever, *a fortiori*, they presuppose no of processes in groups; and, since there is no such thing as a group mind, historians must explain processes in groups by explaining the individual acts of which they are composed.

Historians, therefore, cannot explain processes in groups unless they can resolve them into individual acts or classes of such acts. Two kinds of reduction are of particular importance. Some processes in groups, like a run on a bank, or a party vote in the House of Commons under a three-line Whip, consist of all or most of the members of a group doing the same thing for the same reason, or from one or another of a very few reasons. When there is a run on a bank, it is easy to reconstruct in our own minds the purposes of the people whose collective action took that form (*IH*, 310): each of a large group of depositors, having become apprehensive of the soundness of the bank, withdraws his deposit in order to secure it. The collective action which took that form might have a result which those who acted neither foresaw nor desired, e.g. that of causing a bankruptcy which otherwise might have been avoided. The doctrine that because every process in groups is composed of individual purposive acts, therefore the result of every such process has been intended by somebody, a doctrine which Professor Popper has happily called 'the conspiracy theory' of society,[1] is a dangerous fallacy which Collingwood was careful to avoid (*IH*, 316).

Other processes in groups which historians try to explain are more complex. A depression, or an outbreak of war, are not collective actions in which all or most of the members of a group do the same thing for the same reasons. Depressions, as economic historians of every school explain them, consist of collective actions by a number of different groups, the members of each of which do the same thing as other members of the same group, but not the same thing as the members of the other groups that are involved. Thus, a given depression might be explained in terms of different common actions by bankers, farmers, industrial firms, and wage-earners, the members of each group doing something different from those of any

[1] K. R. Popper, *The Open Society and its Enemies*, vol. ii, pp. 94–96.

of the other groups, and in all probability none of them foreseeing or desiring what their interaction would bring upon them.

It is even more complex when the groups studied are not classes of like-minded individuals, but institutions. A kingdom does not declare a war, a union a strike, or a firm a lock-out because all or most of its subjects, its members, or its shareholders act in a certain way. The acts of an institution are the acts of such of its members as are empowered to act for it. A declaration of war is made by a monarch, or by the comparatively few men who form a government; many strikes are called by union officials; and lock-outs are ordered by boards of directors: yet wars, strikes, and lock-outs are carried out by whole states, whole unions, and whole companies. Explaining a war, a strike, or a lock-out is therefore largely a matter of explaining why a monarch or a government or the officials of a union or the directors of a company acted as they did. While in some cases it may be necessary to explain why their subordinates continued to obey, in most it is not: subordinates for the most part obey because they accept their position as subordinates. Only if they have brought themselves to ask and answer the question whether or not they shall continue to do so is it necessary to explain why they do.

Although Collingwood was a methodological individualist, he did not hold a view which, as Popper has shown, is often wrongly identified with individualism, namely, that historical processes can be analysed into facts about individuals, without mentioning their social situation and membership of institutions.[1] Popper has called this position 'psychologism'.[2] In illustrating his theory of historical explanation, Collingwood frequently gave examples in which either the agent's *causa ut* or his *causa quod* had to do with some group or institution to which he belonged. Thus he held that Caesar's crossing of the Rubicon is to be so explained, 'in terms of . . . Caesar's defiance of Republican law' (*IH*, 213). Caesar's action would be unintelligible in terms of his thoughts about other individuals.

These applications exhibit in a small measure the power of Colling-

[1] Cf. Maurice Mandelbaum, in Patrick Gardiner (ed.), *Theories of History*, pp. 476–88; originally published *Brit. Journ. Sociology*, vi (1955), pp. 305–17.

[2] K. R. Popper, *The Open Society and its Enemies*, vol. ii, pp. 88–99; *The Poverty of Historicism*, pp. 152–9.

wood's theory. His own approach was to analyse an explanation of the simplest possible historical act, namely, a simple physical movement which is done for some reason, such as Brutus' stabbing of Caesar. His reason was that, in principle, the theory of the simplest case is the theory of all cases; for complex interactions have no element that cannot be found in the simplest act. The elements of every historical explanation are therefore the same: the *causa ut* and the *causa quod* of each agent or group of agents, and the practical inference each makes from them.

Collingwood appears to have assumed that opposition to his theory would be on a point of principle, the question whether or not explanations in history proper are formally identical with those of natural history. In his British Academy lecture on *Human Nature and Human History*, he warned his audience that 'all kinds of historical fallacies are still current, due to confusion between historical process and natural process: not only the cruder fallacies of mistaking historical facts of culture and tradition for functions of biological facts like race and pedigree, but subtler fallacies affecting methods of research and the organization of historical inquiry . . .' (*IH*, 228). Yet he seems to have been confident that his readers would be able to explore the ramifications of his theory for themselves, and in his *Autobiography* he brusquely declined to pamper them. 'I will not', he wrote, 'offer to help a reader who replies, "ah, you are making it easy for yourself by taking an example where history really is the history of thought; you couldn't explain the history of a battle or a political campaign in that way". I could, and so could you, Reader, if you tried' (*A*, 111-12). It may be so. That perceptive and intelligent readers, with leisure to spare, could do so, I do not doubt; but it was an unreasonable burden to lay on even the most willing of them.

IX

THE PHILOSOPHY OF HISTORY

§ 1. *The Presuppositions of Scientific History*

It was in his *Autobiography* that Collingwood first expounded his conception of metaphysics as an historical investigation into the absolute presuppositions of the natural science or 'physics' of given periods; but neither in the *Autobiography*, nor in any of the books that he wrote after it, did he once ask the question, 'What are the presuppositions of scientific history?'

In his Inaugural Lecture, 'The Historical Imagination', which he delivered three years before he wrote his *Autobiography*, he implied that the foundations of scientific history could be established *a priori*. History, he declared, is 'wholly a reasoned knowledge of what is transient and concrete' (*IH*, 234), in which the criterion of truth is 'the idea of history itself: the idea of an imaginary picture of the past' (*IH*, 248). That idea is *a priori* in the Kantian sense; for it is not an inference from what is observed. Every man possesses it 'as part of the furniture of his mind, and discovers himself to possess [it] in so far as he becomes conscious of what it is to have a mind' (*IH*, 248). In a measure as history is the interpretation of traces or relics of the past in the light of that idea, it is a 'self-dependent, self-determining, and self-justifying form of thought' (*IH*, 249).

The idea of an imaginary picture of the past must be distinguished from any particular imaginary picture of it. The former is abstract and formal, the latter concrete. An imaginary picture of the past, since it can only be verified by reasoning from evidence, must be *a posteriori*; but the abstract idea of such a picture, since it depicts no historical fact, may be *a priori*. While all scientific historians have the same idea of an imaginary picture of the past, in that they all conceive the historical past according to the same general principles, each of them will have a different imaginary picture of it. No two historians work with exactly the same evidence, or interpret their evidence in exactly the same way. Their agreement about the idea of an imaginary picture of the past is a matter of principle, a philosophical matter as it were; their disagreements about which imaginary picture of the past is true are not matters of principle at all, but disagreements as historians about what follows from the available evidence.

An *a priori* idea of an imaginary picture of the past must not be confounded with an absolute presupposition about it. Although absolute presuppositions are *a priori* in the sense that they are not empirical, they are not *a priori* in the Kantian sense; for no absolute presupposition is part of the furniture of every mind. What one man or one group presupposes another may not. Collingwood's doctrine in 'The Historical Imagination' that the historian's idea of an imaginary picture of the past is *a priori*, 'part of the furniture of his mind', is in fact incredible. While it is true that you could not be said to have a mind unless you had some idea of before and after, past and future, it does not follow that you must have an idea of an imaginary picture of the past which would afford an adequate criterion of truth for history. Collingwood maintained that the historian's idea requires that any admissible imaginary picture of the past must be localized in space and time, consistent with itself, and founded on evidence (*IH*, 246). However, in *The Idea of History*, by describing the mythical and theocratic quasi-historical conceptions of the past which 'dominated the whole of the Near East until the rise of Greece' (*IH*, 16), he himself showed that men who have not possessed a modern historian's idea of an admissible picture of the past have nevertheless been conscious of the past, and presumably of themselves as thinkers.

It is not unreasonable, then, to infer that Collingwood tacitly revised his position in 'The Historical Imagination' in the light of his Theory of Presuppositions, relinquishing the doctrine that the historian's idea of an imaginary picture of the past is *a priori* in the Kantian sense, and replacing it with the doctrine that historians presuppose that idea (cf. also *EM*, 63–64). In the main body of *The Idea of History* he treated it as a presupposition of scientific history that:

1. *There is an historical past, that is, a past consisting of events localized
   in space and time, the occurrence of which can be ascertained by inference from evidence.*

In terms of the Theory of Presuppositions in the *Essay on Metaphysics*, historians do not merely presuppose this, but absolutely
presuppose it. They do not affirm it as an answer to any question
they ask as historians. However, as I have already shown (in Ch. IV,
§ 2), Collingwood's further conclusion in the *Essay on Metaphysics*,
that what is absolutely presupposed is neither true nor false, does
not follow. A scientific historian's conception of the past is valid;
an ancient Sumerian's mythical conception of it is not.

Collingwood's analysis of the historical past in 'The Historical
Imagination' was deliberately incomplete: in it, he set out to establish that historical thinking is autonomous, by showing that its
principles are independent of those of any other discipline (*IH*,
234–7). For this, it sufficed to show that historians work with an
a priori idea of an imaginary picture of the past, or with absolute
presuppositions about it, which are not derived from immediate
perception or natural science. It was not necessary to distinguish
between the historical past and past natural events. To draw that
distinction further presuppositions must be laid down.

In his *Autobiography* Collingwood narrated how he came to discover the most important of these further presuppositions, although
he did not call them that. In logical order, as opposed to the chronological order in which he discovered them, they are are follows.

2. *The historical past is made up of actions, and the inner side of every
   action is a thought.*

This presupposition distinguishes the subject-matter of history
proper from that of natural history. Collingwood expressed it in the
epigram, 'All history is the history of thought' (*A*, 110).

If history is at bottom the history of thought, then historians
must in some way have access to past thoughts. According to
Collingwood's analysis of scientific history, the only access they
have is by way of inference from evidence. But historians can only
interpret their evidence by systematic questioning, and in their
questions they make conjectures about past thoughts.

If someone, hereinafter called the mathematician, has written that twice two is four, and if someone else, hereinafter called the historian, wants to know what he was thinking when he made those marks on paper, the historian will never be able to answer this question unless he is mathematician enough to think exactly what the mathematician thought, and expressed by writing that twice two are four. (*A*, 111.)

This gave Collingwood a further presupposition:

3. *Past thoughts can be re-enacted in the minds of historians* (cf. *A*, 112).

With this presupposition goes a fourth:

4. *The past thoughts which an historian studies are not dead, but although known to be past, they in some sense still live in the present* (cf. *A*, 97).

Of the four presuppositions I have extracted from Collingwood's reflections on scientific history, the first two, once they have been understood, have seldom been doubted. Even of those who question the scientific value of a study of past actions, most will concede that, for better or worse, history is such a study. The third and fourth are in a different position. Although Collingwood formulated the fourth as early as 1920, he himself later confessed that his original interpretation of it was unsatisfactory. As for the third, vestiges of the realism in which he had been trained as an undergraduate prevented him even from formulating it until the two years following the summer of 1928, when he first sharply distinguished history proper from natural history (*A*, 107, 115). Nor was realism his only adversary. Idealism, as represented in the work of F. H. Bradley, was utterly hostile to the conception of a past, which, while living in the present, is nevertheless genuinely past.

There is a short way with such difficulties. Scientific history exists. The Copernican revolution brought about by Niebuhr, Ranke, and their successors is now itself a matter of history. To argue that scientific history is impossible because its presuppositions are false, is like trying to argue the hind leg off a donkey. Both realist and idealist objections to certain of the presuppositions of scientific history might be dismissed on the ground that, since scientific history has established itself, any philosophical theory which denies its validity is *eo ipso* false.

Yet Collingwood condemned such violent refutations as unphilo-sophical. 'If your donkey has four visible legs', he once remarked, 'and you can prove that it ought to have three, the discrepancy is a reason not for ceasing to think about the donkey's anatomy, but for thinking about it again: revising, not merely ignoring, the original argument.'[1] In *The Idea of History* he therefore set out to explode the errors which had seduced some philosophers into reject-ing his third and fourth presuppositions, not only in the forms in which those errors appeared in the writings of his contemporaries and predecessors, but also in those in which they had infected his own thinking. Consequently, in a remarkable Epilegomenon, 'His-tory as Re-enactment of Past Experience' (*IH*, 282–302), he put into the mouths of a series of imaginary objectors the difficulties which had frustrated him, and patiently elicited the confusions from which they proceeded.

§ 2. *Re-enactment and Intuition*

Ironically, in 'History as Re-enactment of Past Experience', Colling-wood has often been taken, not to have been trying to demolish philosophical objections to certain of the presuppositions of scientific history, as he said he was (*IH*, 283–4), but to have been advocat-ing a new theory of historical method: a theory, moreover, which flatly contradicts his own analysis of scientific history as 'Baconian'.

This misunderstanding may be dispelled by a careful analysis of the misunderstood passage. In it Collingwood began by stating the point in his conception of history which was the first target of his imaginary objector's attack, namely that an historian can re-think or re-enact the identical thoughts which constitute the inner side of the past acts which it is his task to discover (*IH*, 282). He then illustrated that point by describing two examples of historical research. He was careful to give warning that although his descrip-tions 'call attention to the central feature of all historical thinking', they possess 'ambiguities and shortcomings', and require 'a great deal of amplification and explanation', which he undertook to pro-vide by dissecting imaginary objections (*IH*, 283).

[1] *Journ. Phil. Studies*, iii (1928), p. 217.

One of his examples was that of an attempt to discover the historical significance of an edict in the Theodosian Code.

In order to do that [an historian] must envisage the situation with which the emperor was trying to deal, and he must envisage it as that emperor envisaged it. Then he must see for himself, just as if the emperor's situation were his own, how such a situation might be dealt with; he must see the possible alternatives, and the reasons for choosing one rather than another; and thus he must go through the process which the emperor went through in deciding on this particular course. Thus he is re-enacting in his own mind the experience of the emperor; and only in so far as he does this has he any historical knowledge, as distinct from a merely philological knowledge, of the meaning of the edict. (*IH*, 283.)

His other example was that of reconstructing the thought expressed in a passage by an ancient philosopher. Since it adds nothing to his first example, there is no need to reproduce it. Presumably he included it for emphasis.

In his description of his first example, Collingwood drew attention to 'the central feature of all historical thinking', as opposed to thinking in natural science: an historian must reconstruct the actual thoughts of historical agents, with their *causae ut*, their *causae quod*, and with the rational processes through which they pass from them to decisions to act. It was against this central feature that the philosophical objections against which he had struggled in the twenties had been directed. He did not mention, in this passage, the feature which historical thinking shares with natural science, namely, the Baconian method, because no objection to that had at any time weighed with him in the slightest. Accordingly, neither in his general account of 'the central feature of all historical thinking', nor in his analyses of his illustrative examples, did he say anything about how reconstructions of past thoughts may be tested and verified (cf. *IH*, 289).

Yet even in 'History as Re-enactment of Past Experience' he left no room for doubt that he continued to adhere to the view that historical thinking is Baconian. When he came to discuss not merely what it is we know in knowing the historical significance of an edict in the Theodosian code, but how we come to know it—and how we come to know the philosophical thoughts of Epicurus or Nietzsche, or the political thoughts of Marius—he wrote: 'the evidence of what these men thought is in our hands; and in re-creating these thoughts in our own minds by interpretation of that evidence we can know, so far as there is any knowledge, that the thoughts we create were theirs' (*IH*, 296). Now if Collingwood held it to be by interpreting evidence that historians come to know that 'the thoughts they create' are in fact re-creations of past thoughts, it is quite impossible that he should also have held that evidence is interpreted by means of the re-creation of past thoughts, or that such re-creation is a matter of self-certifying intuition. It is true that in this passage he did not explain what he meant by 'inter-pretation of . . . evidence', but why should he have? Elsewhere he had said all that anybody could require (e.g. *IH*, 9–10, 202–4; cf. *A*, 80–84, *IH*, 252–82).

§ 3. *The Realist Problem: Can Thoughts be Re-enacted?*

Only three years before he discovered it to be a presupposition of scientific history that one man's thoughts can be re-enacted in the mind of another (*A*, 112), Collingwood had denied that the literal re-enactment of a past thought was possible. In an essay on 'The Nature and Aims of a Philosophy of History', which he had pub-lished in 1925, he had conceived history as making the realist assumption that what is known is necessarily external to the mind that knows it, and consequently had assumed that the relation between knower and known is analogous with that between specta-tor and spectacle. He had then argued as follows:

From philosophy, again, history is differentiated by its objectivity. History assumes that there is a world of fact independent of the knowing mind, a world which is only revealed and in no sense con-stituted by the historian's thought: it assumes that this thought establishes a relation of knowledge between two terms, the knowing mind and the world of fact, which pre-exist to the establishment of that relation. How this can be, history does not ask. . . . No doubt the historian's studies bring him into the closest contact with a spiritual life akin to his own; he seeks to study the activities of the human spirit . . . by apprehending them in their full actuality, as they really exist in the world of fact. But these actual happenings are always the object of his thought, and never his thought itself. However closely he sympathizes with the men whose acts he traces, however much akin to himself he feels them, they are no more than akin. . . . He is an historian, and those whom he studies are not historians. . . . Consequently he is always the spectator of a life in which he does not participate: he sees the world of fact as it were across a gulf which, as an historian, he cannot bridge. (*Proc. Aris. Soc.* xxv (1924-5), pp. 164-5.)

In *The Idea of History* Collingwood put yet a further argument into the mouth of an imaginary objector. It was this. If it is true that no one experience can be 'literally identical' with any other, the re-enactment by an historian of a past thought would be impossible. At best an historian's thought could only resemble a past thought, so that 'the doctrine that we know the past by re-enacting it is only a version of the familiar and discredited copy-theory of knowledge' (*IH*, 284). Yet if philosophical realism were true, it would follow that no one experience can be literally identical with another. According to realism, experience has two components, act and object. Thus the 'experience' of thinking that the angles at the base of an isosceles triangle are equal may be analysed into an act of thinking and the object of that act, namely, the proposition that those angles are equal. That the acts of thought in two such 'experiences' are different seems to be 'sufficiently proved by either of the two facts that they are done by different persons and are done at different times' (*IH*, 284). Collingwood's imaginary objector is now in a position to draw his conclusions. Since it is unquestioned that a past thought and an historian's attempt to re-enact it are done for the most part by different persons, and invariably at different times, it follows, by the preceding analysis, that the two acts are different, and that one cannot literally re-enact the other.

Thus Collingwood was confronted with two realist proofs that a past thought and an historian's alleged re-enactment of it cannot be the same. The first, which he had himself offered in his essay of 1925, relied on the premiss that a past thought is merely the object of an historian's re-enactment—a spectacle, as it were, of which he is a spectator. The second, which in *The Idea of History* he put into the mouth of an imaginary objector, reached the same destination by a different but parallel route: since a past thought and its re-enactment are thought by different persons at different times, they cannot be the same. Collingwood was inclined to believe that both of the realist objections ultimately sprang from a common source. The reason why his imaginary objector (who seems at this point to be something more than imaginary) thought it self-evident that a past and present act of thought cannot be the same was that he conceived an act of thought as something having its place in the flow of consciousness, whose being is simply its occurrence in that flow. The flow of consciousness, or, more strictly, the flow of im-mediate consciousness, as we have seen, is nothing but the flow of feeling inasmuch as one is conscious of it (cf. *IH*, 291; *NL*, 4. 22–4. 24). According to the objector, once a thought has 'happened', the flow of consciousness carries it into the past, whence nothing can recall it: another thought of the same kind may happen, but not that one again (cf. *IH*, 286). The conception of acts of thought as having their place in the flow of immediate consciousness also lay behind his essay of 1925; for his position in that essay, that an historian is a spectator of past thoughts, may be traced to his early doctrine that history is at bottom a matter of perception. When, a year later, he remarked in *Speculum Mentis* that 'History is . . ., as a specific form of experience, identical with perception' (*SM*, 205), he expressly affirmed that doctrine; for objects of perception, as we have seen, are objects in the flow of feeling which have been raised to consciousness.

Collingwood's task in 'History as Re-enactment of Past Experi-ence' was twofold: to prove that a past thought and an historian's re-enactment of it could be the very same act, and to dispose of the various objections to it, real and imaginary. The former was com-paratively easy. Assuming that solipsism, i.e. the position that knowledge of past thoughts is impossible, must be false, he had only to show that unless past thoughts could literally be re-enacted, solipsism was inescapable. His argument was as follows.

The objector . . . maintains that although the object of two people's acts of thought may be the same, the acts themselves are different. But, in order that this should be said, it is necessary to know 'what

someone else is thinking' not only in the sense of knowing the same
object that he knows, but in the further sense of knowing the act by
which he knows it. . . . But to do this involves the repetition by one
mind of another's act of thought: not one like it (that would be the
copy-theory of knowledge with a vengeance) but the act itself. (*IH*, 288.)

This argument rests on the fact that you cannot know another
man's thoughts as you can know his physical movements, by perception. Merely perceiving another man's utterances and gestures
will not disclose to you what he thinks; to discover it you must
interpret those utterances and gestures: that is, think for yourself
what they mean. That is why in *The Idea of History* Collingwood
declared that 'thought can never be mere object' (*IH*, 288). Utterances and gestures can be mere objects, because you can perceive
others making them without making them yourself; the reason why
thoughts cannot be mere objects is that you cannot perceive them
at all: you cannot become aware of the thoughts of others except
by thinking them for yourself. The doctrine of *Speculum Mentis*, that
history, as a specific form of experience, is identical with perception, and its derivative, the doctrine that to historians past thoughts
are an objective spectacle, are therefore both false. If either were
true, scepticism would be inevitable.

That is not all. Collingwood believed that the doctrine that history is at bottom a matter of perception was connected with the
doctrine that all experience is perceptual, a flow of feeling raised to
consciousness by attention. If historians can literally re-enact past
thoughts, then mind cannot be a flow of immediate consciousness.
Feelings are successive states in a flow; and, once past, they cannot
be recalled. You can think about both past feelings and past
thoughts, but there is a fundamental difference between the two
cases. When you think of a past feeling, that feeling does not reappear. You need not become angry again in order to think of your
past anger: 'the actual past anger . . . is past and gone; that does
not reappear, the stream of immediate experience has carried it away
for ever; at most there reappears something like it' (*IH*, 293).

It is otherwise with thought. 'To think at all about [a] past
activity of thought', Collingwood argued, 'I must revive it in my
own mind, for the act of thinking can be studied only as an act'

(*IH*, 293). By this distinction between immediate experience and thought he crudely anticipated his own developed analysis of the orders of consciousness in *The New Leviathan*. Yet his later analysis confirmed his earlier contention. The only element in the life of the mind that can be strictly described as a flow of immediate consciousness is the flow of first-order consciousness. Even second-order consciousness, which isolates continuing objects of feeling by selective attention, is not merely a flow; and acts of consciousness of higher orders cannot intelligibly be described as states in a flow at all (cf. *NL*, 6. 58).

Once he has abandoned the doctrine that all experience is a flow of immediate consciousness, Collingwood's imaginary objector has lost his fundamental philosophical ground for believing that a past act of thought cannot be re-enacted (cf. *IH*, 286–7). Yet the idea that if acts of thought are done by different persons or at different times then they must be different can be advanced independently, as mere common sense. By putting the following argument into the mouth of his imaginary objector, Collingwood gave this common-sense assertion philosophical form. When we distinguish two things and yet say that they are the same, as we often do, we mean that they are different instances of the same universal. There is only one kind of identity in difference, namely, specific identity in numerical difference. Therefore, the only kind of identity there can be between a past thought and an historian's re-enactment of it is specific identity in numerical difference; and so the two must be numerically different (*IH*, 285).

Since Collingwood's rejoinder to this interesting but muddled argument was itself muddled and question-begging (cf. *IH*, 286–7), I shall pass over it. Argument and rejoinder both derive from the same error, that specific identity is non-numerical. All identity and all difference are numerical. You can ask whether two things belong to the same species (i.e. to one species) or to different species (i.e. each to a different one of two species), but identity and difference of species are as numerical as identity and difference of individuals. The expressions 'numerical identity' and 'numerical difference' are pleonastic: they mean nothing more than 'identity' and 'difference' simply.

Collingwood's mistaken belief that there is such a thing as numerical difference, as opposed to specific difference, goes with an even more dangerous error, that there can be *mere* numerical difference. Once it is clear that numerical difference is just difference, and numerical identity just identity, it also becomes clear that the concepts of identity and difference, taken by themselves, are incomplete. To ask whether this and that are the same or different would be senseless unless you specified, explicitly or implicitly, some concept under which they both fall, in terms of which your question was asked. Was the conflict in which Nelson fought at Trafalgar the same as that in which Napoleon fought at Austerlitz, or were they different? The answer turns on whether that question is asked about a war or a battle. The war in which each fought was the same, but not the battle. The question is therefore ambiguous until it is made clear whether the concept of conflict in terms of which the question is asked is that of a war or of a battle. In the same way the question, 'Are a past thought and an historian's re-enactment of it the same or different?' is senseless until both the past thought and the historian's re-enactment are both brought under some concept; and, if the concept specified is that of an act, it is ambiguous; for 'act' may mean both what is done, and the doing of it (i.e. its 'enactment' or performance).

If both act and re-enactment are brought under the concept of the doing of an act (or its 'enactment'), they are obviously different enactments. Collingwood made this plain in his terminology, when he described historians as *re*-enacting, *re*-thinking, or *re*viving past thoughts. Considered as enactments, an enactment and its re-enactment are not the same. That, however, was not in question. Collingwood did not ask whether the past enactment of a thought and an historian's re-enactment of it were the same enactment, but whether in both enactments the same thing was done. To distinguish between an act of thought and its various enactments is not sophistical hair-splitting.

That Collingwood believed that this distinction could not be drawn for any acts except acts of thought is shown by his remark that 'Euclid and I are not (as it were) two different typewriters which, just because they are not the same typewriter, can never perform the same act but only acts of the same kind' (*IH*, 287–8). This, however, was a mistake. If two different typists strike the letter *A* on two different typewriters, they both strike the same letter; and, if striking the same letter were the act in question, they would both have performed the same act. The objection that no two typewriters are exactly identical in their physical structure is beside the point. If the act in question was striking a certain letter, they must be said to have performed the same act, namely, that of striking the letter *A*; if it had been striking a certain letter on a certain typewriter, they would have performed different acts.

It is in this sense that Collingwood's arguments show that the same act of thought can be performed at different times by different persons. Although he was muddled about what the distinction between an act and its enactment is, and because of his muddle thought that distinction to be inapplicable to physical acts, he was clearly right in applying it to acts of thought.

When I read Plato's argument in the *Theaetetus* against the view that knowledge is merely sensation, [he wrote] I do not know what philosophical doctrines he was attacking. . . . Plato's argument must undoubtedly have grown up out of a discussion of some sort, though I do not know what it was, and been closely connected with such a discussion. Yet if I not only read his argument but understand it, follow it in my own mind by re-arguing it with and for myself, the process of argument which I go through is not a process resembling Plato's, it actually is Plato's, so far as I understand him rightly. (*IH*, 301.)

Plato's enactment of that process and my re-enactment are different enactments, but there is one process which is acted and re-enacted. In the same way, if you strike the letter *A* on a typewriter and then I do so, although our reasons for doing so may be different, although you may tap lightly and I bang hard, we both perform the same act; that of striking the letter *A*. If the act in question had not been that of striking a certain letter, but that of striking a letter with a certain finger, then our acts might have been different; for you might have used one finger and I another.

§ 4. *The Idealist Problem: Can the Past Live?*

Although his own early difficulties with his third presupposition of scientific history proceeded in the main from his realist preconceptions, Collingwood did not delude himself that the anti-realist idealism of the school of Green was any less hostile to scientific history than Cook–Wilsonian realism. Accordingly, the second series of philosophical objections to his presuppositions of scientific history which he chose to examine in 'History as Re-enactment of Past Experience' were of idealist origin. The first of those objections was as follows.

Suppose it granted that an experience could be identically repeated, the result would only be an immediate identity between the historian and the person he was trying to understand, so far as that experience was concerned. The object (in this case the past) would be simply incorporated in the subject (in this case the present, the historian's own thought); and instead of answering the question how the past is known we should be maintaining that the past is not known, but only the present. (*IH*, 284.)

The root of this objection is that a re-enactment of a past thought must be a present experience. Clearly, 'mere re-enactment of another's thought does not make historical knowledge; we must also know that we are re-enacting it' (*IH*, 289). But in that case, 'the knowledge that we are re-enacting a past thought, is in the nature of the case impossible; since the thought as re-enacted is now our own, and our knowledge of it is limited to our own present awareness of it as an element in our own experience' (*IH*, 289). This objection is not to the third presupposition, that past thoughts can be re-enacted, but rather to the fourth, that although known to be past, thoughts can yet live in the present. Its point is that even if a past thought could be re-enacted, it could not be known to be past. What lives in the present cannot be past.

Collingwood believed that Professor Michael Oakeshott had followed this line of reasoning in *Experience and its Modes*.[1] Oakeshott there, as Collingwood interpreted him, offered the following

[1] Cambridge, 1933.

dilemma. The object of historical thought is either present or past: the historian thinks of it as past, but there he is wrong; for if it were past, he could not think it. As Oakeshott himself wrote, 'History, because it is experience, is present . . .' (op. cit., p. 111). If, on the other hand, the object of history is really present, then the historian ,in conceiving it *sub specie praeteritorum*m, isconceives it. As an historian he makes the philosophical mistake of referring to the past what is in fact present experience. As long as he remains an historian, he is in philosophical error; and as soon as he corrects his error, he ceases to think as an historian (*IH*, 155–7).

Collingwood's way out of Oakeshott's dilemma was between its horns. Oakeshott had presupposed that there are only two possibilities: either that past thoughts are irrecoverably lost, or 'dead', as Collingwood liked to put it; or that they are present, and in no way past at all. This would be true if all experience were feeling: for past feelings are indeed irrecoverably lost, and cannot be felt again; and that present feelings, being in no way past, can at best resemble past feelings. But, as we have seen, Collingwood's whole later philosophy of mind repudiated such an identification of experience with feeling. The fact that I cannot feel a past feeling does not entail that I cannot think about one; and even less does it entail that I cannot both think a past thought and know that it is past (*IH*, 158).

Experiences are not exhaustively divisible into those which are past and dead, and those which are present and alive. Some experiences live even though they are past: namely, past thoughts revived by historical thinking. Although Collingwood had, as early as 1920, grasped the principle that 'the past which an historian studies is not a dead past, but a past which in some sense is still living in the present' (*A*, 97), at that time, because he lacked a theory of the re-enactment of past thought, he could not adequately explain how the past could live. By 1930, however, he was in a position to allow for what is true in such dicta as Oakeshott's 'History, because it is experience, is present', and Croce's 'All history is contemporary history' (*IH*, 202), without denying that historical knowledge is knowledge of past actions.

Past thoughts do not live of themselves. They are not ghosts which haunt historians; they do not force themselves willy-nilly upon anybody. They are live, not as spiritualists suppose dis-embodied spirits to be alive, but as anything is alive which is unextinguished, unabated, or unforgotten. This sense of the word is illustrated by Macaulay's description of certain agitators as striving 'to keep discontent alive'. A past thought lives when an historian succeeds in re-enacting it. In order to re-enact a past thought, an historian must have evidence that it was thought. Yet evidence alone is not enough. The thoughts of Cicero would not be alive if his writings remained but the Latin language was not understood; and even though the Pont du Gard remained standing, the thoughts of its Roman engineers would not be alive if nobody understood the principle of the arch, or what an aqueduct was. The past lives, not simply because its relics and traces remain, but because the thoughts without which they cannot be interpreted 'are still in existence as ways in which people still think' (A, 97). It is not, however, necessary that those ways of thinking should have survived continuously. By systematic questioning of evidence ways of thinking which have been lost have been recovered: they 'have died and been raised from the dead, like the ancient languages of Mesopotamia and Egypt' (A, 97).

Collingwood's philosophy of history accordingly stands between the idealism and the realism which divided his contemporaries and immediate predecessors: while it inherits elements from both, it cannot be reconciled with either. From idealism he adopted two doctrines: first, that every thought is 'immediate', in the sense that 'it occurs at a certain time, and in a certain context of other acts of thought, emotions, sensations, and so forth' (IH, 297); and secondly, that a thought's relations with its context 'are not those of an item in a collection, but those of a special function in the total activity of an organism' (IH, 300). From 'those who have opposed the "idealists", ' he adopted the conception of thought as objective or 'mediate', and not necessarily altered by alterations of the context in which we think it (IH, 300).

This realist doctrine, together with his own principle that a thought is not an element in the flow of immediate consciousness, but an act of higher order, enabled Collingwood to maintain that, besides occurring in a given immediate context, a thought can 'sustain itself through a change of context and revive in a different one' (*IH*, 297; cf. 300). When a thought is revived, its original context of other thoughts and feelings has been lost, and a new context has replaced it.

> The first discovery of a truth, for example, differs from any subsequent contemplation of it, not in that the truth contemplated is a different truth, nor in that the act of contemplating it is a different act; but in that the immediacy of the first occasion can never again be experienced: the shock of its novelty, the liberation from perplexing problems, the triumph of achieving a desired result. . . . (*IH*, 297–8.)

In turning his back on idealism, Collingwood foresaw the challenges that would be thrown down to him. F. H. Bradley had thought it self-evident that any experience 'torn from its context is thereby mutilated and falsified; and that in consequence, to know any one thing, we must know its context, which implies knowing the whole universe' (*IH*, 298; cf. 141). To defend his realist position that thoughts need not be altered by alterations of the context in which we think them, he had to break decisively with Bradley's doctrine that to isolate a thought from its context is to mutilate it. He did so with two devastating arguments.

In the first he showed that Bradley's view entailed complete scepticism. If it were true, no thought whatever could be discussed, much less proved or disproved; for any attempt to state what was to be discussed would tear it from its original context. Although Bradley himself did not deny that on his principles any attempt to think at all must be self-frustrating, he ought either to have done so or to have revised his principles. Collingwood refused to consider it a genuine possibility that the exercise of reason should be in conflict with itself (*IH*, 299).

In his second argument Collingwood attacked Bradley's premiss directly. It is simply untrue that a thought is mutilated or falsified by tearing it from its context of other thoughts and feelings, because that context has nothing to do with its character as a thought, that is, with what it affirms, which Collingwood called its 'objectivity' or its 'mediacy'. Bradley failed to allow for the fact that not all the content of experience is immediate. A thought is not what it is because it involves awareness of a certain immediate flux of feeling, or because it has a context of other thoughts (*IH*, 141). Its 'objectivity' or 'mediacy', as he later demonstrated in *The New Leviathan*, derives from its character as a linguistic act. Every act of thought is a linguistic act of a certain kind, and is what it is in virtue of the meaning of what is said in that act.

It is true that no act of thought would be intelligible without some appropriate context of other thoughts. For example, a significant theoretical thought can only arise in a context of methodically ordered questions and answers. Bradley would have been right if his claim had been only that a thought would be mutilated and falsified unless it occurred in some appropriate context or other; his mistake was to imagine that only one context could be appropriate. For any thought many different contexts are appropriate; and as long as it is re-enacted in one of them, it will be neither mutilated nor falsified (*IH*, 301).

§ 5. The 'Positivist' Problem: History and Determinism

Idealism and realism are not the only philosophical systems with which scientific history, as Collingwood conceived it, cannot be reconciled. In concluding his British Academy Lecture, *Human Nature and Human History*, in which he rehearsed his principal ideas about the nature of scientific history, he remarked that throughout it he had found it necessary 'to engage in a running fight with what may be called a positivistic conception, or rather misconception, of history, as the study of successive events lying in a dead past, events to be understood as the scientist understands natural events, by classifying them and establishing relations between the classes thus defined' (*IH*, 228).

This jejune Comtist theory, however, was not the misconception he had in fact controverted. In his own criticism of Comte, he had demonstrated that natural scientists do not explain past events by classifying and correlating them. On the contrary, their method is Baconian. They try to penetrate, by systematic questioning of observable fact, to the laws which underlie all merely empirical correlations (cf. *IH*, 126–7). The alternative which jeopardized Collingwood's conception of history was not Comtism, but genuine naturalism: the doctrine that past actions are to be understood as natural scientists really do understand past natural events, that is, by natural history.

We have already considered Collingwood's argument, in *The Idea of Nature*, that natural science 'exists and always has existed in a context of history, and depends on historical thought for its existence' (*IN*, 177; see above, Ch. VIII, § 1). That argument, when taken in conjunction with his demonstration that in scientific history past actions are not explained as past natural events are explained in natural history, undoubtedly demolishes the naturalistic conception of existing scientific history. But that is not enough. The present state of the theoretical sciences is not perfect. May it not be that past actions in principle can be studied, and ought to be studied, as natural history studies past natural events?

Ultimately, this question raises the metaphysical problem of the relation between nature and mind. We must defer our examination of Collingwood's attempt to solve that problem to a later chapter (XI, § 2). In his British Academy lecture he did not carry his 'running fight' to the metaphysical citadel of naturalism. Instead, he chose to dispute a key naturalist position, namely, that all past actions can in principle be explained by subsuming them under general laws of nature.

This position may be conveniently referred to as 'scientific determinism'. It is unfortunate that Collingwood described his sustained criticism of it as a fight with 'a positivistic conception'; for neither scientific determinism nor naturalism is essentially positivistic. Comtist positivism was not truly naturalistic, because it misconceived what natural science is; and modern logical positivism, which in at least some of its forms has an adequate conception of natural science, is essentially distinct from naturalism. There are two reasons for this. First, the fundamental tenet of logical positivism is the empirical criterion of meaning, which does not in any of its more plausible forms entail that naturalism is true. Although most logical positivists are naturalists, that is not because they are logical positivists. Secondly, even if most logical positivists are naturalists, not all naturalists are logical positivists. For example, the non-positivistic conception of laws of nature defended by Professor Kneale in his *Probability and Induction* is perfectly compatible with naturalism and scientific determinism.

Scientific determinism is empirically neither verifiable nor falsifiable. Even supposing that every known event could be explained by means of established laws, it would remain possible that further observation might falsify those laws; and even supposing that no known event could be so explained, that might be because the required laws had not been thought of. The only arguments which bear on either side of the question are philosophical, and it is discouraging to record that, on both sides, the vast majority of those customarily offered are extraordinarily bad. Although the confusions in the arguments against determinism are widely known, being analysed in most manuals of elementary philosophy, those in the arguments for it are not. Why this is so I cannot imagine.

The arguments for scientific determinism reduce to two. The first, which appeals to the progress of natural science, is as follows. All attempts to restrict the events which can be explained by the methods of natural science are arbitrary, and many of them have already been made ridiculous by scientific progress. To exclude human action from the province of natural science is as obscurantist as were past attempts to exclude biological processes. Human actions, therefore, like all other natural happenings, must admit of explanation by natural science, i.e. explanation according to general laws of nature, even if the laws required have not yet been discovered.

The second argument for scientific determinism is *a priori*, and makes no predictions about the future of natural science. It rests on two philosophical premises: first, that human actions are not unintelligible chance occurrences; and secondly, that if human actions could not be explained in accordance with general laws of nature, their occurrence would be an unintelligible matter of chance. From these premises it immediately follows that all human actions can be explained in accordance with general laws of nature. This proof has been ingeniously refined by the following proof of its first premiss: the common-sense belief that human actions are free is true beyond doubt, but human actions could not be free if they occurred by chance; therefore, human actions are not chance occurrences. The original argument together with its refinement purports to show not only that scientific determinism is true, but that free-will implies determinism and is inconceivable without it.[1]

The *a priori* argument for determinism transparently begs the question. The Christian philosophical tradition, which on this point has passed over into uninstructed common sense, distinguishes between human actions and chance events by affirming that, whereas the latter have no cause, the former are brought about by rational beings. A rational being is one who has the power of deciding which action he will perform of the various ones he recognizes as possible for him on a given occasion. For such decisions he may have reasons or he may not. Even if he does not, his action is not therefore a chance occurrence.

If a man who enjoys both golf and tennis equally, and has had the opportunity to spend an afternoon playing either, has chosen 'for no particular reason' to play golf rather than tennis, it would be an abuse of language to describe his action as a matter of chance. He did not aimlessly drift into a game of golf, but deliberately decided to play it rather than tennis. It is a sufficient explanation of his act to say, 'That is what he chose to do'.

Even when a man has a reason for a decision, a similar point holds. Why act on that reason rather than on another? There may or may not be a further reason; but, whether there is or not, such chains of reasons must come to an end. When the ultimate reasons upon which a man has acted have been reached, he may be able to vindicate them by showing that they are intrinsically reasonable; but that is not the same thing as explaining the fact that he acted in accordance with them. You may believe that it is self-evidently unreasonable to tell a lie to somebody who, without coercing you in any way, asks you a question; but it does not follow, because you believe it, that you always tell the truth under such circumstances. You may lie on a malicious impulse, knowing that it is wrong and unreasonable. There is a difference between thinking a reason

---

[1] This echoes the title of an essay by R. E. Hobart (Dickinson Miller) in *Mind*, xliii (1934), pp. 1–27.

adequate, and acting in accordance with it. History explains a man's actions by referring to the reasons upon which he actually chose to act, not to the reasons which he thought most adequate. Whether a man has acted upon reasons which he believes adequate, or upon others, an irreducible component of the explanation of his act is that he chose to act upon those reasons.

A scientific determinist might rejoin: 'The fact that such choices are not chance occurrences shows that they must have some explanation; and if they have no historical explanation in terms of reasons or purposes then they must have a non-historical explanation, an explanation in accordance with general laws of nature'. The first step in this argument is a *non sequitur*. Traditionally it was supposed that a rational being is one which has the power to survey different reasons for acting, and to choose to act in accordance with one reason rather than another. Such choices were taken neither to require nor to admit further explanation. In a brilliant youthful essay which he published in a collaborative volume entitled *Concerning Prayer* (B. H. Streeter and others, London, 1916), Collingwood remarked that, 'To the question "Why do people go wrong?" the only answer is "Because they choose to"'. He defended his answer as follows.

To a mind obsessed by the idea of causation, the idea that everything must be explained by something else, this answer seems inadequate. But action is precisely that which is not caused; the will of a person acting determines itself and is not determined by anything outside itself. Causation has doubtless its proper sphere. . . . But . . . [it] cannot be applied to the activity of the will without explicitly falsifying the whole nature of that activity. An act of the will is its own cause and its own explanation; to seek its explanation in something else is to treat it not as an act but as a mechanical event (loc. cit., p. 459).

It is, of course, open to scientific determinists to deny the traditional presupposition that, when a man makes an ultimate choice, there's an end on't. Civilizations have existed in which this presupposition has not been made (cf. *NL*, 13. 49), and doubtless others will exist in the future. Collingwood was the last man to deny that a traditional absolute presupposition might be jettisoned. It is not legitimate, however, for scientific determinists to pretend that nobody has ever made or could ever make the traditional presupposition, or that it is logically absurd to make it.

In his analysis of scientific history, Collingwood implicitly showed how a thoroughly Baconian science of human action could be reconciled with the traditional conception of man as a free agent. Unhappily, in 'History and Freedom', an excerpt from *The Principles of History*, he went farther. Partly owing to an error about the nature of the compulsion which situations exert upon actions, he mistook their compatibility for a necessary connexion. '[S]imultaneously with [the] discovery of his own freedom as historian', he wrote, the historian 'discovers the freedom of man as an historical agent. Historical thought, thought about rational activity, is free from the domination of natural science, and rational activity is free from the domination of nature' (*IH*, 318). This would only be true if, in order to be successfully studied by the method of history, human actions had necessarily to be recalcitrant to those of natural science. Yet Collingwood not only proved no such thing, in *The New Leviathan* he expressly stated that any and every physical happening, including even the physical movements which express rational activity, can be investigated by natural science (*NL*, 2. 44). The fact that history is free from the domination of natural science entails only that rational actions can be explained scientifically without subsuming them under laws of nature. It shows that it is *possible* that rational action should be free from the domination of nature, but not that it must be.

And so we return to the first argument for scientific determinism: the argument from the progress of natural science. Does not the progress of natural science, its extension to more and more fields of inquiry, afford adequate reason for the conclusion that all human behaviour will in the end be brought under its sway? To this argument Collingwood replied that projected natural sciences of human activity are not of recent origin. From the time of Locke and Hume 'a science of human nature' has been a favourite with both philosophers and scientists. Yet all the many attempts to develop such a science have failed (*IH*, 206–8).

It is true that the theoretical structure of some social sciences (e.g. economics) resembles that of a natural science. Laws of economic behaviour are propounded which can be tested by applying them to observed behaviour. However, the resemblance between the social and the natural sciences is superficial. As Collingwood pointed out,

A positive science of mind will, no doubt, be able to establish uniformities and recurrences, but it can have no guarantee that the laws it establishes will hold good beyond the historical period from which its facts are drawn. Such a science (as we have lately been taught with regard to what is called classical economics) can do no more than describe in a general way certain characteristics of the historical age in which it is constructed. If it tries to overcome this limitation by drawing on a wider field, relying on ancient history, modern anthropology, and so on, for a larger basis of facts, it will still never be more than a generalized description of certain phases in human history. It will never be a non-historical science of mind. (*IH*, 223–4.)

The force of Collingwood's criticism may be underrated because he neglected to distinguish between laws and statements of trends or of patterns of behaviour. As Popper has emphatically protested, the two are fundamentally different: 'A statement asserting the existence of a trend is existential, not universal. (A universal law, on the other hand, does not assert existence; on the contrary: ... it asserts the impossibility of something or other.)'[1]

Natural events are not explained by laws alone, but by laws together with statements about initial conditions. Scientific determinists are not committed to holding that any set of initial conditions must recur. In some cases, e.g. the movements of the planets relative to the sun, they do. But scientific determinism would not be refuted if it were shown to be unlikely that in human affairs any set of initial conditions should ever recur. If none did, there would be no 'recurrences' or repeated trends in human activity; but it would not follow that there were no natural laws applicable to it. Now there are 'recurrences' or repeated trends in human activity, and Collingwood did not deny it; but the fact that they are confined to certain phases in history does not entail that there are no laws of nature which apply to human activity.

Collingwood's reference to classical economics shows that his

[1] K. R. Popper, *The Poverty of Historicism*, p. 115.

criticism did not rest upon this confusion. The laws of classical economics (or of any of the various post-classical economic systems) are not statements of trends. Collingwood claimed that no system of laws of human behaviour in any department of life would hold good in all periods of human history. The system of classical economics does not assert the absolute impossibility of certain forms of economic behaviour, as it would if economic laws were genuine laws of nature; it affirms only a conditional impossibility, namely, that those forms of behaviour are impossible provided that men act in accordance with the fundamental laws of the system. Since theoretical economics, by common consent among scientific determinists, is the social science which most nearly approximates to their ideal, what holds of it holds also for the less developed social sciences.

Nor will it do to say that many of the laws of nature applicable to human activity are 'so trivial, so much part of our common knowledge, that we need not mention them and rarely notice them'.[1] The specimens of such laws which are commonly offered are plainly not what is demanded. Thus Popper once proposed this: 'If we say that the cause of the death of Giordano Bruno was being burnt at the stake, we do not need to mention the universal law that all living things die when exposed to intense heat.'[2] However, neither this explanation nor this law belongs to history proper, but to the natural situation within which human action takes place.

Sometimes the non-historical character of the offered law is disguised, as in another specimen Popper has offered, namely, 'You cannot, without increasing productivity, raise the real income of the working population'.[3] Assuming a society in which the labour force is fully employed, whose total income is equitably distributed, and which is not in a position to beg, borrow, or steal from its neighbours, this law is simply an application of the law of conservation of energy. In the circumstances specified, the goods which constitute real income can only be produced by the labour force available. If, as is presupposed, that force is expending its maximum of energy it follows that more goods can be produced only by a more efficient

---

[1] Popper, *The Poverty of Historicism*, p. 145.   [2] Ibid., p. 145.
[3] K. R. Popper, in Patrick Gardiner (ed.) *Theories of History*, p. 282.

employment of that energy, i.e. by greater productivity. Except for such examples as these, which, although laws, are not laws of rational human activity, the putative laws to which scientific determinists appeal commonly turn out either to apply only to some phases of human history, as does another of Popper's examples, 'You cannot have a full employment policy without inflation',[1] or to be guarded generalizations, which, since they are not susceptible of empirical falsification, are not laws of nature at all, e.g. 'Strict Orthodox Jews fast on the Day of Atonement'.[2]

The progress of the social sciences, therefore, affords no support to scientific determinism. It owes nothing to the deterministic methods of the natural sciences, although there is an illusion that it does; partly because laws applicable to natural processes have been mistaken for laws of human action, and partly because the laws of such social sciences as theoretical economics have been interpreted as universal laws of nature. Once those errors have been corrected, the illusion vanishes that the social sciences are becoming more like natural sciences.

The argument for determinism from the progress of the natural sciences may take yet another form. Instead of looking to the social sciences, determinists may look to progress in existing natural sciences such as neuro-physiology. If neuro-physiology can already explain many bodily changes, may it not one day be able to account for all of them, every movement of the limbs and tongue, every change in facial expression? That this is *a priori* possible, there can be no doubt. However, as intimated above, I shall not inquire whether the non-deterministic character of the sciences of human activity tends to show that no natural science can account for all bodily movements, until we examine Collingwood's metaphysical theory of the relation of mind to nature (cf. Ch. XI, § 2).

Scientific determinism must be distinguished from the speculative forms of determinism propounded by idealist philosophers like Kant and Fichte, though not by Hegel (*IH*, 98–102, 109, 114), by materialist philosophers like Karl Marx (*IH*, 122–6), and by visionary historians like Spengler and Toynbee (*IH*, 181–3, 159–65). In our

---

[1] Ibid., p. 282.
[2] Michael Scriven, in Patrick Gardiner (ed.), *Theories of History*, p. 465.

time, no political or social movement hostile to liberty or rational inquiry has neglected to encourage its adherents by assuring them that success is predetermined, that it is inevitable that free societies will disintegrate, and disinterested inquiry be suppressed. Collingwood wasted little energy in refuting such theories. Intellectually, arguments that humble the pretensions of a sophisticated theory like scientific determinism suffice with something to spare for caricatures of it. Yet rational criticism seldom weakens the fascination of speculative determinism for its adherents. Whether it prophesies ultimate victory or inevitable defeat, it tells them what in their hearts they want to believe; and so it 'partakes the solidity of its indestructible foundations'[1]—the gullibility and vanity of man.

In criticizing Spengler, Collingwood drew attention to the unscrupulous falsifications of fact to which speculative determinists commonly resort (*IH*, 182–3). But that was not his fundamental criticism. By studying the course of history simply to find and 'pigeon-hole' the various trends that take place in it, Marx, Spengler, and Toynbee refuse to investigate why those whose actions they study acted as they did. Collingwood put the point in a memorable metaphor: 'In order to pigeon-hole historical facts, the living body of history must first be killed (that is, its essential character as process must be denied) so that it may be dissected' (*IH*, 163–4). Yet, when this butchery has been committed, and the mangled trends duly pigeon-holed, the resulting predictions, however interesting they may be, are scientifically worthless. Because events in contemporary history resemble portions of some pigeon-holed group of past trends, it does not follow that their sequel will accord with those trends. 'A positive science of mind will, no doubt, be able to establish uniformities and recurrences, but it can have no guarantee that the laws it establishes will hold good beyond the historical period from which its facts are drawn' (*IH*, 223–4).

§ 6. *History and Practical Wisdom*

The outbreak of the First World War, and the 'sheer ineptitude' of the treaty which ended it, indelibly impressed Collingwood with

---

[1] Cf. A. E. Housman, *D. Iunii Iuvenalis Saturae* (2nd ed., Cambridge, 1931), p. xii.

the 'contrast between the success of modern European minds in controlling almost any situation in which the elements are physical bodies and the forces physical forces, and their inability to control situations in which the elements are human beings and the forces mental forces' (*A*, 90). One reason why he believed that those who live the life of the mind could no longer afford to neglect history was that only by the methods of history can purposive human action be understood, and only by understanding what others have done and are doing can you master the situations in which you find yourself. 'Well-meaning babblers talked about the necessity for a change of heart. But the trouble was obviously in the head. What was needed was not more goodwill and human affection, but more understanding of human affairs and more knowledge of how to handle them' (*A*, 92).

The first gift which history can bestow upon a man of action is a trained eye for his situation. Anybody who wishes to discover why those with whom he must deal act as they do must follow historical method, asking questions about what they think, and verifying or falsifying proposed answers to those questions by referring them to such evidence as may be available. However, a training in history does not merely bring knowledge of that method. Everybody follows historical method to some extent, although not everybody is aware that he does so. What historical training can confer, which the untrained employment of historical methods in everyday life cannot, is exact knowledge of the range of past responses to the profuse variety of past situations. Everybody acts in accordance with what he knows, and a large part of what he knows, whether he be a soldier, a manufacturer, a politician, or a philosopher, is how his predecessors have solved their problems: their ways of thinking are still in existence as ways in which he thinks (cf. *A*, 97).

As Collingwood's own analysis of human action has shown, nobody necessarily acts in the same way as anybody else has done. Even if he knows what others have thought in similar situations, he may still have formed conclusions of his own. Nobody who has learned what history has to teach will assume that those with whom he deals must act in the same way as any of their predecessors. The commander of an army must be ready to encounter a Napoleon or a Marlborough, as well as a Joffre or a Haig. Yet even the boldest thoughts of a genius take their rise from those of their predecessors; and you will understand them more readily if you have understood those earlier thoughts. By comparison with a non-historian, an historian who is trying to understand how somebody else will act in a certain situation, and who knows how others have dealt with similar situations, is 'as the trained woodsman is to the ignorant traveller' (*A*, 100).

It might seem that a trained eye for situations is a small gift. After all, a man may grasp what his situation is without being able to master it. Many would be dissatisfied with anything short of a set of rules by which to act in any situation that may arise. Collingwood's first comment on this demand was as follows.

[I]f ready-made rules for dealing with situations of specific types are what you want, natural science is the kind of thing which can provide them. The reason why the civilization of 1600–1900, based upon natural science, found bankruptcy staring it in the face was because, in its passion for ready-made rules, it had neglected to develop that kind of insight which alone could tell it what rules to apply, not in a situation of a specific type, but in the situation in which it actually found itself. (*A*, 101.)

It ought to be remarked that in this passage Collingwood did not deny that such ready-made rules would be useful, but only that they would be useful without the insight into situations which history can furnish.

He did not, however, inquire into the kind of ready-made rules that natural science can provide. They would, presumably, be technological rules, that is, rules which lay down that if, in a situation of a certain kind, a certain end is to be sought, then that end can be brought about in a certain way. For example, if you are confronted with a river fifty yards wide, flowing between rocky banks fifteen feet high, and if you propose to throw a footbridge over it, then civil engineers can tell you of various ways to accomplish your purpose. In giving you this information, they will draw upon technological rules which ultimately rest on laws of nature. Provided that in describing your situation no factor that must be taken into account has been forgotten, and provided that the steps to be taken in constructing the bridge have been adequately specified, then it will be possible to deduce, by means of established laws of nature, that if those steps are taken, then the river will be bridged (cf. *A*, 103).

Collingwood seems to have been oblivious of the fact that his own analysis of scientific history shows that it too can yield ready-made rules of a kind. Historical situations recur, just as natural situations do (*IH*, 223-4, 265). Military history, for example, provides students of tactics and strategy with knowledge of what types of tactical and strategic situations may be expected to recur. Provided that such a situation has been adequately specified, including the thoughts of each of the relevant agents or groups of agents, then it will be possible directly to deduce that, if certain steps are taken, certain results will follow. Deductions of this kind do not employ general laws; for, as Collingwood's analysis of historical inference has shown, premisses about thoughts can entail conclusions about actions without the mediation of such laws. There is, however, a difference between the genuinely technological rules in a manual of civil engineering and the rules in a manual of military tactics, which may be marked by calling the latter 'quasi-technological'. The rules for constructing on a specific site a certain kind of bridge provide for every change in the situation that may be caused by the various steps taken in constructing it; but the rules for capturing a specific kind of military position will only provide for the responses the defenders make to the various steps taken in capturing it, if those responses follow some previous pattern. Manuals of tactics can show you how to deal with responses which have been thought of before, but not with surprises improvised on the spot.

Whether you are an engineer or military tactician, you must control changing situations; but if, like an engineer, you must control situations which are merely natural, you have an important advantage. Ideally, all the changes in a natural situation can be calculated, by means of natural laws, from a specification of its state at any one time, and from information about the extraneous factors, including what you may do as an engineer, that may enter into it. On the other hand, the changes in an historical situation can only be calculated conditionally. Historical situations consist of human actions and reactions, which can only be predicted by rulers when those who perform them think as others have thought in situations of the same kind. Should they strike out on new paths, the situation which must be controlled will not be predictable. In order to control historical situations, then, you must make plans with many branches: plans which allow for anything that may be done by those whose actions you must control. You will not be able to do so unless you are at least as fertile in improvisation as they.

Collingwood more than once pointed out that historians can only reconstruct past thoughts which they have sufficient intellectual capacity to re-think (*IH*, 218–19; *A*, 112). European historians in the eighteenth century found the Middle Ages barbarous and unintelligible because they were unequal to the task of re-thinking the thoughts which were fundamental to the life of those Ages. An historian today could not write a true history of Napoleon's campaigns, or of the modern theory of gravitation, unless he were equal to re-thinking Napoleon's military thoughts or Einstein's scientific thoughts. He need not, of course, be able to originate them; but he must be able to reconstruct what they were when provided with evidence that Napoleon and Einstein thought them. Since the thoughts behind the significant actions of great statesmen, scientists, philosophers, generals, and business-men are seldom commonplace, nobody can become a scientific historian without accustoming himself to working 'against the grain' of his own mind: to reconstructing thoughts which he himself either could not or would not originate.

A scissors-and-paste man, especially if he writes as a propagandist, is under no such discipline. A scientific historian will usually have an opinion about which side in a given historical conflict was the better, and he should not try to conceal it. The discipline of scientific history, however, will help him to resist propagandist temptations, whether they be to suppress what was bad in the intentions of those who belonged to his own side, or to calumniate those who opposed it. The fault of propagandist historians like Hilaire Belloc is neither that they favour one side rather than another, nor that their conclusions are always false. Belloc himself was gifted with remarkable historical insight, and not a few of his contentions have worn better than those of his Whig and Protestant adversaries. Yet, because he began with reconstructions of the past which fulfilled his propagandist purposes, and sought evidence solely in order to confirm them, his results were scientifically worthless. He could never be compelled, by the failure of his preconceived reconstructions, to attribute to the historical agents of whom he wrote any thoughts which he would neither have thought for himself nor have expected in those who opposed him. Belloc's historical heroes think as he did and his villains think as he imagined his contemporary adversaries in politics and religion to do. If he had been more scientific as an historian, he might have been more successful as a politician; for he would have accustomed himself to seeking out how others think, even when their ways of thinking were altogether at variance with his preconceptions.

For these reasons, Collingwood held that scientific history, 'the science of human affairs', would enable man to control human relations as natural science had enabled him to control nature, by bestowing two gifts upon him: first, an eye for human situations, developed by an extensive acquaintance with past ways of thinking that may be revived in present actions (A, 100); and secondly, a mind trained to seek out the thoughts contained in actions, free from the illusion that those thoughts must be familiar or congenial (A, 115–16). He did not notice, as he might have, that along with an eye for situations there goes a certain equipment of quasi-technological rules for dealing with them, so long as they develop on the pattern of earlier situations.

In urging these conclusions, Collingwood expressly stated that our most serious practical problems are how to control situations, not for what ends they are to be controlled. The First World War happened, not because 'any except at most the tiniest fraction of the combatants wanted it', but because a situation 'got more and more out of hand' (A, 90). Not man's heart was at fault, but his head (A, 92). Yet, at the close of the very chapter in which he made those statements, Collingwood went on to claim that action at a high 'potential' must be done, not from Desire, not from Self-Interest, not even from the moral rules of Right Conduct, but from the agent's insight into his situation; and he implicitly identified the insight required with that provided by scientific history (A, 105–6). Now it is manifest that historical insight is not a substitute for a principle of action, whether self-interest or morality. Hitler displayed profound, if narrow, historical insight in divining how weak-willed were his British and French opponents in 1938–9, and how out of date their military thinking in 1940;[1] but this insight, which for a time gave him power to control his military and political situation, did not teach him to use that power well or even prudently.

How came Collingwood to confound historical insight with moral? A brief and puzzling passage in his *Autobiography* (A, 104–6), and four highly condensed chapters in *The New Leviathan* (Chs. 15–18) contain our only clues. In both, he espoused the idealist doctrine that a fully rational moral judgement must be concrete, not abstract: that is, it must lay down that a certain individual action, *individuum omnimodo determinatum*, ought to be done (A, 106; *NL*, 17. 51–17. 55). The morality of observing rules, which he disparaged as 'the low-grade morality of custom and precept' (A, 106), is abstract; for it does not prescribe that this or that individual act be done, but only some act or other of a certain kind (*NL*, 16. 61–16. 63). In *The New Leviathan* he declared that a moral agent is immediately conscious, in any concrete situation, that there is one and only one concrete action which it is his duty to do (*NL*, 17. 56–17. 58). Since no rule or set of rules can prescribe more than some action of a certain kind, you cannot find out from them what your duty is; and, if you try, you will find that so many rules must be taken into account that you cannot in practice use them (A, 105). It would seem to follow that the highest stage of ethical thinking must be intuitive, and that appears to have been Collingwood's conclusion in his *Autobiography*; for he described that stage as one of 'improvising, as best you can, a method of handling the situation in which you find yourself' (A, 105).

In *The New Leviathan* he retracted this suggestion. While continuing to maintain that a moral agent is immediately conscious that some individual act is what he ought to do, he now emphatically denied that it is possible to find out by intuition what that act is.

[1] Alan Bullock, *Hitler: A Study in Tyranny* (New York: Bantam Books, 1961), pp. 291, 396–9, 526.

'To answer that question', he declared, 'demands a process of logical thinking, over and above the intuitive or immediate process which answers the question: "Have I got any obligations, never mind what?" ' (*NL*, 17. 58). This twofold doctrine, that obligations are concrete, but that they can only be discovered by logical thinking, is self-contradictory in view of his own analysis of logical thinking as conceptual (*NL*, 11. 35). All concepts are abstractions (*NL*, 7. 22, 7. 62–7. 67). It is therefore plain that if a concrete obligation cannot be fully specified by abstractions (*NL*, 17. 53–17. 56), then it cannot be determined by logical thinking, because logical thinking is by its very nature abstract.

Although this contradiction first came to the surface in *The New Leviathan*, it was latent even in the *Autobiography*. There Collingwood had denounced, as subverting civilization itself, the doctrine that guidance in the problems of life is not to be sought from thinkers or from thinking, from ideals or principles, but from people who are not thinkers, and from processes that are not thinking (cf. *A*, 48; *EM*, 138). Now, on one side, ideals and principles are abstract, and thinking employs abstractions; and on the other, intuition is not abstract. Intuition, therefore, is not thinking; and a man who is guided solely by it is not a thinker. While the particular heresy Collingwood had in mind was the subordination of reason to passion, his anathema also falls on its subjection to intuition.

What has gone wrong? If the general tendency of Collingwood's later thought is sound, he was not mistaken in maintaining that thinking is conceptual, or that our duties must be ascertained by logical thinking. His error must therefore have been to think that in any concrete situation you are immediately aware that there is some concrete action which it is your duty to do. I cannot explain Collingwood's conviction that he was aware of such duties, except as a relic of philosophical idealism. He himself warned us that yesterday's controversial theses are apt to become today's self-evident axioms (*A*, 65).

No proposition whatever is infallibly known to be true, because every application of a concept to an object of consciousness may theoretically involve a mistake (*NL*, 11. 35). The concept of a concrete duty is abstract, like any other concept (*NL*, 17. 56). If our immediate consciousness does not corroborate Collingwood's conviction that in every situation where a concrete duty, then we are entitled to examine his writings for unacknowledged reasons for it. He expressly associated it with the presupposition that a truly moral action must be 'completely rational in principle', in the sense that its every concrete detail must be rational (*NL*, 17. 55). If that be so, then no action which is done merely in observance of a rule can be truly moral; for a rule does not specify down to the last concrete detail what is to be done, but only its general character (*NL*, 16. 63). What Collingwood did not notice was that no action whatever is rational down to the last concrete detail. However rational a certain bodily action may be, e.g. your having given a friend by word of mouth some accurate and useful information, it would not have been less rational if your wording had been slightly different, or you had spoken a little more loudly. Yet what words you used, and how loudly you spoke, are concrete details of what you did.

That no action is rational down to the last concrete detail was not the only point Collingwood overlooked. He also seems to have presupposed that a truly moral action is a response to a whole concrete situation. An example in his *Autobiography* shows this.

[E]verybody has certain rules according to which he acts in dealing with his tailor. . . . But so far as he acts according to these rules, he is dealing with his tailor only in his capacity as a tailor, not as John Robinson, aged sixty, with a weak heart and a consumptive daughter, a passion for gardening and an overdraft at the bank. The rules for dealing with tailors no doubt enable you to cope with the tailor in John Robinson, but they prevent you from getting to grips with whatever else there may be in him (*A*, 104–5).

Here, Collingwood implied that unless in your dealings with John Robinson you take account of whole concrete individuality, then you fall short of your full duty. Yet is it not plain that when John Robinson presents you with his bill, many of his features as a concrete individual, for example, his age and his passion for gardening, have nothing whatever to do with what your response ought to be? Collingwood's conception of duty in his *Autobiography* and in *The New Leviathan* is therefore mistaken in two respects. He wrongly believed that only one concrete act can fulfil all your obligations in a given concrete situation, and that the whole of your concrete situation has a bearing on what your obligations are. In fact, only some features of any situation are morally significant, and a variety of concrete acts will fulfil the obligations that arise from those features. In the example quoted from his *Autobiography* Collingwood made a further blunder, which is inexcusable even on his own principles. Supposing that you ought, in paying your bills, to take account of everything else there may be in John Robinson besides a tailor, it is quite false that the rules for fair-dealing with tailors prevent you from doing so. They prohibit you from nothing but cheating. It is just possible that Collingwood may have intended to insinuate that, in some circumstances, it might be your duty to cheat; but I find that hard to believe, in view of his caustic and sensible criticism in *The New Leviathan* of supposed conflicts between moral rules (*NL*, 16. 64–16. 75).

So far as it rests on direct consciousness, I question Collingwood's theory of duty because my moral consciousness does not corroborate his; and so far as it rests on the presupposition that an action done from duty must be rational in every concrete detail, I question it as flouting common sense. I have already intimated that it is also incompatible with his own philosophy of mind in *The New Leviathan*. In both his *Autobiography* and *The New Leviathan* Collingwood emphatically declared that moral questions cannot be answered except by logical thinking (*A*, 48; *NL*, 17. 58). Consequently, if his doctrine in *The New Leviathan* is true, that logical thinking is abstract (*NL*, 11. 35), the hope that moral questions may be answered by 'concrete' thinking or insight is chimerical. Moral insight is necessary for prompt decisions; but it is always subject to abstract rational scrutiny.

We are now in a position to answer the question, 'How was Collingwood led to confound historical insight with moral?' At bottom, it was because, under the influence of idealism, he failed to draw a logical conclusion from his own analysis of the nature of thought: namely, that reason cannot oblige you in any situation to do a given concrete act, *individuum omnimodo determinatum*, but only an act of a certain kind. He could not relinquish his idealist conviction that, in each situation in which you find yourself, there is one and only one concrete act which it is your duty to do.

This false ethical theory had unfortunate consequences in Collingwood's conception of theoretical reason, because of his obsession in later life with directly practical action. He became persuaded that a man's theoretical attitude towards things other than himself merely reflected his practical attitude to his own actions (*NL*, 18. 2). Theoretical science is 'a picture of the outer world, painted in colours that the painter has already learned to use for his self-portrait' (*NL*, 18. 51). Applying this rash and unsupported generalization to the history of science, he interpreted Greco-Medieval natural science, which was teleological, as reflecting 'a teleological or utilitarian view of human action', and the 'regularian' natural science, which arose in the seventeenth century, as reflecting 'a regularian or legalistic view of human life' (*NL*, 18. 33, 18. 45). He would allow neither utilitarian nor regularian morality, both of which are abstract, to be a suitable basis for history, the theoretical science of man. For that, only the morality of concrete duty would do: 'history is to duty what modern [natural] science is to right, and what Greco-Mediaeval science was to utility' (*NL*, 18. 51).

A remarkable corollary of this position is that historical and moral insight are one and the same. A man's consciousness of his concrete duty is his awareness of one and only one individual action which, in his unique situation, he ought to do; and an historian's consciousness of a past act is his awareness of that act as being, for the man who did it, the only and only one individual action which, in his unique situation, he ought to have done (cf. *NL*, 18. 52). In other words, an historian understands past acts as done from duty; and, if it be granted that a man is morally obliged to do what he thinks it his duty to do, to explain an act historically is the same as to justify it morally. Now this is plainly false. Collingwood tried to make it a little more palatable by maintaining that only dutiful actions are truly free, i.e. truly acts (cf. *NL*, 17. 8); but such a conception of free choice collapses from very eccentricity.

If that were not enough, the notion that all historical explanations are in terms of duty is incompatible with Collingwood's own analysis of historical explanation in his *Autobiography* and *Idea of History*.

According to that analysis, historians explain actions in terms of the thoughts which constitute their inner side; and all thought is conceptual, i.e. abstract. Historians therefore presuppose that the actions they explain do not have for their inner side a non-abstract concrete insight.

This morass of contradictions can only be avoided by discriminating historical from moral insight. To discriminate them, however, was not my main purpose. I hope to have shown that in his *Autobiography* and in *The New Leviathan* Collingwood fell into the error of identifying historical and moral insight because he tried to graft upon his fundamentally sound philosophy of history two false doctrines: namely, that duty is concrete, and that theoretical reasoning simply reflects practical reasoning. It is of the last importance that those false doctrines be recognized to be as incompatible with the principles of his philosophy of history, as they are with his general philosophy of mind. Fortunately, they contaminate but a small part of the *Autobiography* (pp. 104–6, 147–67) and *The New Leviathan* (pp. 104–29), and are wholly absent from *The Idea of History*, except for the fragments of *The Principles of History* which are incorporated in it.

PART III

METAPHYSICS

X

THE REFORM OF METAPHYSICS

§ 1. *Absolute Being as the Object of Thought of the Second Degree*

IN 1932 Collingwood denied that the theory of science and the theory of history are parts of science and history. ' [I]f scientists and historians study these things', he remarked, 'they study them not in their capacity as scientists or historians, but in their capacity as philosophers' (*EPM*, 1–2). Four years later, he transformed this remark into a definition of philosophy. 'Philosophy', he declared, 'may . . . be called thought of the second degree, thought about thought. For example, to discover the distance of the earth from the sun is a task for thought of the first degree, in this case for astronomy; to discover what it is exactly that we are doing when we discover the distance of the earth from the sun is a task for thought of the second degree, in this instance for logic or the theory of science' (*IH*, 1).

The phrase 'thought about thought' does not convey exactly what Collingwood meant by 'thought of the second degree'. History, after all, is about past thoughts, and in 1936 he did not identify philosophy with history. To distinguish thought of the second degree from history he had to add to his description of it. In *The Idea of History* he explained that although thought of the second degree is about thought, it is never concerned with thought by itself; it is always concerned with thought's relation to its object. It is therefore concerned with the object as much as with the thought (cf. *IH*, 2). By contrast, history can be conceived as being concerned with thought by itself. An historian of astronomy would thus investigate what conclusions past astronomers have arrived at, and how they arrived at them, but not whether those conclusions were true, or whether they were reached by sound methods. The same distinction can be drawn between the history and the philosophy of history itself. An historian of history would be said to investigate only what past historians have in fact thought; but a philosopher of history would be required to investigate both what past historians have thought and whether their thinking was well done (cf. *IH*, 3).

Since thought of the second degree is a criticism of the first degree, doubts intrude whether this distinction will serve to separate philosophy even from the natural sciences, much less from history. Collingwood himself recognized that the great natural scientists constantly reflected on their methods; and he even laid it down that, 'A man who has never reflected on the principles of his work has not achieved a grown-up man's attitude towards it; a scientist who has never philosophized about his science can never be more than a second-hand, imitative, journeyman scientist' (*IN*, 2). It would seem to follow that the philosophy of natural science, as thought of the second degree, is nothing but the reflective and critical phase of the various natural sciences. Nor is that all. When he wrote the lectures which form the bulk of *The Idea of History*, he certainly believed that historians must criticize the thoughts they investigate. After describing the 'task of discovering (for example) "what Plato thought" without inquiring "whether it is true"' as a 'self-contradictory' one (*IH*, 300), he protested that 'if I am to know Plato's philosophy', I must be able 'both to re-think it in my own mind and also to think other things in the light of which I can judge it' (*IH*, 301). On this conception of history, an historian of natural science must think critically about scientific thought in relation to its object, and an historian of history about historical thought in relation to its object. Historical thought would therefore be thought of the second degree, and philosophy, as thought of the second degree, would be indistinguishable from the critical phase of history.

Collingwood's position in the *Essay on Philosophical Method* allowed him to escape these conclusions. There, he maintained that critical inquiries into the various departments of thought of the first degree will converge, because no department of thought, taken by itself, is self-sufficient. Critical thought begins by determining the conditions on which each of the special sciences is valid, and goes on to set itself 'the task of thinking out the idea of an object that shall completely satisfy the demands of reason' (*EPM*, 125). This object, Collingwood believed, is the object of metaphysical thought, and therefore of philosophical thought in general; for he held that 'every philosophical science partakes of the nature of metaphysics, which is not a separate philosophical science but a special study of the existential aspect of that same subject-matter whose aspect as truth is studied by logic, and [whose] aspect as goodness by ethics' (*EPM*, 127). That subject-matter can be nothing but Being itself; for, as Spinoza pointed out, it is '*omne ens*' that is '*unum verum bonum*' (*EPM*, 33, 127).

There are various forms of mental activity, each of which is directed upon some form of being. Both the series of forms of mental activity and the series of forms of being are ordered in scales, in which the higher forms explain the lower, and the lower are appearances of the higher (*EPM*, 86–88). Philosophy, as the highest form of mental activity, will therefore explain the conditional necessity and value of each of the lower forms of it, which, in *Speculum Mentis*, he specified, in descending order, as history, natural science, religion, and art. The mind, so far as it is philosophical, is absolute; so far as it is merely historical, scientific, religious, or artistic, it is an appearance of mind (*SM*, 293–5). Collingwood regarded the forms of being as correlative with the forms of mental activity, or rather, he regarded both as aspects of the same scale of forms; for, as he remarked in *The Idea of History*, 'Philosophy cannot separate the study of knowing from the study of what is known' (*IH*, 3). Hence he concluded that the objects of art, religion, natural science, and history are only fully intelligible in terms of Being itself, the object of metaphysical thought; and that Being itself is the reality of which they are appearances (cf. *SM*, 310–14).

Since from this point of view, what absolutely *is* is the same as what the mind conceives completely to satisfy the demands of reason, Collingwood could not escape inferring that the Ontological Proof of St. Anselm is substantially valid (*EPM*, 124–5, 127). To diminish the scandal of this result, he tried to divest it of its religious and theological colouring by protesting that what St. Anselm had in fact proved to exist was not the God of Abraham, Isaac, and Jacob, but rather absolute being, the *ens realissimum* (*EPM*, 127). He had done so, Collingwood asserted, by combining the 'Platonic principle that when we really think . . . we must be thinking of a real object' with 'the neo-Platonic idea of a perfect being (something which we cannot help conceiving . . .)' (*EPM*, 124). However, neither the Platonic principle nor the neo-Platonic idea, taken in isolation from the other, would have sufficed. The former alone does not prove the existence of anything, because it may be doubted whether we ever really think; and the latter, taken by itself, is only an idea, which no more guarantees the existence of its object than the idea of a gorgon or a harpy does. The point of St. Anselm's proof as Collingwood interpreted it, was that when we conceive of the neo-Platonic idea, as we cannot help doing, we must really be thinking; and that therefore, by the Platonic principle, we must be thinking of a real object. At bottom, what St. Anselm discovered was that the Platonic principle is 'latent' within the neo-Platonic idea (*EPM*, 124).

At the present time most philosophers would probably dispute the 'Platonic principle' which forms the major premiss of Collingwood's reconstruction of the Ontological Proof; and, even granting a distinction between real thinking and what customarily passes for it, it does not seem to follow that 'when we really think . . . we must be thinking of a real object' (*EPM*, 124). Yet simply to controvert what another philosopher holds as a first principle is barren. Whether a principle is sound or not can usually be determined by following out its consequences. Let us therefore examine, not the premiss, but the conclusion of the Ontological Proof, namely, that the *ens realissimum* exists. What sort of proposition did Collingwood take it to be?

One thing is clear: it is a philosophical proposition; and Collingwood maintained that all philosophical propositions are both universal and necessary (*EPM*, 111–16). Disregarding compound propositions, the most familiar necessary truths are those in which, as in *Every effect has a cause* and *No plane figure is enclosed by fewer than three straight lines*, whatever may fall under one concept (e.g. whatever is an effect, whatever is a plane figure) is said either to fall under another (e.g. to have a cause) or not to fall under another (e.g. not to be enclosed by fewer than three straight lines). Many hold that all non-compound logically necessary propositions connect or divide concepts in this way. However, no such proposition asserts the existence of anything. *Every effect has a cause* is universal and necessary whether or not there are any effects. In other words, propositions which merely connect or divide concepts do not affirm that anything whatever falls under those concepts. Hence they can be thought of as hypothetical: as asserting that *if* anything falls under a certain concept, *then* it must fall under (or outside) a certain other one.

The conclusion of the Ontological Proof, however, is not in this sense hypothetical. Even if it connects the concept of the *ens realissimum* with some other concept, which is questionable, that is not all it does. Its main purpose is to affirm that something falls under the concept of the *ens realissimum*, and that is not hypothetical. In this respect, Collingwood maintained the conclusion of the Ontological Proof typical of all philosophical propositions. '[U]nlike mathematics or empirical science', he declared, 'philosophy stands committed to maintaining that its subject-matter is no mere hypothesis, but something actually existing' (*EPM*, 127). Its propositions are therefore not merely universal and necessary, but also categorical (*EPM*, 136).[1]

If a 'categorical' proposition be defined as one which commits those who affirm it to maintaining that its subject-matter is no mere hypothesis, but something actually existing, then Collingwood's view that philosophical propositions are both universal and categorical traverses the logic which has come to dominate the schools since Collingwood's death, that is, the logic of Whitehead's and Russell's *Principia Mathematica*. According to *Principia Mathematica*, the simplest propositions which are 'categorical' in the sense defined above are expressed by sentences in which a predicative expression is joined with a logically proper name. Since not all predicative expressions yield statements when joined with logically proper names, those which do may be distinguished, following Frege, as 'first-order predicates'.[2] The expression '. . . is a politician'

---

[1] See Note on Sources at the end of this Section, p. 261 below.

[2] P. T. Geach and Max Black (eds.), *The Philosophical Writings of Gottlob Frege* (Oxford, 1952), p. 50; P. T. Geach, *Mind*, lix (1950), p. 469.

is such a predicate; for when joined with such logically proper names as 'Gladstone' and 'Dickens' it yields statements, one true and one false. A logically proper name is an expression which, in its context of use, stands for a bearer. The expressions 'Gladstone' and 'Dickens', which I have mentioned in my last sentence but one, I presume all my readers will take to name the greatest of English Liberal statesmen and the author of *The Pickwick Papers*.

The propositions expressed by the sentences 'Gladstone is a politician', and 'Dickens is not a politician' are categorical, because 'Gladstone' and 'Dickens' are used as logically proper names. Although the expression 'logically proper name' is a term of art, the distinction between genuine and spurious logically proper names is perfectly familiar. Anyone who, having remarked that Gladstone, although a politician, was a man of sense, went on to say, 'But Harold Transome was a fool', would lay himself open to the question, 'And who was Harold Transome?' If he were to reply, 'Nobody at all, I used the first name that came to my head', he would convict himself of frivolous deceit. By using a word as though it were a logically proper name, he committed himself to maintaining that it has a bearer.

One of the uses of the word 'exist', when joined to a proper name, is now clear: it is to affirm that the proper name in question is a logically proper name, i.e. that it has a bearer. In this use of 'exist', the expression 'does not exist', when joined to a proper name, would result in a statement that the proper name lacks a bearer. Certainly, the sentence 'Harold Transome does not exist' cannot mean that the name 'Harold Transome' has a bearer, but a non-existent one!

Nor is this the only use of 'exist' when joined to a proper name. You may say, 'Gladstone no longer exists, but Churchill is yet with us'. Here 'exists' is equivalent to 'is alive': *vivere viventibus est esse*. 'Exist', in this use, can also be joined to the names of non-living things, e.g. 'Leonardo's cartoon, *The Battle of Anghiari*, no longer exists'. When used in this way, 'exist' is essentially temporal: its purpose is to affirm or deny that the bearer of a logically proper name is alive or extant at a given time. Since, whether or not it exists, the subject-matter of Collingwood's philosophical propositions presumably neither comes into being nor passes away, he did not have this temporal use of 'exist' in mind when he said that a categorical proposition commits those who affirm it to maintaining that its subject-matter is something actually existing. Accordingly, I have mentioned the temporal use of 'exists' only to distinguish it from its non-temporal uses, which are what matter. 'Exists' as it is used in 'Gladstone exists', when that is taken to mean, 'The name "Gladstone" is a logically proper name', is non-temporal. Even though the bearer of the name 'Gladstone' is dead, the name remains a name.[1]

None of Collingwood's universal categorical propositions, that is, none of his philosophical propositions, is expressed by a sentence containing a logically proper name. His own examples of meta-physical propositions, apart from 'The *ens realissimum* exists', were 'Matter exists' and 'Mind exists'. In the system of *Principia Mathematica* such statements are analysed in terms of statements composed of logically proper names and first-order predicates. Let us begin with a simple case: the statement 'Politicians exist'. According to *Principia Mathematica* it can be constructed out of the statement,

1. Gladstone is a politician,

in two steps. First, replace the logically proper name, 'Gladstone', by a variable, which can take any logically proper name as its value. In *Principia Mathematica* the letters 'x', 'y', 'z' are used as such variables. This step yields,

1_1. x is a politician,

a formula which is not a statement at all. However, it may be transformed into a statement by 'quantifying over' the variable. This gives us:

1_2. For some value of 'x', 'x is a politician' is true,

which is customarily abbreviated to,

1_{2a}. $(\exists x)$ x is a politician.

The proposition expressed by (1_2) and (1_{2a}) is true, because when

<hr>

[1] I owe my analysis of the uses of 'exist' to P. T. Geach, 'Form and Existence', in *Proc. Aris. Soc.* lv (1954–5); Geach acknowledges a debt to Wittgenstein, *Philosophical Investigations*, i, §§ 40–41.

the logically proper name, 'Gladstone', is substituted for 'x', the formula 'x is a politician' becomes the true statement, 'Gladstone is a politician'. Moreover, the proposition expressed by (1_2) and (1_{2a}) is the same as that expressed by 'Politicians exist'; for what can that mean except that at least one man, Gladstone or another, is a politician?

Can Collingwood's metaphysical propositions be analysed in this way? Do the statements 'The *ens realissimum* exists' and 'Matter exists' mean 'For some value of "x", "x is the *ens realissimum*" is true', and 'For some value of "x", "x is material" is true'? There is an enormous obstacle to such analyses. As we have seen, Collingwood held that his propositions were universal and necessary; but the equivalents which *Principia Mathematica* offers for them are particular and contingent.

The complex expression, 'For some "x", "x . . ." is true', and its abbreviation '$(\exists x) \, x \ldots$', are certainly not logically proper names; for they stand for no bearer. Neither are they first-order predicates; for, when combined with logically proper names, they do not yield statements. However, 'For some "x", "x . . ." is true' and '$(\exists x) \, x \ldots$' do yield statements when combined with first-order predicates. I shall therefore follow Frege and Geach in calling them 'second-order predicates'.[1] Now it seems impossible that any statement formed by joining the second-order predicate '$(\exists x) \, x \ldots$' to a first-order predicate should be necessarily true. It could only be necessarily true if there were a connexion between the senses of the two predicates, i.e. if one were contained in the other. Unfortunately, the sense of the purely formal '$(\exists x) \, x \ldots$' cannot possibly contain the sense of any first-order predicate; nor can it be contained in the sense of any first-order predicate, because even if some concepts contain propositions, they do not contain propositions about themselves. The statement '$(\exists x) \, x$ is the *ens realissimum*' says that the concept of the *ens realissimum* applies to something; but that it applies to something cannot be said to be part of the content of the concept without a vicious infinite regress.

In order to uphold his doctrine that, as well as being categorical,

---

[1] Geach and Black (eds.), *The Philosophical Writings of Gottlob Frege*, p. 50; Geach, *Mind*, lix (1950), p. 472.

metaphysical statements like 'The *ens realissimum* exists' are universal
and necessary, Collingwood had no choice but to propose an alternative to the analysis of categorical propositions in *Principia Mathematica*. Unhappily, having failed to appreciate Russell's revolutionary theory of quantification, which Frege had anticipated, he
was ill-equiped to improve on it. I suspect that his counter-theory
dissatisfied him; for neither in the *Essay on Philosophical Method*, nor
in his letters to Ryle about Ryle's Russellian criticisms of it,[1] did
he offer more than hints of what it was.

The *Essay on Philosophical Method* yields four major clues for reconstructing Collingwood's alternative to Russell. The first is
his statement that philosophy has a subject-matter, the existential aspect of which is studied by metaphysics (*EPM*, 127);
and the second is his endorsement of the traditional view that
Being itself is that subject-matter (*EPM*, 123–5). A third clue
is that he does not seem to distinguish between the subject-
matter of philosophy and the true subject of philosophical propositions (cf. *EPM*, 125–7). I therefore conclude that he held the
true subject of the metaphysical statement 'The *ens realissimum*
exists' to be 'Being itself', and that he conceived the statement
as a whole to be equivalent to 'Being itself is the *ens realissimum*'.
This statement he regarded as universal, because 'Being itself'
is equivalent to 'being as such', and so to Spinoza's '*omne ens*'. In
the same way, 'Mind exists' and 'Matter exists' may be rendered
as the universal statements 'Being itself is mental' and 'Being itself
is material'. A fourth clue is his description of a philosophical proposition true in virtue of the nature of its subject, i.e. of what is
'necessary in [its] concept' (*EPM*, 116). From this it follows that if
any of his specimen metaphysical statements, as I have analysed
them, are true, it will be because their predicates '. . . is the *ens
realissimum*', '. . . is mental', '. . . is material' are necessary in the concept of Being itself.

The objections which would be advanced by defenders of *Principia Mathematica* are readily imagined. If 'Being itself' is the subject
of necessary truths, then the innumerable beings which are the
subject-matter of contingent propositions, and which bear the

[1] See Note on Sources, p. 261 below.

logically proper names of ordinary discourse, must fall outside
Being itself. Are they then nonentities? Or is Being itself but one
being among others? Presumably Collingwood would reply by invoking his doctrine of the scale of forms. The various contingent beings,
from shoes and ships to sealing-wax, which can bear ordinary
logically proper names, all fall under one or other of the lower forms
on the scale which constitutes the concept of Being. Those lower
forms, however, cannot without qualification be either identified
with or distinguished from the highest form, the concept of 'an
object that shall completely satisfy the demands of reason' (*EPM*,
125). The highest form is the concept of that reality, and the lower
are concepts of its appearances (*EPM*, 87–90). Hence my left shoe,
say, is neither a nonentity nor a further being alongside Being itself.
In one sense, it does not really exist, because it falls short of Being
itself; but in another sense, it not only exists but must exist, because
Being itself necessarily appears exactly as it does.

If this was indeed what Collingwood would have replied to a
Russellian, then he would merely have echoed F. H. Bradley.

Universal judgements [Bradley had declared] are relative or absolute. If relative, they are the same as particular judgements. If
absolute, they are either hypothetical or categorical. In the first the
ostensible subject is an abstraction: in the second it must be the
ultimate reality. Particular categorical judgements may all be reduced
to abstract or hypothetical universals, and these again to categorical
universals. In the end all truth, if really true, is true of the ultimate
non-phenomenal fact. (*Principles of Logic*, Oxford, 1928, vol. i, p. 193.)

But a Russellian's strongest objection is yet to come. What of
the very highest form on the scale which constitutes the concept of
Being? Let it be granted that the lower forms are appearances of the
higher, i.e. that they are concepts of what less completely satisfies
the demands of reason; it still remains to ask, 'Does anything fall
under the highest form?' Is it true that, for some value of '*x*', '*x* is
Being itself' is true? Is Bradley's ultimate non-phenomenal fact a
fact? And, if it is a fact, how on earth can it be a necessary fact?

Collingwood did not ask himself these questions. Presumably he
did not think them to arise at all. Is there not something absurd
about the question, 'Does Being itself exist?' Of course, if there is

something absurd about that question, he ought to have assured himself that his own analysis of the concept of being did not permit it to arise. Yet he took no such precaution. In his correspondence with Ryle in the spring and summer of 1935 he betrayed no doubts whether his theory of the categorical universal proposition was sound; and Knox has reported that, as late as 1936, 'he still believed in the possibility of metaphysics as a separate study . . . of "the One, the True, and the Good"' (*IH*, x–xi).

Note on the Sources of Chapter X, §1

Although my interpretation of Collingwood's brief reference to 'the categorical universal [judgement] of philosophy' (*EPM*, 136) is adequately supported by the text of the *Essay on Philosophical Method*, I should not have hit upon it without help. After Professor Ryle, in 'Mr. Collingwood and the Ontological Argument', had confessed his inability to 'make head or tail' of what Collingwood had meant (*Mind*, xliv (1935), p. 141), Collingwood wrote him a long letter in which he elucidated the passage in question, along with others. Professor Ryle has kindly permitted me to transcribe the following portions of Collingwood's letter, which is dated '9 May, 1935'. References are to the pages of Collingwood's holograph. The headings and the two passages in (iii) which I have placed in square brackets are my interpolations.

(i) *The nature of metaphysical propositions*. 'I believe that such propositions as "God exists", "mind exists", "matter exists", and their contradictories, do not assert or deny particular matters of fact; nor do I believe that they assert or deny anything which can be adequately described as collections or classes of matters of fact. To assert or deny propositions of this kind, with reasons given for the assertion or denial, seems to me the business of constructive or destructive metaphysics; and what, I suppose, I am objecting to . . . is a question-begging assumption that Hume was right when he divided all possible subjects of discourse into (*a*) ideas & the relations between them and (*b*) matters of fact . . .' (p. 4).

(ii) *Categorical universal propositions*. (*a*) '. . . [Y]ou seem to hold (and wrongly to ascribe to me) the view that *no* universal judgment . . . can be categorical, so that when you find me now saying that the philosophical judgment is categorical you assume me to be contradicting my statement on p. 111 that it is universal' (p. 5). (*b*) 'Your theory is that *only a singular proposition can be categorical*. . . . Therefore you foist upon me the doctrine that "every philosophical proposition is or contains or rests on a genuine singular proposition." . . . You find yourself unable to "make head or tail" of my notion that there are categorical universal judgments in philosophy, as well as categorical singular judgments in history, because, once more ascribing to me a doctrine which I do not hold & have in fact been at pains to repudiate, you assume that, when I said that the universal judgments *of exact & empirical science* are merely hypothetical, I meant that *all* universal judgments are merely hypothetical' (p. 7).

(iii) *Categorical universal propositions and traditional universal propositions.* 'I will admit for the sake of argument that there are any-propositions [i.e. propositions of the same form as "Any horse is a quadruped"] and every-propositions [i.e. propositions about every single member of an enumerated class]; but I contend that there are also all-propositions, or (as some logicians have called them) "true universals" having a categorical character, i.e. they are *not* enumeratives, and yet they are not indifferent to the existence of the things to which they apply, but are of such a kind that their truth depends on that existence. I regard such propositions as especially characteristic of philosophy. . . . At the same time, I am committed to the view that the subject-matter of philosophy is not a mere assemblage of matters of fact' (pp. 25–26).

§ 2. *The Reformation: Metaphysics as an Historical Science*

Those who had studied the *Essay on Philosophical Method* when it appeared, and had been acquainted with Collingwood's stubborn unpublished defences of it, must have been astonished and bewildered when they were first confronted with the opinions about the nature of metaphysics he espoused in his *Autobiography*. In neither of the philosophical works which he wrote in 1937, *The Principles of Art* and a paper on 'The So-Called Idea of Causation', had he betrayed any dissatisfaction with what he had maintained from 1932 to 1936. Yet in the *Autobiography*, which he wrote in 1938, he implicitly abandoned his conception of metaphysical propositions as categorical and universal, and substituted for it the doctrine that they are historical, i.e. categorical and singular (*A*, 66; cf. *EPM*, 136).

Worse still, he claimed to have reached this view during the First World War, and to have embodied it in a manuscript, *Truth and Contradiction*, which was rejected by a publisher in 1917, and which he destroyed after writing the *Autobiography* itself (*A*, 74; cf. 42–43, 99 *n*.).[1] 'It became clear to me', he wrote, 'that metaphysics . . .

---

[1] 'I did not really feel any great desire to expound the philosophical ideas I have been setting forth in these chapters [i.e in *A*, Chs. 5–7], whether to my colleagues or to the public. As I have said, I tried to expound them; but when *Truth and*

is primarily at any given time an attempt to discover what the people of that time believe about the world's general nature; such beliefs being the presuppositions of all their "physics", that is, their inquiries into its detail. Secondarily, it is the attempt to discover the corresponding presuppositions of other peoples and other times, and to follow the historical process by which one set of presuppositions has turned into another' (*A*, 65–66). Metaphysics, then, is not an attempt to establish categorical universal propositions about Being itself, but categorical particular propositions about what this or that people at this or that time have believed. As such, it is 'purely historical' (*A*, 66). Kant had asked, 'How can metaphysics become a science?' Collingwood's answer, which in the *Essay on Metaphysics* he audaciously claimed to be 'the reform of metaphysics, long looked for and urgently needed', was: 'By becoming more completely and more consciously what in fact it has always been, an historical science' (*EM*, 77).

Since not even in the *Essay on Metaphysics* did Collingwood acknowledge that he had abandoned the position he had taken up in the *Essay on Philosophical Method*, he disabled himself from justifying his change of opinion. He did indeed admit that metaphysics has long been considered to be the science of being as such: in Aristotle's phrase, of τὸ ὄν ᾗ ὄν (*EM*, 9). But, in expounding this traditional conception of metaphysics, Collingwood broke utterly with his exposition of it in the *Essay on Philosophical Method*. Instead of representing Being itself as the highest form on a scale of forms of being, but *not* as the genus of the lower forms, he refused to consider any possibility but that the concept of Being itself, of 'pure being', is 'the limiting case of the abstractive process', namely, the concept of what is left when all that differentiates one thing from another is abstracted from it (*EM*, 14). If such a conception were the only alternative to his reformed metaphysics, there would be some reason to accept the reformation. But since in his *Essay on Philosophical Method* Collingwood himself had set forth a

Contradiction was rejected by a publisher and my attack on "realist" principles ignored by my colleagues, I felt justified in turning to the far more congenial task of applying them and thus testing them empirically' (*A*, 74). Here Collingwood plainly implied that in *Truth and Contradiction* he had expounded the theory of metaphysics of *A*, Chs. 5–7.

third possibility, readers of the *Essay on Metaphysics* may be excused for finding its argument less than conclusive.

Some readers have even doubted the truth of Collingwood's statement that he had anticipated his position in the *Autobiography* in a manuscript written during the First World War. Unfortunately, by destroying the manuscript, he made direct verification impossible. However, Knox has testified that 'the philosophy which "emerged" after 1936 was not an entirely new growth but had its roots in its author's past' (*IH*, xi). This is confirmed by a passage from *Ruskin's Philosophy*, an address which Collingwood delivered to the Ruskin Centenary Conference at Coniston in August 1919. In it, after asserting that in each of us there exists a 'central core of convictions' which is 'the nucleus and basis' of our several lives, and that 'in that sense every one of us has a philosophy', he went on to say this.

[F]or the most part we do not know that we possess [a philosophy]: still less do we know what are the convictions which constitute it. The fact seems to be that a man's deepest convictions are precisely those which he never puts into words. . . . It may seem strange that our deepest . . . convictions should habitually go unexpressed. But this is still stranger, that we are often quite mistaken as to what these convictions are. If you ask a man to state his fundamental beliefs, and then carefully watch his actions and sayings, you will generally find that these are based on a set of beliefs quite different from the ones which he has stated. . . . Now it is the attempt to discover what people's philosophy is that marks the philosopher. Much as everybody has a brain, but only the anatomist sets himself to discover what it looks like and how it works, so everybody has a philosophy, but only the philosopher makes it his business to probe into the mind and lay bare that recess in which the ultimate beliefs lie hidden. (pp. 7–8.)

The fact that Collingwood had developed this conception of philosophy as a young man does not explain why he reverted to it in his maturity. To find such an explanation we must inquire into the merits of his proposed reform, if any.

Both in the early *Ruskin's Philosophy* and in the *Essay on Metaphysics*, as we have seen, Collingwood maintained that philosophy had always been historical, i.e. an attempt to discover the ultimate presuppositions or convictions by which men have lived. Yet in the *Essay on Metaphysics* he continued to recognize St. Anselm's Ontological Proof as a major philosophical achievement (*EM*, 189–90). He was, therefore, obliged to interpret that proof as a specimen of reformed metaphysics, and incidentally to overthrow his interpretation of it in the *Essay on Philosophical Method* as a specimen of ontology. To do so is plainly difficult. After all, St. Anselm solemnly undertook to prove that whoever says in his heart, 'There is no God' is a fool; and he professed to have done so by a purely analytical argument, namely, by revealing a hidden contradiction in the statement 'The being *quo maius cogitari nequit* does not exist'. Prima facie, to describe such a proof as historical would be perverse.

Collingwood's strategy was nevertheless ingenious. What St. Anselm proved, he argued, was 'not that because our idea of God is an idea of *id quo maius cogitari nequit* therefore God exists, but that because our idea of God is an idea of *id quo maius cogitari nequit* we stand committed to belief in God's existence' (*EM*, 190). But although it is clever, this is nonsense. It would be no less absurd to contend that when Euclid argued that, provided our idea of a triangle accords with his axioms and definitions, the interior angles of a triangle must equal two right angles, what he really proved was that, provided our idea of a triangle accords with his axioms and definitions, we stand committed to believe that the interior angles of a triangle equal two right angles. The fact that our idea of a triangle accords with Euclid's axioms and definitions could not commit us to any belief whatever about triangles, did not the truth of that belief logically follow from those axioms and definitions. In the same way, St. Anselm's proof could not show that we stand committed to belief in God's existence, did not the truth of that belief logically follow from the definition of God as *id quo maius cogitari nequit*.

When he turned from the proof itself to St. Anselm's rejoinder to Gaunilo's objections, Collingwood fared better. Gaunilo had complained that St. Anselm had only proved the existence of God to those who believed it already, and St. Anselm replied that he had intended no more. From this Collingwood concluded that whatever may have been in St. Anselm's mind when he invented his proof, 'on reflection he regarded the fool who "hath said in his heart, There is no God" as a fool not because he was blind to the actual existence of *un nommé Dieu*, but because he did not know that the presupposition "God exists" was a presupposition he himself made' (*EM*, 189). In other words, even if St. Anselm had imagined, when he invented his proof, that it demonstrated the existence of God by combining the neo-Platonic idea of a perfect Being with the Platonic principle that when we really think we must be thinking of something (cf. *EPM*, 124); by the time he replied to Gaunilo, he had come to acknowledge himself merely an anatomist of the recesses of the mind where ultimate beliefs lie hidden.

To this, however, there is a conclusive objection. When St. Anselm conceded Gaunilo's objection that his proof convinces only those who already believe its ostensible conclusion, was he speaking of those who consciously believe it, or of those who are unwittingly committed to believing it? Collingwood could only interpret him as speaking of the latter; for he held that the point of the Ontological Proof is that you cannot conceive of God as *id quo maius cogitari nequit*, and deny that He exists, unless you are a fool, that is, unless you have failed to discern that that conclusion follows from your conception. Here Collingwood overlooked the crucial distinction between conceiving and presupposing. Because St. Anselm's proof cannot convince those who do not share the conception of a being *quo maius cogitari nequit*, he inferred that it cannot convince those who do not share St. Anselm's presuppositions. But to form a concept is not to presuppose anything. Provided that the concept of a being *quo maius cogitari nequit* conceals no contradiction, and provided that his reasoning was sound, St. Anselm's proof that God exists must convince all who can understand it, no matter what they may presuppose.

Even though his position that metaphysics 'has always been' an historical science (cf. *EM*, 77) has proved untenable, it still remained open to Collingwood to defend his proposed reform. Metaphysics may not have been an historical science, but perhaps it ought to have been transformed into one. Collingwood's arguments for reform, however, were disappointing. In the *Autobiography* he offered nothing but sceptical commonplaces (*A*, 65–67; see below, § 4); and in the *Essay on Metaphysics* he invoked a theorem from his Theory of Presuppositions which I have already exploded (see above, Ch. IV, § 2), namely, that absolute presuppositions are neither true nor false. If indeed absolute presuppositions were neither true nor false, and if the ultimate beliefs on which each man's intellectual life depends were absolute presuppositions, then Collingwood would have been in a strong position to argue that any inquiry into such ultimate beliefs except an historical one would be pointless. The questions asked of an ultimate belief by traditional metaphysics are 'Is it true?' 'What evidence is there for it?' 'How can it be demonstrated?' 'What right have we to believe it if it can't?' But, since all these questions presuppose that ultimate beliefs are propositions rather than absolute presuppositions, on Collingwood's premises they must be dismissed as nonsensical (*EM*, 33, 47). Any answers to these nonsense questions which traditional metaphysics may provide must also be dismissed as nonsense. They are 'neither metaphysical truths nor metaphysical errors', but 'pseudo-metaphysics' (*EM*, 47–48). However, no argument can be stronger than its premises; and one of the premises of this argument, as we have seen, is false.

I have now shown that Collingwood failed to justify his proposed reform of metaphysics, but I have not shown that it was unjustifiable. On his own showing, however, it was paradoxical. In *The Idea of History* he had described the 'task of discovering (for example) "what Plato thought" without inquiring "whether it is true"' as 'self-contradictory', and had gone on to declare that, 'What is required, if I am to know Plato's philosophy, is both to re-think it in my own mind and also to think other things in the light of which I can judge it' (*IH*, 300–1). Yet the task of his historical science of absolute presuppositions is nothing other than to discover what the people of a given time think about the world's general nature, and to do so without inquiring whether what they think is true (*A*, 65–66). Hence, in his *Autobiography*, he set reformed metaphysicians a task which in *The Idea of History* he had pronounced self-contradictory.

It is true that in the *Autobiography* he retracted the position he had taken up in *The Idea of History*, arguing that, since historians can only ascertain a man's past thoughts by reconstructing the problems he was trying to solve from traces of his attempts to solve them, they cannot find out what anybody who has failed to solve a problem has thought about it. By failing to solve it, he is 'bound' to have mixed up his tracks so completely that neither his problem nor his would-be solution can be recovered. Therefore, since Villeneuve at Trafalgar failed to carry out his tactical plan, nobody will ever know what it was (*A*, 69–70). It also follows that there are not two questions, 'What did Plato think?' and 'Is it true?' If you can reconstruct Plato's thought, then Plato must have solved his problem, i.e. his thought must have been true (*A*, 72).

This line of thought removes one difficulty by creating another. If past thoughts can only be ascertained by reconstructing the problems which they solved, then how can absolute presuppositions, which are not answers to questions, be recovered at all? Conversely, if absolute presuppositions can be recovered, it must be possible to ascertain past thoughts which are not successful solutions of problems.

Moreover, not even in the *Autobiography* did Collingwood consistently maintain that only thoughts which succeeded in solving problems could be discovered. When he came to recount his historical work on Roman Britain, he claimed to have discovered what Caesar's purpose had been in invading Britain, even though Caesar 'had failed to achieve it' (*A*, 131). Again, as Knox has pointed out, Collingwood was prepared to say that in analysing the form of the *polis*, Plato 'seems to have thought' that it was 'the one and only ideal of human society possible to intelligent men', whereas in fact it was only 'the ideal of human society as that ideal was conceived by the Greeks of Plato's own time' (*A*, 62–63; *IH*, xii). No historian could long maintain that history can make sense of success and victory, but not of defeat and disappointment.

§ 3. *Presupposing and Consciousness*

Collingwood's project for an historical science of absolute presuppositions was paradoxical in yet other ways. As he described them, the methods of his projected science would not have been historical; and, more astonishingly still, its subject-matter, the making and changing of absolute presuppositions, would have fallen outside the subject-matter of history.

Since a presupposition is defined as what you are committed to accept by asking a question (see above, Ch. IV, § 1), presupposing something must be distinguished from asserting or deliberately assuming it, just as logically implying something must be distinguished from actually drawing a conclusion. You may mistake or be unaware of what your questions commit you to accept, just as you may mistake or be unaware of what your statements imply. It follows that an inquiry into what a given person has presupposed about a given topic must first establish what questions about it he has asked or considered legitimate; and secondly, by purely logical analysis, it must elicit what those questions commit him to accept. The first part of such an inquiry, while unquestionably historical, would be comparatively easy; for most of the questions with which an historian of absolute presuppositions would occupy himself would be explicitly asked by natural scientists in their writings. Collingwood therefore neglected the historical part of his projected science for the logical. '[A]s regards procedure and the qualifications necessary to carry it out', he declared, 'there is no difference whatever between metaphysical analysis and analysis pure and simple as I have been hitherto describing it' (*EM*, 40); and thitherto he had been describing it as logical (*EM*, 38–39; cf. 22).

For the most part Collingwood's *specimina philosophandi* in the *Essay on Metaphysics* bear out his description of metaphysical method as logical. Sometimes, indeed, they do not: as when he argued that eighteenth-century natural scientists presupposed what Kant had said they did, on the ground, not that their questions logically committed them to doing so, but that they and their successors accepted what Kant had said. Yet, even in that case, he took pains to intimate that his reasoning was 'not necessarily conclusive' (*EM*, 332–3). Except for his instructions on how to interview a reluctant natural scientist about his absolute presuppositions (*EM*, 43–45), which it is hard to take seriously, he seems always to have taken it for granted that only the analytic method was conclusive.

Of that method, the most arresting specimen Collingwood gave was his criticism of Aristotle as a metaphysician. After showing that Aristotle's absolute presuppositions as a natural scientist, by his own account of them, diverged on two fundamental points from those of modern science, Collingwood maintained that the discrepancy arose, not because modern natural science has diverged from Aristotelian, but because Aristotle was mistaken about his presuppositions as a natural scientist: he was 'not so much failing to anticipate the absolute presuppositions of a future age as failing correctly to define his own' (*EM*, 214). It was by analysis, not by historical reasoning, that Collingwood demonstrated Aristotle's failure correctly to define the presuppositions of his own, i.e. of Greek, natural science. Not only did he not try to show that Aristotle had consciously accepted the presuppositions he had failed correctly to define, he took it for granted that Aristotle had not even formulated them. Having established that, on the points in question, Aristotle asked exactly the same questions as modern scientists now ask, he was content to demonstrate by analysis that all who ask those questions, Aristotle among them, are committed to accepting what modern metaphysicians say that modern natural scientists presuppose (*EM*, 215, 218).

Not only is the method of reformed metaphysics analytical rather than historical, if history is the history of thought, as Collingwood believed, then absolute presuppositions do not belong to the subject-matter of history. Since presupposing something is being committed to accept it by the questions you ask, it is no more an act of consciousness, and therefore no more an act of thought, than logically implying something. You may mistake, or simply overlook, what the questions you ask commit you to accept. Collingwood did not fail to perceive this.

[I]n our less scientific moments [he remarked] . . . we are not even aware that whatever we state to ourselves or others is stated in answer to a question, still less that every such question rests on presuppositions, and least of all that among these presuppositions some are absolute presuppositions. In this kind of thinking, absolute presuppositions are certainly at work; but they are doing their work in darkness, the light of consciousness never falling on them. (*EM*, 43.)

Unfortunately, this crucial passage is negligently expressed. If one of your absolute presuppositions does its work in darkness, that is not because you are ignorant of the supposed general truth that every question rests on presuppositions some of which are absolute, but because you do not know that this or that question you ask presupposes it.

Although Collingwood clearly saw that the light of consciousness need not fall on a presupposition, he did not see that that is because presupposing is not an act of thought. Instead, he came to the conclusion that presuppositions on which the light of consciousness does not fall are the objects of 'repressed' or unconscious acts of thought. According to his philosophy of mind, since every act of consciousness has an object which it brings to consciousness, it is impossible to perform an 'unconscious' act of consciousness, in which you do not become conscious of anything. However, it is perfectly possible, having become aware of something disturbing, so promptly and completely to withdraw attention from it that by no ordinary higher order act of reflection can you become aware that you ever were conscious of it. It was in this way that Collingwood interpreted the 'unconscious' or repressed fears and desires with which Freud credited his patients (NL, 5. 86–5. 89).

In *The Principles of Art* he had shown that acts of consciousness do not cease to exist when they are repressed.

> The feeling from which attention is distracted [he wrote] . . . does not lapse from attention altogether. Consciousness does not ignore it; it disowns it. Very soon we learn to bolster up this self-deceit by attributing the disowned experience to other people. Coming down to breakfast out of temper, but refusing to allow that the ill humour so evident in the atmosphere is our own, we are distressed to find the whole family suffering agonies of crossness. (*PA*, 218.)

Collingwood could therefore allow that 'unconscious' or repressed desires and thoughts might be genuine forces, and even that they might metaphorically be described as in equilibrium or not. Having mistaken presupposing for an act of thought, his theory of repression invited him, first to treat most acts of presupposing as unconscious thoughts, and then to interpret changes in what is presupposed along the lines of Freudian morbid psychology (*EM*, 48 *n*.).

Unconscious acts of presupposing, like other unconscious acts, may be assumed normally to be in equilibrium. A natural scientist's absolute presuppositions will therefore normally form a 'constellation', that is, a set of 'consupponible' presuppositions (*EM*, 66). Presuppositions are said to be 'consupponible' when it is logically possible to presuppose them together. In Collingwood's opinion, no constellation of absolute presuppositions strong enough to give rise to an advanced natural science can be wholly stable, any more than a legal or constitutional system can be (*EM*, 77). Every such constellation arises out of the questions which are sanctioned in a given phase of natural science; but good natural scientists are sometimes inclined to ask questions the presuppositions of which contradict those of orthodox questions. In a measure, 'strains' of this sort can be 'taken up' by the existing system: by slightly modifying either the new or the old questions, or perhaps both, their conflicting presuppositions can be mutilated into consupponibility. However, strains become very severe when orthodox questions are suspected of being unfruitful and a hindrance to devising others more fruitful; and when those strains become too great, 'the structure collapses and is replaced by another, which will be a modification of the old with the destructive strain removed' (*EM*, 48 *n.*).

In accordance with his mistake that presupposing is an act of consciousness, Collingwood ascribed changes in what is presupposed in natural science to changes in the equilibrium of unconscious forces in the minds of natural scientists. Both their orthodox and their unorthodox questions he took to arise from repressed acts of presupposing, which, like other repressed thoughts, retain their power even though they are disowned. Scientific revolutions, most of which consist in modifications of the questions it is considered legitimate to ask, come about when the repressed thoughts which give rise to unorthodox questions become too powerful to be taken up by the old system. Collingwood therefore declared that such revolutions are 'not consciously devised but created by a process of unconscious thought' (*EM*, 48 *n.*).

In announcing this conclusion, Collingwood unwittingly declared bankrupt his project for an historical science of absolute presuppositions. Scientific history treats only of utterances and deeds which express thoughts, and it explains why a man said or did this rather than that by ascertaining his reasons for having done so. To explain what somebody has said or done as proceeding from unconscious forces would deprive it of the status of an expression of thought. 'The mind, regarded in this way, ceases to be a mind at all' (*A*, 93). As Knox was quick to point out, such explanations belong not to history, but to psychology (*IH*, xiv).

Is it then impossible to find historical explanations of why the presuppositions of natural science have changed from generation to generation? By no means. However, in order to explain how it is possible, the error from which Collingwood's psychological interpretation sprang must be exposed and corrected. As I have already pointed out, that error was to mistake presupposing for an act of thought, whereas it is no more than a logical correlate of the act of asking certain questions, just as implying is no more than a logical correlate of making certain statements. Having mistaken presupposing for an act of thought, it is natural to go on to mistake presupposing something without knowing what you presuppose for a repressed and disowned act of thought; and thence to infer, as Collingwood did, that such repressed acts stir rebelliously in the unconscious mind. In fact, as our analysis of presupposing has shown, nothing happens when you presuppose something you know not what, except that you ask a question without noticing what it commits you to accept. This unromantic result dissolves the cobwebs of Collingwood's theory of unconscious presuppositions. A presupposition of which you are unaware no more lurks, unseen but powerful, in the recesses of your unconscious mind than does a conclusion you have failed to draw.

An historical explanation of why certain absolute presuppositions of natural science changed from Aristotle's time to Galileo's, and from Galileo's to Einstein's, must begin with the acts of thought of which those presuppositions are logical correlates: that is, with the questions asked by Aristotle, Galileo, Einstein, and their fellows. Since asking a question is an act expressing a thought, it can be investigated by the ordinary methods of scientific history.

It may be objected that I have intolerably simplified what happens in science. Most natural scientists, like most other men, swim with intellectual currents they have not set in motion. Confronted with a new phenomenon, either they ask about it the questions they have been accustomed to ask about familiar phenomena which they take to be analogous with it, or, lacking a familiar analogue, they abandon hope and turn to another problem. If you inquire of them why they ask of familiar phenomena the questions they do, they will either 'blow up right in your face' (*EM*, 31), or they will tell you that those questions and only those have been found fruitful, they know not how or by whom. If an historian of science were to confine his attention to such 'average' scientists, he would no doubt find the changes from generation to generation in the questions they ask altogether inexplicable; and he might even be tempted to take refuge in Collingwood's mythology of unconscious 'strains' in order to explain them.

Those who bring about scientific revolutions, however, are not 'average' scientists. They are men who insist on asking questions the presuppositions of which conflict with those of the questions they have been taught to ask. Nobody who is capable of seriously asking a question will change any important question he asks unless he has some reason for doing so; and his reasons will bear either directly on the questions themselves, or indirectly on what he believes to be their presuppositions. No presupposition which is changed for a reason can be absolute; for whoever changed it must have asked and rationally answered a question of the form, 'Which of the incompatible presuppositions, p_1 or p_2 or ... p_n, shall I accept?' and presuppositions which are answers to questions are relative.

The major changes in the absolute presuppositions of European natural science were made by men to whom they were not absolute presuppositions at all. When Bacon and Galileo argued that natural scientists ought to ask 'regularian' rather than teleological questions, they no longer absolutely presupposed nature to be teleological, but neither did they absolutely presuppose it to be regularian. Which of the two it is, regularian or teleological, was to them a question, a question to which they sought a rational answer. Their arguments for the regularian view were so convincing that many of their successors came to hold it as an absolute presupposition, and some of them to imagine their absolute presupposition to be self-evident (*A*, 65).

Bacon and Galileo themselves were under no such delusion: they knew that the regularian view had to be established by argument, and between them they gave two powerful arguments for it. Both of them showed that teleological explanations were largely barren, and that regularian ones were more fruitful, both in predictions and in practical applications. Then Galileo showed that regularian explanations could actually be found; and he did so in the most impressive way imaginable: that of finding some. Bacon expressed the first of these arguments in his gibe that the teleological method '*tanquam virgo Deo consecrata, nihil parit*'; and Collingwood himself acknowledged that Bacon's contempt for the barrenness of teleology was 'typical' of the whole scientific movement in the seventeenth century (*IN*, 93).

Historical investigations of changes in thought about the foundations of natural science, as such works as Butterfield's *Origins of Modern Science* show, differ in no way from those of changes in other fields of thought. The major movements in the history of civilization have come about, not because of eruptions in the unstable depths which lie beneath the unconscious minds of scientists and men of action, but because a few great men have succeeded in identifying and questioning the absolute presuppositions of their predecessors, so converting them into relative ones. Scientific revolutions, like those in morals and politics, can be studied by scientific history, because they are made not in darkness, but in light.

§ 4. Coincidentia Oppositorum: *Scepticism and Dogmatism*

In his early *Speculum Mentis* Collingwood had contended that any characterization of reality or being by one of the opposites it contains is bound to commit 'suicide' by generating its own opposite, because in the end such opposites coincide (*SM*, 197–8, 310). Although in the *Essay on Philosophical Method* he did without the phrase *coincidentia oppositorum*, he resorted to the doctrine it expresses when he argued that any thoroughly sceptical philosophy must be covertly dogmatic because it can neither justify nor doubt the grounds upon which it rests (*EPM*, 147–8). By pointing out that the would-be science of absolute presuppositions abolishes itself by a *coincidentia oppositorum*, in which the liabilities of its scepticism are counterbalanced by heavy drafts of dogmatism, Knox showed that the argument of the *Essay on Philosophical Method* refutes the project of the *Essay on Metaphysics* (*IH*, x–xix).

The sceptical side of Collingwood's reformed metaphysics derives from his theorem that absolute presuppositions are neither true nor false. Although in his *Autobiography* he had scoffed at 'philosophers' convictions about the eternity of problems or conceptions' as being 'as baseless as a young girl's conviction that this year's hats are the only ones that could ever have been worn by a sane woman' (*A*, 65), he was offended when a correspondent imputed to him the opinion that changes in absolute presuppositions are merely changes in fashion (*EM*, 48 *n*.). Yet his grounds for denying the charge were weak. He found nothing better to plead than that a change in his absolute presuppositions is 'the most radical change a man can undergo', which a change in his style of hat is not; and that, whereas fashions would not change if individuals did not deliberately choose new styles of dress, changes in absolute presuppositions are made unconsciously (*EM*, 48 *n*.).

Such a defence hardly deserves a reply. If a change is merely a change of fashion, it is neither because it is about something trivial, nor because it results from conscious choices; rather, it is because it is a change for change's sake which is sanctioned by a group. From Collingwood's theorem that absolute presuppositions are neither true nor false it follows inexorably that no good reason can be given for preferring one to another; and, if that is so, then changes in absolute presuppositions must be made either for bad reasons or for change's sake. Any change in absolute presuppositions which is sanctioned by a group and which is not made for bad reasons must therefore be a change of fashion.

Neither in his *Autobiography* nor in the *Essay on Metaphysics* did Collingwood discern a further sceptical consequence of his theorem that absolute presuppositions are neither true nor false, namely, that answers to questions that arise from them are also neither true nor false. However, in his unpublished *Principles of History*, he not only saw it, but embraced it. Having laid it down that 'natural science . . . starts from certain presuppositions and thinks out their consequences', he inferred that, 'since these presuppositions are neither true nor false, thinking these together with their consequences is neither knowledge nor error' (*IH*, xii–xiii). Hence, by his own subsequent admission, his position in the *Autobiography* and *Essay on Metaphysics* was self-contradictory. Having denied either the truth or the falsity of absolute presuppositions, he could not consistently affirm it of answers to questions that arise from them (cf. *EM*, 23–25).

The same contradiction appears in his specimens of reformed metaphysics. When he compared a possible 'pan-magical' constellation of absolute presuppositions with that of modern European science, he urged his fellow modern Europeans to recognize 'the arbitrary character' of their classifications (*EM*, 195). Although he conceded that a primitive conception of the world like the pan-magical one could be shaken, he acknowledged only two ways of shaking it, neither of which was rational: one was 'through the influence of a very powerful tribesman who found himself taking a different view'; the other was 'by the prestige of some other community, accepted and revered in the first instance as extremely powerful magicians, and later found to reject and despise it' (*EM*, 194.) Such a 'very powerful tribesman' could have had no reason for the 'different view' he 'found himself' taking; nor could the community as a whole have justified their veneration for the other community, once it had been found to despise and reject the pan-magical view.

Yet, instead of denying that the absolute presuppositions of modern science are an advance upon a pan-magical conception of nature, as this position obliged him to do, Collingwood decried 'the feeling of hostility to science as such', and warned his readers that it 'may be "rationalized" through an obscurantist philosophy which by sophistical arguments pretends to prove that the advances which are actually being made are in fact no advances' (*EM*, 342). Far from pretending or intending to prove any such thing, he professed a deep attachment for European science and civilization (*EM*, 140–1, 197–8, 341–3), and reprobated all whom he took to be its enemies. They were, he declared, 'traitors to their academic

calling' (*EM*, 342). Some of them, the realists, were 'reactionary
thinkers, wedded to the errors of the past, enemies of modern
science, and obstructors of all progress whether in metaphysics or
in science, natural or historical'; others, the psychologists, were
'irrationalist agents', who availed themselves 'of the privileges
accorded to science by a rationalist civilization in order to undermine the entire fabric of that civilization' (*EM*, 341, 136–7). If he
forbore to denounce these evildoers as conspirators plotting 'to
destroy civilization', his reason was that they were less depraved
than diseased. In his view, they were afflicted with 'a kind of epi-
demic withering of belief in the importance of truth and in the
obligation to think and act in a systematic and methodical way'
(*EM*, 134–5).

In these fervent deprecations Collingwood did not fall into the
rhythm and diction of the pulpit inadvertently. Having renounced
the backing of reason for the absolute presuppositions of modern
science, he could only champion them as a man of faith. 'The only
attitude towards them that can enable us to enjoy what they have
to give us', he declared, '. . . is an attitude of unquestioning acceptance. We must accept them and hold firmly to them; we must insist
on presupposing them in all our thinking without asking why they
should be thus accepted' (*EM*, 173).

The guardianship of the absolute presuppositions of modern
science, as opposed to their discovery, must on this view be vested
not in philosophy but in religion. Religion, in fact, is nothing but
clinging to a constellation of presuppositions by a sheer act of faith,
'whether or not we know what they are, whether or not we work
out their consequences'; and the function of religious institutions is
to consolidate those absolute presuppositions in believers, and to
perpetuate them in their posterity (*EM*, 197). As Knox has observed,
this doctrine 'has affinities with Kierkegaard and even Karl Barth'
(*IH*, xvii).

Such a coincidence of scepticism and dogmatism is disastrous.
After denying the truth or falsity of absolute presuppositions,
Collingwood could only persevere in his adherence to modern European science by resorting to dogmatism. By a cruel trick of history,
he had condemned that way out of his difficulties before he became

aware that he would be obliged to take it himself. In the first Part of the *Essay on Metaphysics*, having distinguished what Newtonian, Kantian, and Einsteinian physics each absolutely presupposed about causation, he had remarked that an unreformed metaphysician would try to find out which is true, in order to know which of these three schools of physicists was on the right lines (*EM*, 51). And although in the third Part of that same *Essay* he was to go on to announce his own 'unquestioning acceptance' of the Einsteinian school (cf. *EM*, 173, 333), in the first Part he had contemptuously dismissed as 'an irresponsible and dogmatic person' any philosopher who would 'pronounce loudly and confidently in favour of one alternative' (*EM*, 51).

§ 5. *Loss and Gain*

The time has come to strike a balance between what Collingwood lost by his reform of metaphysics and what, if anything, he gained. We have found that his proposals for reform were inconsistent, and his arguments for them feeble and confused. He projected an historical science of absolute presuppositions. But not only was the method he prescribed for it not historical but analytical, on his own principles, since absolute presuppositions are not acts of thought, they are not proper objects of historical inquiry. Furthermore, as though he had foreseen the latter of these objections, he explained that absolute presuppositions only fail to satisfy his specifications of acts of thought because ordinarily they are unconscious. By this manœuvre he transformed his projected historical science into a sort of depth psychology. To crown these tergiversations, on perceiving his doctrine that absolute presuppositions are neither true nor false to collide with his passionate devotion to European science and civilization, he tried to reconcile his dogmatism with his scepticism by protesting that, although he accepted without question whatever absolute presuppositions his unconscious mind might visit upon him, he was not so credulous as to think any of them true (*EM*, 173–4).

Collingwood's projected reformation was therefore too riddled with confusions and contradictions to stay afloat; and no considerable part of its wreckage can be salvaged. If it be judged solely by reference to what it affirms, then our reckoning must show a heavy loss with no compensating gain. However, not all contributions to philosophy are affirmative. Philosophers as great as Locke and Bradley have hoped less to attain to philosophical knowledge than to clear away the rubbish that obstructs the road to it (*A*, 16). If the unreformed metaphysics of the *Essay on Philosophical Method* had bequeathed Collingwood any liabilities, then their discharge must be entered as an asset. The negative side of the reformed doctrine that metaphysics is an historical science of absolute presuppositions is that metaphysics is not what it is said to be in the *Essay on Philosophical Method*, namely, the science of Being itself. If that view is rubbish lying in the road to knowledge, then the proposed reformation was a gain as well as a loss.

As we have seen, Collingwood at different times advanced two distinct conceptions of the putative science of Being itself: one of them he defended in the *Essay on Philosophical Method*, the other he assailed in the *Essay on Metaphysics*. The latter conception was indeed indefensible. It rested on four presuppositions, namely:

1. That all science is of the universal and abstract.
2. That there is potentially at least a science of every universal.
3. That there are degrees of universality or abstractness, and that these give rise to a hierarchy of universals and a corresponding hierarchy of sciences.
4. That a generic universal is not only the indispensable presupposition of the specific universals subordinate to it, but their sufficient logical ground. (See *EM*, 12,)

If these presuppositions are legitimate, then the science of Being itself must be the First Science; for according to (3) the abstract universal *being* would be the highest universal in the hierarchy, and according to (4) the science of Being would be the logical basis of the sciences of the special forms of being. Collingwood's objection to such a science was conclusive.

The universal of pure being [he pointed out] represents the limiting case of the abstractive process. Now even if all science is abstractive, it does not follow that science will still be possible when abstraction has been pushed home to the limiting case. Abstraction means taking out. But science investigates not what is taken out but what is left in. To push abstraction to the limiting case is to take out everything; and when everything is taken out there is nothing for science to investigate. (*EM*, 14.)

Why did Collingwood take seriously a conception so ridiculous? One reason was that he attributed it to Aristotle (*EM*, 9–13, 17). Why he did so I cannot explain; for it was Aristotle who first demonstrated that Being is not a genus at all, and so, *a fortiori*, not the *summum genus*. All the differentiae of any genus must have being. But, Aristotle held, it is impossible for a genus, taken apart from its species, to be predicated of its own differentiae. If the differentiae *rational* and *brute* divide the genus *animal*, then it is impossible that *animal*, when taken apart from the species *rational animal* or *brute animal*, should be predicated either of *rational* or of *brute*. If being is a genus, Aristotle therefore argued, it follows both that its differentiae must have being, and that being must not be predicated of them. Now since that is self-contradictory, the hypothesis that being is a genus must be false (*Metaphysics* B, 998b, 21–27).

In the *Essay on Philosophical Method* Collingwood himself had shown that Being itself, the object of metaphysical thought, could not be abstract Being, although his argument was less perspicuous than Aristotle's beautiful proof. It ran as follows:

These three predicates, unity, reality, and goodness, are assigned by traditional metaphysics to every *ens* or being. But if all concepts were arranged in a table of classification, each divided at each stage into mutually exclusive species, the highest term in the table would be the most abstract of all possible abstractions: simple, abstract being. If being has necessary determinations such as according to this doctrine unity, reality, and goodness are held to be, it follows that these determinations are somehow exempt from the rules of classification. Just as Aristotle showed that the concept of good overlaps or transcends or diffuses itself across the divisions of the categories, so, according to [the] traditional formula, there is a similar overlap or transcendence or diffusion in the concepts of unity and reality. (*EPM*, 33.)

The implication is that Being itself cannot be abstracted from the various forms of being as their *summum genus*, because its 'necessary determinations', unity, reality, and goodness, can be abstracted neither from the various forms of being, nor from one another, nor from Being itself. Being itself, therefore, cannot be 'simple, abstract being'.

Why then, in the *Essay on Metaphysics*, did Collingwood not even mention the possibility of a non-abstract concept of Being? I have already urged (Ch. I, § 3) that we ought not to ascribe his silence to illness or negligence unless we despair of finding any reason for it; and a reason is ready to hand. From *The Principles of Art* to *The New Leviathan* he steadily maintained that all thinking is conceptual and that all concepts are abstract (see above, Ch. III, §§ 1–2). He therefore excluded even the possibility of a non-abstract concept of Being. If there were to be a science of Being itself, distinct from the various sciences of things that are, it could only be of abstract being.

If our sole object were to explain why the conception of metaphysics Collingwood had championed in the *Essay on Philosophical Method* disappeared from his writings after *The Principles of Art*, there would be no need to prolong this analysis. But were Collingwood's second thoughts better than his first? Was his earlier conception of metaphysics in truth untenable?

According to the *Essay on Philosophical Method*, as we have seen, metaphysical propositions are both categorical and universal, and their subject-matter is Being itself, *omne ens*. The character of metaphysical propositions like *God exists* and *Mind exists* is therefore better displayed by the wording, 'Being itself is divine', and 'Being itself is mental'. It is not difficult to see that such propositions might be taken to be universal. To Collingwood in 1933, the concept of Being itself was the supreme philosophical concept (*EPM*, 124–7). The propositions that God exists and that mind exists would indeed be universal if they should assert that the properties of being divine and of being mental belong to Being itself as 'necessary in [its] concept' (cf. *EPM*, 116). It would not, however, follow from those propositions that all beings (*omnia entia*) are divine and mental; for the concept of being in virtue of which we speak of many beings is a lower form. The many beings of ordinary discourse are but appearances of Being itself; and the concepts by which we think of them are ordered on a scale, to the highest form of which they vainly strive to be adequate (*EPM*, 86–89).

In order to establish that his metaphysical propositions are categorical as well as universal, Collingwood had to show that although their subject-term is a universally quantified concept, they are nevertheless categorical, that is, about something existing (*EPM*, 127). It would not be enough that the concepts of deity or of mind should be implicit in that of Being itself; for although mathematics abounds in propositions which rest on the fact that one concept is implicit in another, 'it is not necessary to believe', in mathematics, 'that the subject of discourse has any actual existence' (*EPM*, 117).

The difficulty is that in this respect Collingwood's metaphysical necessary truths appear to resemble those of mathematics. Although they differ from ordinary generic and specific concepts in resolving into scales of forms, and in that the classes of things which fall under them overlap, Collingwood's philosophical concepts are universal; and a universal concept is simply one which is, truly or falsely, applicable to or predicable of more than one thing, a 'one in many'. Its counterpart in discourse is what Frege called a 'first-order predicate'. Even first-order predicates like '. . . is omnipotent', which can be truly predicated of at most one thing, can be significantly predicated of many. A Satanist might dispute with a Christian which is omnipotent, Satan or the God of Abraham; but he could not do so unless they both understood the statements, 'Satan is omnipotent' and 'The God of Abraham is omnipotent' equally well. Now if '. . . is Being itself' is a first-order predicate, then the proposition that Being itself exists may be analysed, following *Principia Mathematica*, as 'Something is Being itself', or, more technically, as '$(\exists x)x$ is Being itself'. But, as we have seen (§ 1), the sense of the second-order predicates '. . . exists', 'something is . . .', and '$(\exists x)x$ . . .', cannot possibly be implicit in the sense of any first-order predicate, not even in that of 'Being itself'.

This result is calamitous for the conception of metaphysics in the *Essay on Philosophical Method*. It shows that it is not necessary to believe, of any statement whose subject can function as a first-order predicate, that what it is about has any real existence. Moreover, it is impossible to escape by denying that 'Being itself' can function as a first-order predicate. If it makes sense to suppose that such first-order concepts as that of deity and that of mind are 'necessary in' the concept of Being itself, then that concept must itself be of the first order. Collingwood was caught in a dilemma: a metaphysical proposition could not be universal unless its subject was a first-order concept; but propositions whose subjects are first-order concepts are not necessarily about anything that really exists.

The theory of concepts which Collingwood developed in *The Principles of Art* and *The New Leviathan* holds good only of first-order concepts. It enabled him to perceive that the conception of metaphysics in the *Essay on Philosophical Method* is incoherent, because it treats the concept of Being itself as both belonging and not belonging to the first order; but it could carry him no further. In none of his later works did Collingwood venture to analyse any of the concepts signified by the various forms and derivatives of the words 'be' and 'exist'. Nor does he seem to have recognized how delicate such analyses must be. The fundamental work of Russell and Whitehead on 'exist' used as a second-order predicate, and Wittgenstein's brilliant analyses of 'object', 'property', 'function', 'number' and the like as signifying what he called 'formal concepts', made no impression on him. Hence he could throw little light on the great traditional questions about the nature of existence, and about realistic as opposed to nominalistic theories of universals. Once he divined that those questions could not be answered as Bradley had answered them, by invoking the concept of a non-abstract universal, he turned away from them altogether.

Instead of hoping that one day philosophy would find true answers to the traditional questions of ontology, Collingwood came to suspect that it was those very questions that had led him and his predecessors astray. On this point Frege, Russell, and Wittgenstein would no doubt have agreed with him. But whereas they reformulated the traditional questions, by means of an improved logic, as fundamental questions about meaning, Collingwood denied their philosophical character, and interpreted them as being historical, so far as they made sense at all. Such a doctrine, brought forth hastily and in illness, inevitably was radically mistaken. Yet Collingwood was not mistaken in abandoning the conception of metaphysics he had defended in the *Essay on Philosophical Method*. A new beginning had to be made.

QUAESTIONES DISPUTATAE

§ 1. Collingwood's Refutation of Realism

COLLINGWOOD did not live to make the new beginning in metaphysics which his philosophy of mind demanded. Nor did he in *The New Leviathan* formally retract his conception of metaphysics as an historical science. Yet *The New Leviathan* contains a daring and important attempt to solve the traditional metaphysical problem of the relation between mind and body; and neither the problem nor the solution proposed is historical. Furthermore, even in the first flush of reformation, when it seemed that the obstacles to converting philosophy into history would be easily overcome, he resurrected an attack on the realist theory of knowledge which he had read to his Oxford colleagues soon after the First World War, and placed it prominently in his *Autobiography* (*A*, 44–45). Again, neither the theory attacked nor his attack on it was historical.

Besides grappling with these traditional philosophical problems, Collingwood turned again and again in his later writings to the question whether philosophy can justify, or even endure, the claims of religion; and for the most part he did not treat it as historical. Our examination of his later metaphysical views may fittingly be brought to an end by investigating his answers to these genuinely philosophical and non-historical disputed questions.

His attempt to refute the realist theory of knowledge is the most curious and least happy of these *specimina philosophandi*. Realism appears to have haunted him as King Charles's head haunted the unfortunate Mr. Dick. In *Speculum Mentis*, where he summed up the realist theory of knowledge 'in the negative formula that knowledge can make no difference to its object' (*SM*, 283), he attacked it on the ground that it rests on an abstraction, and that to abstract is to falsify. 'The fact is', he wrote, 'that modern realism is

essentially inconsistent. It is . . . a confused running to and fro between two principles, the abstract concept and the concrete fact. It
springs from the scientific realism which asserts reality in the form
of the abstract concept and, by implication, reduces the opposite of
the concept, namely immediacy or sensation, to the level of mere
appearance' (*SM*, 285). By the time he wrote *The Principles of Art*
he could no longer make this criticism; for he himself had come to
agree with the realists that abstract concepts and concrete objects
were distinct 'principles', and that nevertheless the abstract propositions of natural science were true.

Although in the *Essay on Philosophical Method* he avoided the subject of realism, he returned to it in *The Idea of Nature*, where he
satirically recorded that 'strict members of the realist faction'
regarded Whitehead as a 'wobbler' because if you had put to him
'the realist's shibboleth', the question, 'Would a rose be red if there
was nobody looking at it?' he would have answered, very mildly,
'No; the whole situation would be different' (*IN*, 167; *A*, 45). While
Oxford realism was a theory of knowledge rather than of perception,
Collingwood plainly would have approved an answer like Whitehead's to the question, 'Would a rose which you know to be red be
red if you did not know it?' Yet it is not clear whether he approved
of Whitehead's reason, namely, that since reality is an organism,
the same order of nature which contains the rose also contains
human beings with their minds; so that the colour of the rose is
located, not in the rose, but in the society of which it is an organic
part (*IN*, 166–7).

In the early refutation which he revived in his *Autobiography* he
followed a different line of thought. His own summary of it was as
follows:

I argued that anyone who claimed, as Cook Wilson did, to be sure
[that knowing makes no difference to what is known], was in effect
claiming to know what he was simultaneously defining as unknown.
For if you know that no difference is made to a thing θ by the presence
or absence of a certain condition c, you know what θ is like with c,
and also what θ is like without c, and on comparing the two find no
difference. This involves knowing what θ is like without c; in the
present case, knowing what you defined as the unknown. (*A*, 44.)

Collingwood did not hesitate to brand realism as 'the undischarged bankrupt of modern philosophy' on the basis of this argument (*A*, 45). In form, it is a *reductio ad absurdum*. From the realists' claim to know that no difference is made to θ by knowing it, it purports to derive the self-contradictory conclusion that θ is both known and unknown to them. Its cardinal step is that if they know what θ is like in the absence of the condition of being known, then it follows that they both know θ and do not know it.

If you know what θ is like in the absence of a certain condition, it certainly follows that you know θ; but does it follow, from the fact that you know what θ is like when it is not known, that θ is unknown to you? I do not think it does. If it did, then by parity of reasoning it would follow that if you know what you are like when you are not at leisure, then you are not at leisure. It would be awkward indeed if you lost all knowledge of your own working habits as soon as you left your study!

Collingwood fell into this blunder because he assimilated knowing to seeing. This is shown by his assertion that 'if you know that no difference is made to a thing θ by the presence or absence of a certain condition c, you know what θ is like with c, and also what θ is like without c, and *on comparing the two* find no difference' (*A*, 44; my italics). He evidently supposed that the only ground on which you could legitimately assert that the presence or absence of c makes no difference to θ would be that you had compared θ in the presence of c with θ in the absence of c, and had found no difference. Comparing two states of a thing and finding no difference is certainly analogous with looking at them both and seeing no difference; and it would be odd to claim that you have seen a thing as it is when it is not seen.

Yet it was outrageous to foist upon Cook Wilson and his followers the notion that you can compare the state of a thing you have come to know with its state before you knew it. The classical statement of Cook Wilsonian realism is the chapter on Knowledge and Reality in H. A. Prichard's *Kant's Theory of Knowledge* (Oxford, 1909); and the reasons Prichard there gave for the proposition that 'what is known exists independently of being known' (op. cit., p. 118) were not empirical. He did not claim to have compared the state of any object as known with its state as unknown. Instead, he reasoned analytically from the concept of knowledge. 'Knowledge', he protested, 'unconditionally presupposes that the reality known exists independently of the knowledge of it, and that we know it as it exists in this independence. It is simply *impossible* to think that any reality depends upon our knowledge of it, or upon any knowledge of it. If there is to be knowledge, there must first *be* something to be known. In other words, knowledge is essentially discovery, or the finding of what already is' (ibid.).

While Collingwood might with some justice have complained of Prichard's dogmatic and hectoring tone, he could not possibly have objected that Prichard implicitly claimed to know what he had simultaneously defined as unknown (cf. *A*, 44). We do have a concept of knowledge, which a philosopher is in duty bound to analyse. At first sight, to know a thing is to know it as it is in itself; and if knowing it affected its nature, it could not be known at all.

Analysis confirms this impression. Collingwood's position, that when you know θ, its nature is affected by being known, reduces to an absurdity. If it were true, then one or another of two equally repugnant conclusions would follow. When you know θ, it may be that you know it, not as it is in itself, but as it is having been affected by your knowing it. Alternatively, it may be that you did know it as it was in itself, but that, having been affected by your knowing it, it is no longer what it was. In neither case can anything whatever be known. By the former alternative, the mind distorts what it tries to know, and so cannot know it; by the latter, at the very moment the mind contrives to know something, it changes it into something else, so that nothing remains which it knows. Hence, if knowing affects or 'makes a difference to' the nature of what is known, the very concept of knowing something is self-contradictory. But that is absurd.

The realist doctrine which Collingwood assailed is therefore, as Prichard took it to be, unconditionally presupposed by the very concept of knowledge. 'It is simply impossible to think that any reality depends upon our knowledge of it, or upon any knowledge of it.' Why Collingwood should have rescued from oblivion his abortive youthful attack on this doctrine is puzzling. In assuming that knowing is analogous with seeing, he flatly contradicted the analysis of thinking which he had advanced in *The Principles of Art*, and which he was, in the main, to confirm in *The New Leviathan* (see above, Ch. IV, § 6). He may have feared that unless he could disprove the realists' epistemology, he would be obliged to accept their ethical doctrine that because moral philosophy is only the theory of moral action, it cannot make any difference to its practice (*A*, 48). If that was his fear, it was groundless. The two doctrines have no connexion whatever. Supposing it to be a fact that killing an enemy in war is morally permissible, realist epistemology holds that it remains a fact whether it is known or not; but it does not follow from this that a man's actions in war will be the same whether he knows that fact or not.

§ 2. *Mind and Nature*

Collingwood's attempt in *The New Leviathan* to solve what is perhaps the fundamental disputed question of modern philosophy, the nature of the relation between mind and body, is much more important than his last fling against realism. He traced the problem itself to Descartes's supposition that natural science is distinct from the sciences of mind because it studies one substance, *res extensa*, whereas the sciences of mind study another, *res cogitans*. At once the question arose: By what science is man to be studied? Since a man's body is an extended thing, it presumably falls within the domain of natural science, as animal bodies do; and since his feelings and thoughts are not extended, they presumably fall within the domain of the sciences of mind. But a man is not a body *and* a mind. Some of his bodily movements are said to express thought, and some of his feelings and thoughts are caused by his bodily states. To which Cartesian science do they belong?

Descartes tried to reconcile his theory with what we ordinarily say and think by asserting that in man *res extensa* and *res cogitans* interact, the organ of their interaction being the pineal gland (*IN*, 6–7, 103–4). However, that does not answer the scientific question. No interaction of *res extensa* with *res cogitans* is intelligible either to natural science or to the sciences of mind. Nor does it help to add together the findings of both. The one treats of *res extensa* in terms of extension, the other of *res cogitans* in terms of thought; but if an interaction between an extended thing and a thinking thing is neither a physical movement nor a thought, neither is it a physical movement *and* a thought. To a strict Cartesian it must fall outside the domain of science altogether, as a miracle produced directly by God (*IN*, 7).

Stung by gibes like Collingwood's, that you will find no takers if you challenge Psycho-Physical Interactionists to put forward an account of interaction which any physicist will accept, as regards the physical end, for anything except nonsense (*NL*, 2. 37), Descartes's successors became more and more reluctant to invoke interaction to explain everyday occurrences like voluntary bodily movements or feelings of bodily pain. Yet within the Cartesian tradition the only alternative to Interactionism is what is called 'Parallelism': the doctrine that although every mental event is caused by other mental events, and every physical event by other physical events, the sequence of mental events in a given man's mind is so in 'harmony' with the sequence of physical events in his body that his body and mind appear to interact. But what explains this harmony? Until they answer that question in scientific terms, Parallelists cannot escape the reproach that they have done no more than substitute a new miracle, pre-established harmony, for the old one, interaction (*IN*, 110–11).

Both these theories Collingwood derided as 'old wives' tales', that is, as stories 'that can only survive by ignorance of [their] subject-matter' (*NL*, 2. 15; cf. 2. 25, 2. 35). Descartes and his followers were reduced to accepting one or another of them, he believed, because although they saw through the unsophisticated old wives' tale of traditional folk-lore, that 'a man's mind [inhabits] his body somewhat as he inhabits a house' (*NL*, 2. 1–2. 11), they did not see to the bottom of it. They saw that a man's mind is more intimately connected with his body than an inhabitant with his house (*NL*, 2. 21), but not 'that nothing can inhabit a house made of matter except something else made of matter' (*NL*, 2. 13). Hence their ignorance of what they were talking about was of that fundamental kind which proceeds from what Ryle has called a 'category mistake'; for anybody who imagines that a mind can 'inhabit' or 'interact with' a body misunderstands what can be significantly said about minds. He is mistaken about what the concept of mind is.

The category-mistake from which Collingwood believed these old wives' tales to derive is that mind and matter are two distinct substances. As Spinoza had seen, there is one world, which may be investigated in various ways. Natural science is one such way. The material world, or 'nature', is simply the world inasmuch as it is knowable by natural science. Nature, so understood, is divided into different realms. There are phenomena which can be successfully investigated by physics, and others which at present can be successfully investigated only by physiology. Whether it will ultimately turn out that these realms overlap, and that physiology, like chemistry, will be reduced to a province of physics, Collingwood did not inquire in *The New Leviathan*, although he implied that it cannot be decided *a priori*. It could be so decided only if animate and inanimate matter were definable *a priori*, which they are not. It would be an 'egregious blunder' to define physics in terms of inanimate matter, or physiology in terms of life; for that would imply not only 'that people know what matter is without studying physics . . ., and what life is without studying physiology', but also 'that this non-scientific . . . knowledge . . . can never be corrected by anything science can do' (*NL*, 1. 5–1. 52).

A second way of investigating the world is 'by expanding and clarifying the data of reflection' (*NL*, 2. 45): that is, by examining both your own acts of consciousness, and the expanded range of data furnished by historical inquiry (*NL*, 9. 22–9. 23). Inasmuch as the world is knowable by this method, which Collingwood, following Locke, called 'the historical plain method' (*NL*, 9. 1; cf. *IH*, 220), it consists of minds; and, just as you must not define physics in terms of matter, so you must not define history in terms of mind. Mind is what history finds it to be, by investigating what actual minds have in fact done (*NL*, 9. 16–9. 18).

The problem of the relation between body and mind as it arose in post-Cartesian philosophy is therefore bogus; for there is no direct relation between them. Those who pose the problem presuppose that man is partly body and partly mind, but man is not divisible into such parts (*NL*, 2. 4–2. 42). His body and mind are not two different things. 'They are one and the same thing, man himself, as known in two different ways' (*NL*, 2. 43).

Although there is no direct relation between body and mind, there is an indirect one. Body is man as knowable by natural science, mind is man as knowable by history, and natural science and history are related. Hence body and mind are indirectly related through the sciences by reference to which their respective natures are defined. An inquiry into the relation between the natural sciences and the historical sciences ought therefore to be substituted for 'the make-believe inquiry into the make-believe problem of "the relation between body and mind"' (*NL*, 2. 49).

Ryle, who in *The Concept of Mind* approached the mind-body problem in much the same way, described Collingwood's pioneer work very justly in his Inaugural Lecture. After remarking that the problem of man's place in nature is 'roughly the problem of co-ordinating the questions which govern laboratory researches with the questions governing the researches prosecuted in libraries', he went on to say this:

> Professor Collingwood saw more clearly, I think, than did his most eminent predecessors in the philosophy of history that the appearance of a feud or antithesis between Nature and Spirit, that is to say, between the objectives of the natural sciences and those of the human studies, is an illusion. These branches of inquiry are not giving rival answers to the same questions about the same world; nor are they giving separate answers to the same questions about rival worlds; they are giving their own answers to different questions about the same world. (*Philosophical Arguments*, Oxford, 1945, p. 4.)

Two relations between the natural sciences and the human studies, i.e. the historical sciences, call for investigation: one is the relation between their methods, and the other is the relation between the objects which can be fruitfully studied by the methods of either or both. Collingwood's views on the former topic can be inferred from his inquiries into natural science in *The Idea of Nature* and the *Essay on Metaphysics*, and into scientific history in his *Autobiography* and *The Idea of History*.

The result of those inquiries was that any bodily movement may be studied by the methods of natural science, and that a sub-class of them, those which can be interpreted as expressions of thought, may be studied by the methods of history. In the former case they are conceived as purely physical changes, which can be explained by showing how they arose from other physical changes according to laws of nature. Neuro-physiology and strict behaviourist psychology conceive changes in the human body in this way, although unfortunately some behaviourists are not strict, and introduce into their work concepts which are covertly historical. By contrast, the historical sciences interpret such bodily changes as they investigate as acts of consciousness, or, in other words, as expressions of thought (*NL*, 1. 61–1. 66).

Logically, according to Collingwood, there is no conflict between history and natural science, between the concept of man as mind and the concept of man as body. Both history and neuro-physiology can investigate the bodily movement which Brutus made when he stabbed Caesar: neuro-physiology as a purely physical movement, history as an act of thought. The stabbing of Caesar was both mental and physical, and a full explanation of it must take both its aspects into account. In *The New Leviathan* Collingwood was explicit: 'the whole of man is body in so far as he approaches the problem of self-knowledge by the methods of natural science . . . [and] the whole of man is mind in so far as he approaches the problem of self-knowledge by expanding and clarifying the data of reflection', i.e. by the methods of scientific history (*NL*, 2. 44–2. 45).

The question remains, however, whether there is anything in any physical movement which cannot be explained by natural science. Obviously, Brutus could not have stabbed Caesar unless his arm had been functioning normally, a matter of physiology. But could it have been predicted, even in principle, that given the physiological conditions which obtained at the moment before the assassination, Brutus's arm would have made the movement which resulted in Caesar being stabbed? Prima facie, Collingwood's answer appears to be 'yes'. 'Nothing could be sillier' was his verdict on the hope that progress in natural science will stop, as cherished by those who fancy that unless something in man 'proves recalcitrant to explanation by the natural sciences . . . the inference will be that man is all body and therefore has no mind' (*NL*, 2. 47–2. 48).

Yet Collingwood did not leave the matter there. By adding that, 'In the natural sciences, mind is not that which is left over when explaining has broken down; it is what does the explaining' (*NL*, 2. 48), he gave ground for doubt whether he really was persuaded that there is no limit in the physical world to what natural science may find a way to explain. His rejection of the assumption that man is partly body and partly mind (*NL*, 2. 41–2. 42) committed him to hold that human mental acts involve physical processes: mind is not a ghostly inhabitant of a bodily house (*NL*, 2. 1–2. 13). When you explain something, therefore, a physical process takes place; and, according to Collingwood's theory that thinking is a linguistic phenomenon, that process must include the utterance of signs which express your explanation, whether by word of mouth, or on paper, or in whatever form of inner monologue you employ. If there is no limit to the physical processes natural science may find a way to explain, then the utterance of your thought could in principle be explained by, say, neuro-physiology, without any reference to what your thought was.

This is paradoxical, and it is regrettable that Collingwood did not investigate it further. The implication of his position appears to be that a significant physical utterance could be explained to its last physical detail without mentioning its meaning. For example, it would follow that the vocal sounds uttered by Sir Winston Churchill, when he called Mussolini 'this sawdust Caesar', could be explained, down to the tiniest inflexion detectable by the most delicate recording instrument, without mentioning that he was speaking about Mussolini or that he spoke in English, or even that he was speaking, i.e. that his utterances were linguistic, and not meaningless noises. No explanation in natural science can mention any of these things; for, by definition, all references to meaning, i.e. to linguistic activity, fall outside the domain of natural science. If such a complete neuro-physiological explanation could be given, then Sir Winston's defiance of Mussolini would be a miracle of the very same kind as that which Collingwood derided when advanced by Parallelists: a miracle of pre-established harmony (*IN*, 110–111). If the noises Sir Winston made can be explained without reference to what he thought, it is an astonishing coincidence that they can be interpreted as expressing his thoughts, or any thoughts at all.

This point is often overlooked because when philosophers and natural scientists speculate about the future of neuro-physiology, or even of behaviourist psychology, they commonly fall into a jargon which belongs neither to natural science nor to the human studies, the sole function of which appears to be to conceal confusions in their thought. The claim that an explanation in natural science can be given for every physical process implies that the physical utterances which express thoughts can be explained without any reference whatever to the thoughts they express. In such an explanation those utterances would be treated as purely physical processes, like the rustling of leaves or the creaking of a door. That they have meaning is accidental to their nature as physical processes, just as it would be accidental that the thudding of apples shaken from a tree by the wind should spell out 'God save the Queen!' in Morse code.

On one side a naturalist conception of significant utterances incurs the disabilities of Parallelism; on another it incurs those of Epiphenomenalism. If every physical movement can be completely explained by natural science, then in principle there is an explanation in natural science for every physical movement for which, conceived as an act expressing a thought, there is an historical explanation. Now, as Collingwood's analyses of explanation in natural science and in history have shown, of the two, explanation in natural science is logically the more powerful. Historical explanations contain no component which permits, under suitable circumstances, the prediction of future actions or the retrodiction of past ones. The crucial component in an historical explanation is a statement of an individual act of thought; that in an explanation in natural science is a general law of nature.

Suppose that the physical movement Brutus made in stabbing Caesar were to be completely explained both in natural science and in history: then, since the explanation in natural science would be the more powerful of the two, I think that the historical explanation would have to be pronounced superficial. An explanation which connected Brutus' movement with his bodily state, and which showed that according to the laws of neuro-physiology anybody in the same bodily state as Brutus would have made the movement he made, would certainly penetrate more deeply into the character of Brutus' movement than one which lacked such generality. Hence any theory according to which those bodily movements which can be historically explained by referring to thoughts can also be explained by neuro-physiology or some other natural science, necessarily reduces those thoughts to mere epiphenomena of natural processes. Whether the workings of mind are supposed to be private and open only to introspection, or whether they are supposed to be essentially public, the same point holds. If all bodily expressions of thought can be explained in natural science, then although mind has a place in nature, its activity makes no difference to the course of natural events.

It is not to be expected that historians will readily acquiesce in a view of the world according to which Sir Winston Churchill's utterances about Mussolini are to be explained by his bodily state: a view which neither explains nor tries to explain the curious fact that they also expressed thoughts; and which denies that those thoughts made the slightest difference to the noises he uttered. Can anybody but a philosopher with a case to prove acquiesce in it?

Yet, if it is rejected, we seem to be compelled to admit a breach in the order of nature itself. Up to a point, the physical processes which take place in the human body will be explicable in natural science; beyond that point they will not. Clearly it would be intolerable if this point were arbitrary. But might it not be that when a neuro-physiological structure of a certain kind comes into being, some of the physical changes in it can be explained as intelligent responses of the whole organism to its situation, but cannot be explained wholly in terms of the neuro-physiological laws which suffice for the physical changes in structures of a lower order? A theory that neuro-physiological structures of a certain kind may exhibit 'emergent' characteristics which are not, even in their physical aspect, wholly explicable in terms of natural science, does not seem to be logically impossible. Nor do I believe that it is in conflict with the results of either physics or physiology, established or in prospect. I hesitate to assert that a theory of this kind is true, because no purely analytical considerations can establish what natural science will or will not discover in the future. Nevertheless, some such theory is what the present state of natural science and the human studies seems to require.

§ 3. *Credo ut Intelligam*

We must now turn to the last, and perhaps the most difficult, of the disputed metaphysical questions, Collingwood's answers to which I have chosen to discuss. Can philosophy justify religious faith? Is it even compatible with it? These questions are themselves ambiguous, according as the expression 'religious faith' is understood. If it means acceptance of the creed professed by a given religious body, e.g. the Nicene Creed, then the question is: Can philosophy justify certain theological propositions? Even that is not unambiguous; for it may be questioned whether the formula of a given creed adequately defines the faith it was meant to define. In the Nicene Creed, for example, what does 'Maker of Heaven and Earth' mean? What sort of making is intended? And even if that should be clarified, is the phrase itself intended literally or figuratively, as the subsequent phrase 'only begotten Son of the Father' presumably is?

Most religious bodies appoint doctrinal authorities whose function it is to establish the limits within which their orthodox adherents may differ on such questions. Many a philosopher, however, has ignored the anathemas of those authorities. May such anathemas not be mistaken? If a religion is a way of life, may not doctrinal authorities know how to follow that way and yet make mistakes about what following it commits them to believe? If such mistakes are possible, they may take the form either of misinterpreting a sound formula, or of promulgating an unsound one. The misinterpretations which are most easily made, and with most difficulty corrected, would be of figurative formulas. Where they can bear a literal sense, as 'He shall come again in glory to judge both the quick and the dead' can, but 'only begotten Son of the Father' cannot, it is tempting to interpret them literally; and even where they make sense only if taken figuratively, more than one figurative interpretation is often prima facie possible.

Although in *The New Leviathan* Collingwood expressed deep respect for Buddhism and Confucianism (*NL*, 13. 48–13. 49), and grave misgivings about Islam (*NL*, 42. 23–42. 25, 42. 68), the only religion whose claims he considered at length, or took seriously himself, was Christianity. His remarks about it in *The New Leviathan* leave little room for doubt that to the end of his life he adhered to the conviction he had expressed in his early *Speculum Mentis*, that Christianity is 'the one true and perfect religion, the only religion which gives the soul peace and satisfaction by solving the specifically religious problem' (*SM*, 145; *NL*, 13. 49–13. 5, 42. 21, 42. 74). However, his opinions both of the 'specifically religious problem' and of Christianity changed.

In *Speculum Mentis* he had argued that anybody who proposes to live as a Christian thereby commits himself to accepting as literally true a creed which is only figuratively true. Moreover, since the truths which the Christian creeds figuratively express are not religious but philosophical, the Christian religion, like all lesser religions, is false. Yet mankind cannot do without it. '[N]ot many persons, and certainly not any societies', can live philosophically: if they are to free themselves from superstition, therefore, it will not be by philosophy, but by a non-superstitious religion, i.e. Christianity (*SM*, 144–6). Four years later, in a pamphlet entitled *Faith and Reason* (London, 1928), he was less sceptical of the claims of Christianity. He repudiated his conclusion in *Speculum Mentis* that religion depends on protecting a certain region of human life from scientific inquiry (cf. *SM*, 149–52). Far from being committed to accepting as literally true anything that conflicts with science or philosophy, true Christianity is what remains when it has renounced all such 'superstitious' elements. 'We must expect the belief in miracles, whether past or present, to go the way of a good many other beliefs whose antiquity alone made them respectable; and we may be perfectly sure that, as a consequence, religion will not be a penny the poorer' (p. 29). The beliefs of true religion, in short, have come to coincide with what in *Speculum Mentis* he would have described as the conclusions of philosophy.

He did not discuss religion in the *Essay on Philosophical Method*, being careful to divest even St. Anselm's Ontological Proof of any religious or theological colouring (cf. *EPM*, 124). When he returned to it, it was in connexion with natural science. In *The Idea of Nature*, in the *Essay on Metaphysics*, in the fragment of *The Principles of History* incorporated in *The Idea of History*, and in *The New Leviathan*, he argued that the questions which natural scientists ask commit them to certain presuppositions about nature as a whole, and that those presuppositions are set forth, in a figurative form, in the Christian creeds (*IN*, 8–9, 102–3; *EM*, 201–27; *IH*, 255–6; *NL*, 18. 42–18. 44). If he was right, and if modern science is the best of the known ways of investigating nature, then a strong argument for Christianity can be given: namely, that in order to investigate nature scientifically, we must believe it. In *The Principles of History* Collingwood was even prepared to say, 'Take away Christian theology, and the scientist has no longer any motive for doing what inductive thought gives him permission to do. If he goes on doing it at all, that is only because he is blindly following the conventions of the professional society to which he belongs' (*IH*, 255–6). He must believe, in order to understand.[1]

What he must believe, however, is not that the Christian creeds are literally true, but that they are figuratively true. In the *Essay on Metaphysics* Collingwood maintained that the Doctors of the Church, at least, had never interpreted them in any other way (*EM*, 218–19, 222). The profession, *I believe in God the Father Almighty, Maker of Heaven and Earth*, 'with reference solely to the procedure of natural science', therefore means to an instructed Christian no more than: I absolutely presuppose 'that there is a world of nature which is always and indivisibly one world' (*EM*, 225). He went on to declare that the Patristic writers, again with reference to the procedure of natural science, had interpreted their creeds as affirming all four of the absolute presuppositions on which he himself believed modern natural science to rest (*EM*, 219–23; see above, Ch. VI, § 2).

---

[1] The phrase 'Credo ut intelligam' derives from Isaiah vii. 9: 'Et caput Ephraim Samaria, et caput Samariae filius Romeliae. Si non credideritis, non permanebitis' (see C. N. Cochrane, *Christianity and Classical Culture*, p. 402). Collingwood knew of Cochrane's work before it was published (ibid., p. vii), and both the *Essay on Metaphysics* and *The Principles of History* show marks of its influence.

There is a difficulty in this defence of Christianity which Colling-wood overlooked. Even to those Doctors of the Church who inter-preted their creeds as having a reference to natural science, that reference was at best of minor interest. What shall it profit a man to gain the whole world, if he lose his own soul? That God the Father made Heaven and Earth, from the point of view of the religious life, is infinitely less important than that God the Son, for us men and for our salvation, came down from Heaven, and that He shall come again in glory to judge both the quick and the dead. To analyse the Christian creed 'with reference solely to the procedure of natural science' is as ridiculous as it would be to analyse the present corpus of chemical laws solely with reference to the procedure of cookery. If either of the two has such a reference, it is but a minor part of its meaning. For that reason, it is fallacious to argue that in order to follow the procedure of cookery, you must accept the present corpus of chemical laws. At most, you need only accept the tiny fraction of that corpus that is indeed presupposed by the procedure of cookery. In the same way, the procedure of natural science commits those who follow it to accepting no more than that small fraction of the Christian creed, which, figuratively interpreted, is all it pre-supposes.

It may be that Collingwood did not intend his analysis of the Christian creed in the *Essay on Metaphysics* to stand alone. In *Faith and Reason* he had emphatically declared that faith takes practical and emotional forms, as well as a theoretical one, even though he had anticipated the *Essay on Metaphysics* in taking its theoretical form to be scientific: namely, faith that the universe is rational. It is only because we know that the universe is rational, he had re-marked, 'that we can be certain of finding in this or that detail of it a fit and possible object of scientific study' (p. 25).

As practical, however, faith is 'the certainty that life is worth living, that the world into which we have been unwillingly thrust is a world that contains scope for action and will give us a fair chance of showing what we are made of; a world in which, if we turn out complete failures, we shall have only ourselves to blame' (pp. 25–26). As emotional, it consists of 'feelings about the world at large', for example, the feeling that it is 'a familiar place, our home', or else the feeling that it is 'alien and strange, and formidable or menacing in its aloofness' (p. 26).

The most surprising feature of Collingwood's analyses of the Christian faith in both *Faith and Reason* and the *Essay on Metaphysics* is that in neither is 'God' taken to be the name of a distinct individual being. 'The infinite', he wrote in *Faith and Reason*, 'is not another thing which is best grasped by sweeping the finite out of the way; the infinite is nothing but the unity, or as we sometimes say, the "meaning" of finite things in their diversity and their mutual connections' (p. 27). He went on explicitly to dissolve belief in God into a certain kind of belief about the universe. 'If you really believe in God you will behave in detail like a man who believes in God. If you believe in the rationality of the world and the trustworthiness of human thinking (these two beliefs are the same belief stated in different terms) you will embody your belief in detailed scientific inquiries' (p. 28).

The Christian doctrine that God created the world is a stumblingblock to anybody who sets out to analyse the Creeds in Collingwood's way; and even when he wrote *Faith and Reason* he was impatient with it.[1] In the *Essay on Metaphysics* he caused it to disappear by an audacious conjuring-trick. 'When Aristotle says that *God did not create the world*', he explained, 'this means that the existence of nature is not a presupposition of natural science but simply an observed fact' (*EM*, 214–15); when the Patristic writers protested that God did create the world, therefore, they were simply contradicting Aristotle (*EM*, 215): they meant that 'the idea of a world of nature is an absolute presupposition of natural science' (*EM*, 219).

Now this cannot be true. If 'God created the world' simply means 'The existence of a world of nature is absolutely presupposed', then absolutely to presuppose a non-theistic world, e.g. a world consisting solely of atoms in a void, must be self-contradictory. But it is certainly not logically impossible to make such a supposition. Moreover, if Aristotle had meant merely to assert that the existence of a world of nature is a matter of observed fact, and the Patristic writers

---

[1] See his review of Charles Gore, *The Philosophy of the Good Life*, in *The Criterion* x (1930–1), pp. 561–2.

to deny it, why on earth did they not say so? Why should they have misleadingly expressed a proposition about the statement, 'There exists a world of nature', as though it were a proposition about the world? If, as I think, this question admits of no rational answer, we may conclude that Aristotle and the Patristic writers meant what they said.

These extraordinary interpretations of what Christians believe explain the acrimony of Collingwood's attack on Ayer for interpreting a theological statement like 'Jehovah is angry' not as about the universe at large, e.g. 'It is thundering', but as 'about *un nommé Dieu*, a being like a human being in his mental powers and dispositions, but with the powers of a human being greatly magnified' (*EM*, 167). 'These are notions of . . . theology', he scolded, 'which have nothing to do with what . . . great theologians have taught . . . They are simply the foolish ideas many of us invented for ourselves, or picked up from foolish parents or foolish nurses, when we were small children' (*EM*, 167).

'*Sed quae stulta sunt mundi elegit Deus, ut confundat sapientes.*'[1] Collingwood ought to have remembered that not all great theologians have taken the part of the wise against the foolish. If 'greatly magnified' be taken as meaning 'infinitely magnified', then there are great theologians who have not scorned to teach that God is like a human being in his mental powers and dispositions, but with those powers greatly magnified. All Christian theologians teach that God is wise and loving, i.e. that he resembles some human beings in exercising his mental power, and in having a certain virtue; and only very foolish nurses or children have ever imagined either that power or that virtue to be in God in any manner but one befitting an all-powerful being. It is true that only those who have been theologically trained would be likely to express this in the technical formula that God has all the perfections of all finite beings, in a manner befitting an infinite being; or to add with St. Thomas Aquinas that 'in the light of this likeness, it is more fitting to say that a creature is like God than the converse'.[2] But Christian theologians agree

---

[1] St. Paul, 1 Corinthians i. 27.
[2] 'Secundum tamen hanc similitudinem convenientius dicitur Deo creatura similis quam e converso' (*Summa contra Gentiles*, i. 29).

with the most foolish Christian parents and nurses that the likeness exists. Ayer's account of what Christians believe, however tendentious it may be, is closer to the truth than Collingwood's.

The only escape from these objections is to revert to something like the position of *Speculum Mentis*, and to distinguish between what Christians believe, and what their beliefs symbolize. By drawing such a distinction, Collingwood could have defended *Faith and Reason* as analysing, not what Christians think they believe, but what, whether they know it or not, their professions symbolize. In this way, he could have upheld the reasonableness of Christianity exactly as in *The Principles of Art* he had upheld the reasonableness of primitive magic. There, it will be remembered, although he conceded that 'magic and religion are not the same thing, for magic is the evocation of emotions that are needed for the work of practical life, and a religion is a . . . system of beliefs about the world, which is also a scale of values or system of conduct', he added that 'every religion has its magic, and what is commonly called "practising" a religion is practising its magic' (*PA*, 73).

Can we then say that Christianity is the system of beliefs and scale of values outlined in *Faith and Reason*, and that the Church evokes the emotions that are needed in order to live in accordance with those beliefs and values by its ritual practices and professions? In *Speculum Mentis* Collingwood himself foresaw the fatal objection to such a view. The ritual practices and professions of Christianity only evoke emotion in believers because they are taken literally. '[A]ll religion, up to its very highest manifestations, is mythological . . . and . . . mythology is finally extruded from religion only when religion itself perishes and gives place to philosophy' (*SM*, 152). In other words, as soon as a Christian believer comes to accept the non-mythological analysis of his belief which Collingwood provided in *Faith and Reason*, he ceases to be a believer. Christianity has been supplanted by philosophy.

What Collingwood did not perceive when he wrote *Speculum Mentis* was that if religion were so supplanted something would be lost. He was not the first to try to strip popular Christianity of its 'superstitious' accretions, or to maintain that the faithful would be not a penny the worse off afterwards. Matthew Arnold had essayed the same feat in *Literature and Dogma*; and F. H. Bradley's deadly criticism of Arnold can be adapted to *Faith and Reason*, with little but a change of names.[1] 'Is there a God?' asks the reader. 'Oh, yes', replies Collingwood, 'and his existence is a presupposition of natural science and practical living.' 'And what is he then?' cries the reader. 'The fact that the universe as a whole is rational; that the world into which we have unwillingly been thrust is a world that contains scope for action and will give us a fair chance of showing what we are made of', is the answer. 'Well, and God?' 'That is God', says Collingwood, 'there is no deception, and what more do you want?' I suppose we do want a good deal more. Most religious men, certainly the general public which Collingwood addressed, want something they can worship; and his hypostatized copy-book headings do not supply it.

§ 4. *Beati qui non Viderunt et Crediderunt*

The Christian faith, we may conclude, cannot be justified by the plea, *Credo ut intelligam*, at least if that plea be understood in Collingwood's sense. It is simply not true that in engaging in natural science, or acknowledging the moral law, you commit yourself to accepting the Christian creed. Collingwood persuaded himself that you are so committed by considering only those parts of Christianity which have to do with natural science and morality; but taken by themselves those parts not only are not Christianity, they are not even religion.

Ought Collingwood then to have repudiated Christianity? Or ought he to have refused even to try to satisfy the insatiable demands of reason, and simply to have defied it? Theologians are not wanting who boast of believing in the truth of Christianity, not for any reason, but out of sheer passionate determination. From the beginning Collingwood discountenanced such attitudes. He would not renounce the stand he had taken in his early essay, 'The Devil', that 'The type of all false religion is to believe what we will to believe, instead of what we have ascertained to be true; supposing that

[1] The remainder of this paragraph is adapted from a celebrated footnote in F. H. Bradley, *Ethical Studies* (2nd ed. Oxford, 1927), p. 318.

reality must be such as to satisfy our desires, and if not, go to, let us alter it'.[1] In a philosophical book this proposition need not be defended.

The upshot of my criticisms of Collingwood's several attempts to reconcile Christianity and philosophy appears to be that, while he might legitimately have claimed that historically the functions of Christianity were important and even beneficent, philosophically he ought to have pronounced its claims to be doubtful if not false. In *The New Leviathan*, I think, that was his position. There, he acknowledged early Christianity to have been the infancy of modern European civilization (*NL*, 42. 74); but, in the brief classification of religions which he interpolated piecemeal into his survey of the functions of consciousness, he assigned the origin even of Christianity, the highest religion he examined, to the comparatively low third order of consciousness, and to the lowest function of that order— anger.

Of the four concepts of deity which he recognized, the most primitive was that in which a god is 'the ideal self which is the object of a hungry man's appetite' (*NL*, 8. 26). By the Principle of Order, this concept must belong to an order of consciousness higher than that to which hunger belongs; for it involves consciousness of hunger. That is why Collingwood did not say that the concept of God as 'the infinite satisfaction of man's hunger' belongs to the appetite of hunger, but that it is 'born of hunger' (*NL*, 8. 28–8. 29).

The crude notion of gods as objects of hunger is transformed into a concept of them as objects of love, whether satisfied or unsatisfied. In part, Christianity is a religion of unsatisfied love, a religion the God of which is 'utterly and fatally "transcendent"', so that a worshipper 'cries into the dark and gets no echo because there is nothing there' (*NL*, 8. 38–8. 39).

Both the gods of hunger and the gods of love are 'born of' appetite, that is, of second-order consciousness. The higher religions, however, are born of passion. Although the God of Christianity is a God of love, he is not essentially that. Since there are two passions, fear and anger, two distinct concepts of deity are 'born of' passion: that of a being the fear of whom is the beginning of wisdom, the

[1] B. H. Streeter and others, *Concerning Prayer* (London, 1916), p. 474.

God of early Judaism (*NL*, 10. 54); and that of a being who is responsible for all the evil in the world, who cannot be served better 'than
by wreaking on him our inevitable wrath', the God of Job and of
Christianity (*NL*, 10. 55–10. 63). The 'essence of Christianity' is
not that God should be loved, but that his worshippers 'should vent
their wrath . . ., with God's own approval, upon God's own wounded
head' (*NL*, 10. 62).

Much in this classification is obscure. In analysing the primitive
concept of God as an object of hunger, Collingwood invoked his Law
of Primitive Survivals in declaring that the idea of God 'never loses
its first features'; for 'no religion quite forgets that, whatever else
its God may be, he is first and foremost the infinite satisfaction of
man's hunger; man himself become omnipotent' (*NL*, 8. 29). Now
even if originally the idea of an omnipotent being were born of
hunger, it is logically impossible that after that being has come to
be conceived as an object of love, it should continue to be conceived
as an object of hunger. In Collingwood's technical jargon an object
of hunger is *idiomorphic*, a satisfactory state of oneself; an object of
love, on the other hand, is *heteromorphic*, something not oneself.
Only if you could conceive of something both yourself and not yourself could you conceive of a god who is both idiomorphic and heteromorphic, an object both of hunger and of love.

There is no such difficulty in conceiving of the God of Christianity
as an object both of love and of anger. You may be angry with
somebody you love. Yet Collingwood did not explain how the Jew-
ish and Christian conceptions of God as establishing the laws of
nature are connected with the far more primitive notions of a transcendently terrible or a transcendently guilty God. Fear and anger
belong respectively to the second and third orders of consciousness;
the idea of a law of nature is produced by theoretical reason, a function of the fifth order. Probably Collingwood would have explained
the belief that the laws of nature were established by a lawgiver as
a primitive survival of a comparatively low-order concept in one
of a higher order. From the fact that he did not describe any religion as 'born of' one of the higher functions of consciousness, it
is reasonable to infer that he did not consider that those higher
functions—desire, choice, and reason—of themselves give birth to

religion. In acts of consciousness belonging to those higher orders, the concept of deity can only be a primitive survival, and a superfluous one.

All four concepts of deity in Collingwood's classification are at bottom childish. In fact our hunger is satisfied by a variety of things, but we imagine one thing that will infinitely satisfy it. In fact we long to attach ourselves to various things, but we imagine one utterly transcendent thing such that, if only we could attach ourselves to it, we should long for nothing else. We have cause to fear many things, but we imagine one supremely fearful thing. We have cause to be angry with many things, but we imagine one thing which is to blame for all our woe. If these ideas exhaust our concept of God, then we had best abandon religious faith once for all.

Yet not even *The New Leviathan* leaves the impression that Collingwood could long have renounced Christianity. Confronted with the claims of a religion, a philosopher can do no other than stand with the sceptical disciple, and demand evidence. A Christian must retort that although to believe having seen is well, blessed are they who have not seen, and yet have believed. Collingwood was at least inclined to accept this reproof. Like the penitents in *Ash Wednesday*, he was of those 'who will not go away and cannot pray'. It is as though he divined in Christianity something which compelled his veneration, while eluding his ardent attempts to define it.

FINIS

APPENDIX I

PHILOSOPHICAL PUBLICATIONS OF
R. G. COLLINGWOOD (1889–1943)

(EXCLUDING BOOK REVIEWS)

THE following bibliography is based on that of T. M. Knox in *Proc. Brit. Acad.* xxix (1943), pp. 474–5, as amplified in *The Idea of History*, p. vii. The dates given are dates of publication.

(a) *Original books, pamphlets, and articles*

1916 *Religion and Philosophy*. Pp. xii+219 (London, Macmillan).
'The Devil' (an essay in *Concerning Prayer*, by 'Pro Christo et Ecclesia', B. H. Streeter, and others, London, Macmillan).

1920 *Ruskin's Philosophy*. An address (Kendal, T. Wilson).
'What is the Problem of Evil?' (*Theology*, i).

1921 'Croce's Philosophy of History' (*Hibbert Journal*, xix).

1922 'Are History and Science different kinds of Knowledge?' (*Mind*, xxxi).

1923 'Can the New Idealism dispense with Mysticism?' A Symposium with Evelyn Underhill and W. R. Inge (*Aristotelian Society, Supplementary Volume III*).
'Sensation and Thought' (*Proceedings of the Aristotelian Society*, 1923–4).

1924 *Speculum Mentis*. Pp. 327 (Oxford, Clarendon Press).

1925 *Outlines of a Philosophy of Art*. Pp. 104 (London, Oxford University Press).
'Plato's Philosophy of Art' (*Mind*, xxxiv).
'The Nature and Aims of a Philosophy of History' (*Proceedings of the Aristotelian Society*, 1924–5).
'Economics as a Philosophical Science' (*International Journal of Ethics*, xxxv).

1926 'Some Perplexities about Time: with an attempted Solution' (*Proceedings of the Aristotelian Society*, 1925–6).

'The Place of Art in Education' (*Hibbert Journal*, xxiv).

'Religion, Science, and Philosophy' (*Truth and Freedom*, ii. 7).

1927 'Aesthetic' (an Essay in *The Mind*, by Various Authors, edited by R. J. S. McDowall, London, Longmans).

'Reason is Faith cultivating itself' (*Hibbert Journal*, xxvi).

1928 *Faith and Reason* (a pamphlet in the Affirmations series, London, Ernest Benn).

'The Limits of Historical Knowledge' (*Journal of Philosophical Studies*, iii).

1929 'Form and Content in Art' (*Journal of Philosophical Studies*, iv).

'Political Action' (*Proceedings of the Aristotelian Society*, 1928–9).

'A Philosophy of Progress' (*The Realist*, i).

1930 *The Philosophy of History* (Historical Association Leaflet, No. 79, London, G. Bell & Sons).

1933 *An Essay on Philosophical Method*. Pp. xii+227 (Oxford, Clarendon Press).

1935 *The Historical Imagination*. An Inaugural Lecture (Oxford, Clarendon Press).

1936 'Human Nature and Human History' (*Proceedings of the British Academy*, xxii).

1938 *The Principles of Art*. Pp. xii+347 (Oxford, Clarendon Press).

'On the so-called Idea of Causation' (*Proceedings of the Aristotelian Society*, 1937–8).

1939 *An Autobiography*. Pp. viii+167 (London, Oxford University Press).

1940 *An Essay on Metaphysics*. Pp. x+354 (Oxford, Clarendon Press).

'Fascism and Nazism' (*Philosophy*, xv).

1941 *The Three Laws of Politics* (L. T. Hobhouse Memorial Trust Lectures, No. 11; London, Oxford University Press).

1942 *The New Leviathan*. Pp. viii+387 (Oxford, Clarendon Press).

1945 *The Idea of Nature* (ed. T. M. Knox). Pp. viii+183 (Oxford, Clarendon Press). [Posthumous.]

1946 *The Idea of History* (ed. T. M. Knox). Pp. xxvi+339 (Oxford, Clarendon Press). [Posthumous.]

(b) Translations

1913 B. Croce: *The Philosophy of Giambattista Vico* (London, Latimer, later reissued in Allen and Unwin's Library of Philosophy).

1921 (With A. H. Hannay) G. da Ruggiero: *Modern Philosophy* (London, Allen and Unwin's Library of Philosophy).

1927 B. Croce: *An Autobiography* (Oxford, Clarendon Press).
G. da Ruggiero: *The History of European Liberalism* (London, Oxford University Press).

1929 Translation of Croce's article 'Aesthetic' in *Encyclopaedia Britannica*, 14th ed.

APPENDIX II

DATES ON WHICH R. G. COLLINGWOOD'S PHILOSOPHICAL BOOKS AFTER *AN ESSAY ON PHILOSOPHICAL METHOD* WERE COMPOSED

1933–4 Early version of *The Idea of Nature*. Knox records that from August 1933 to September 1934 Collingwood worked on the lectures that became this book; and that he delivered them in Michaelmas Term 1934 and again in 1937 (*IN*, v).

1935 *The Idea of History*, Part V, § 2. This is Collingwood's Inaugural Lecture from the Waynflete Chair: it was delivered on 28 October 1935, and published under the title *The Historical Imagination* (Oxford, 1935).

1936 The greater part of *The Idea of History*. Knox records that during the first six months of 1936 Collingwood wrote the thirty-two lectures which later became Parts I, II, III (except for § 8), IV, and V (except for §§ 1, 2, 3, and 6) of this book. The manuscript fell into two parts: an historical account of how the modern idea of history has developed from Herodotus to the twentieth century, and a series of 'metaphysical epilegomena' (*IH*, v–vi). During this period he also wrote Part V, § 1, which on 20 May 1936 he delivered as a lecture to the British Academy, entitled 'Human Nature and Human History' (*Proc. Brit. Acad.* xxii, 1936).

1937 *The Principles of Art.* 'After settling accounts with my archaeological studies in a way to be described in the next chapter, I wrote in 1937 the second book of my series, *The Principles of Art*' (*A*, 118).

1938 *An Autobiography*. Its Preface is dated '2 October 1938', which is presumably when it was completed (*A*, v).

1938–9 *An Essay on Metaphysics*. Collingwood was granted leave of absence from his University duties during the academic year 1938–9, during which he made 'a voyage from England to Java under perfect conditions' (*EM*, viii). Since his Preface to the

Essay on Metaphysics is dated 'off Cape St. Vincent, 2 April 1939', presumably on the return voyage, I conclude that the voyage out was late in 1938. See also Appendix III (v).

1939 (i) *The Idea of History*, Part III, § 8, and Part V, §§ 3 and 6. Knox records that these sections are excerpts from the incomplete *Principles of History*, which contained only one third of what was planned. It seems to have been written during his stay in Java (*IH*, v–vi). Knox dates it 'in the spring of 1939': presumably the Javanese spring, since Collingwood had reached Cape St. Vincent on the way home by 2 April (*EM*, viii).

(ii) Revised version of *The Idea of Nature*. Knox writes: 'In September 1939 the manuscript of the lectures [which became *The Idea of Nature*] was drastically revised and a beginning was made on rewriting it in book form for publication' (*IN*, v).

1940 Revised version of part of *The Idea of History*. Knox writes as follows. 'In 1940 [Collingwood] revised part of the 1936 manuscript, especially the section on Greece and Rome, and rechristened it *The Idea of History*. But though he meant eventually to make it a companion volume to *The Idea of Nature*, he was unfortunately unable to work on it any further' (*IH*, v).

1940–2 (i) Second revision of *The Idea of Nature*. Knox records that, during the period when Collingwood was 'mainly occupied with *The New Leviathan*', he 'found time to revise [*The Idea of Nature*] a little further, notably the section on Hegel', and that 'he then substituted the short concluding passage on the transition from Nature to History for the sketch of his own cosmology which had closed the original lectures and with which he may have become dissatisfied' (*IN*, v).

(ii) *The New Leviathan*. The Preface is dated '16 January 1942', presumably the date of its completion. Collingwood himself recorded that it was 'written in great part . . . during the bombardment of London' (*NL*, v). The bombardment of London began in September 1940, when it became clear that the R.A.F. had not been defeated by attacks on its airfields. The German High Command hoped that 'Britain might sue for peace if the machinery of government could be paralysed and life to the community made unbearable by an intense bombing of London. . . . By the end of October [1940] London had survived some thirty-eight serious attacks. . . . German losses increased and after a major attack on London on 10 May 1941, Germany withdrew many of her bombers in preparation for the pending attack on the Soviet Union' (Sir A. Longmore, *The New Cambridge Modern History* (Cambridge, 1960), xii, pp. 287–8).

The New Leviathan was the last of Collingwood's philosophical books. He resigned his Professorship in 1941, and eventually retired to Coniston, where he had inherited a house from his father. In January 1943 he died and was buried there (R. B. McCallum, *Proc. Brit. Acad.*, xxix (1943), p. 468).

APPENDIX III

LETTERS FROM R. G. COLLINGWOOD TO
BENEDETTO CROCE

CROCE himself published Italian translations of the following five letters or portions of letters in *Nuove Pagine Sparse* (Naples, 1949), i. 28–33. With great kindness, Dr. Alda Croce has furnished me with typed copies of Collingwood's originals, which are in English; and has granted me permission to reproduce them here. Dr. Croce informs me that other letters from Collingwood to her father are preserved in the Croce Library at Naples, but that, by her father's own express rule, the collection of his letters may not be consulted until twenty years after his death.

Dr. Croce also informs me that, through slips, the letters (ii) and (iii) are misdated in *Nuove Pagine Sparse*.

(i)

Pembroke College, Oxford
May 29—1921

. . . The article is written for England, where I am known as a friend and disciple of your philosophy: hence I have not mentioned the hundred points on which I agree with your view of history, but have concentrated my attention on the hundred and first where I find myself differing from you, or, at least, from what I take to be your view. This I say because some things in the paper look like the observations of a hostile critic, and I should like you to know that that is very far from being the character they were intended to bear. I have no time to write about work to which I feel hostile: I only write about the people whom I most closely agree with. It is only because of the necessity of satisfying the anti-Croce in me that I look so sedulously for the anti-Croce in yourself.

[The article referred to in this letter is 'Croce's Philosophy of History', *Hibbert Journal*, xix (1920–1), pp. 263–78. In *The Idea of History* Collingwood implicitly withdrew most of the criticisms he had made in this article, and showed that he was ultimately converted to many of the views which he had attacked in it (*IH*, 201–4).]

(ii)

From the Librarian,
Pembroke College, Oxford
25—X—26

... I was glad to see your review in *La Critica* of Professor Warner Fite's book; I had read it, with great pleasure in its freshness and spontaneity, and had induced an English publisher to issue an edition here: I was glad therefore to see that you also had enjoyed it.

(iii)

Stapleton's Chantry,
N. Moreton, Wallingford
Jan: 5: 1928

... and the leisure which the chair would give me (by setting me free from the very exacting duties of a college tutor) would enable me to pursue the work on the philosophy of historical method which I regard as my chief task in philosophy.

I have learnt from you to regard philosophy as primarily the methodology of history; and, alone (I think) among English philosophers, I have devoted much time to specialised historical work, in order to train myself for a treatment of philosophy from this point of view—I am now 38 years old, and am ready to begin the work of systematising the problems of historical methodology as they present themselves to me; but I shall never be able to do this until I get free from college teaching.

(iv)

Magdalen College, Oxford
20. IV. 38

My dear Croce

The Clarendon Press is sending you by now a copy of my new book, a treatise on aesthetic called *The Principles of Art*. I hope that you will do me the honour of accepting it in token of the debt (far too great and too complex to be ever acknowledged in detail) which I owe you in every department of thought and more especially in aesthetic. If you should read the book, you will find that the doctrine taught in it is in all essentials your own, as I have learned it from you and reconstructed it in my own mind, in terms of my own experience, over a period of many years: for my central theme is the identity of art and language, and my book is nothing but an exposition of that theme and some of its implications. In a few particulars I have modified or even controverted doctrines maintained in your original *Estetica*, but always in the belief that my modifications are true to the spirit of your own work and to the principles of which you have given us the classical expression. I have mentioned your name hardly at all; but that is in accordance with a method of writing which I inherit from a long line of English philosophers, and it will not disguise from you, or from anyone else who knows anything of the subject, the closeness of the relation which connects my thought with your own.

(v)

a/b. S. S. De Weert, off Sumbawa
29 Jan. 39

My dear Croce

Your letter of 12 December reached me at Macaosar yesterday when I was joining this steamer. All I had time to do was to send a statement of its contents to Hugh Last, who is Camden Professor of Ancient History at Oxford and the leading man in ancient history there, telling him that he could rely on my support in any scheme by which Momigliano could be brought to Oxford. I think that Last, who knows Momigliano, is probably already at work on his case. I wish I could say that so famous and so good a scholar as Momigliano was certain of finding a home with us: but I cannot say that; partly because we have already taken in a number of expelled professors from Germany and it is doubtful how many more we can provide for: partly because, since England became a vassal state of Germany, our government (so I hear in my letters from home) discourages all hospitality towards members of the race which our new masters regard as undesirable.

I am writing from the Netherland[s] East Indies, because just a year ago, while I was working at the proofs of [The] Principles of Art, I was partly paralyzed by a stroke which deprived me of the use of my left arm and left leg. Later, I had another which deprived me of the power of speech. When I was able to leave my bed, the University gave me a year's holiday, which I am spending for the most part at sea. I am making a good recovery: I can use my hand and foot moderately well, and can speak now well enough for the purposes of my profession. I shall go back to work in April. In the mean time, I have brought only two books with me on my voyage to the East: one is the plays of Racine, the other is your new book on History. Each of them offers new beauties every time I read it. I hope you will still have time and strength to write many more books: for this one is the best you have written. It combines the wisdom of age with the vigour of an unexhausted youth. Macte esto virtute.

Yours sincerely
R. G. Collingwood

INDEXES

I. PERSONS AND PUBLICATIONS MENTIONED

(References to Collingwood and his writings are not indexed, nor are merely illustrative references to historical figures)

II. GENERAL TOPICS

Collingwood's name is abbreviated to 'C' throughout

Absolute, the, *see* BEING (1).

abstraction, *see* CONCEPT (1).

academic thinking, 89–90.

academicism (in art), 98–99.

achievements and achievement words, 37–38, 107–8, 202–3.

act, distinguished from enactment, 221.

the same act may be re-enacted on different occasions by different persons, 4, 213, 221–2.

C mistakenly asserted that only acts of thought can be so re-enacted, 222.

action, *see* HISTORY (3), and ETHICS (3).

not reducible to physical movements, 192, 293–7.

two sides of, 192–4, 293.

and intention, 86, 202.

aesthetics, *see* ART.

anger, 66, 82–83, 91.

anthropology, 170–1.

appearance, *see* BEING (1).

appetite, *see* CONSCIOUSNESS (2) Second order.

defined, 64–65.

varieties of, *see* hunger, love.

archaeology:

C's *obiter dicta* about, 197.

C's work in, 1, 3, 5, 197, 199.

C's *obiter dicta* and practice conflict with his theory of scientific history, 198–200.

architecture, 125.

ART, *see* EXPRESSION and IMAGINATION.

(1) In general: to what is the word 'art' truly applicable?, i.e. the problem of usage, 95, 98; usage and tradition, 96–98, 123–7; problem of usage decided by criticism, 99, 122–3.

(2) Criticism of: as identifying what is a work of art and what is not, 95, 102–3, 123–5, 131–2; as judging whether a work of art is good or bad, 125–30, which depends on what art is,

125–6 (*see* corruption of consciousness); how far objective, 113–14, 120–1, 127–9; as judging whether a work of art is major or minor, 131–2; a work of art may be good but not major, 130.

(3) Definition of: (*a*) *false definitions* (*see* craft): as amusement, 96, 97–98, 100–1; as instruction, 102; as magic (*see* oratory), 101; as representation (μίμησις), 100, 102–3; others, 101–2; (*b*) *the true definition*: as imaginative creation, 105, 111–12; imagination and consciousness, 107–8, 127, 131–3; imagination as expression, 107–15; imagination as linguistic, 46, 108, 130–1.

(4) Works of: as existing in the mind ('imaginary'), 116; as linguistic creations which may exist in a physical medium ('imaginative'), 118–19; C failed to distinguish 'imaginary' from 'imaginative' works, 116–19; not necessarily works of craft (*see* craft), 103, 111, but may be, 97–98, 111–12.

associationism, 54–56.

atheism, 301–2.

ATTENTION, *see* CONSCIOUSNESS (2).

(1) And Consciousness: is that by which the preconscious is raised to consciousness, 40; is not introspection, 41; is linguistic, 41–43.

(2) And Abstraction: in *PA*, C held attention to be selective but not abstract, 40, 48–49, 51–52; in *NL*, however, he showed that selection involves abstraction, 49–50, 52–53; in *NL*, C implied, but did not assert, that first-order consciousness comes about by first-order attention, 43, 47–48.

Baconian method, 150, 156, *see* VERIFICATION.

not inductive, 151.

consists in systematic questioning,

Baconian method (*cont.*)

in which all hypotheses but one are eliminated, 150-4, 179-80, 191, 196, 215-16.

requires a principle of simplicity, 81-82, 147.

behaviourism, *see* PSYCHOLOGY (2).

BEING, *see* METAPHYSICS (1).

(1) In *EPM*: C recognized the concept of *being* as philosophical, *see* CONCEPT (2), 6-7, 252-4, 260-2, 281-3, and related to those of *unity*, *truth*, and *goodness*, 6, 10, 253, 281; such philosophical concepts are defined by a scale of forms, in which the lower are appearances of the higher, 7, 260.

(2) In *EM*: C asserted that the concept of *being* is the most abstract of all, 14, 263-4, 280-1; C ignored Aristotle's proof that being is not a genus, 281.

biology, 149-50.

Buddhism, 85, 298.

calculus of classes, 57-58.

categorical propositions, *see* PROPOSITION (1).

category-mistake, 290-1.

causa quod and *causa ut*, see HISTORY (3).

causation:

in natural science, 144-5.

in scientific history, *see* HISTORY (3).

cause of a human act different in kind from a cause in natural science, 230-2.

charge, emotional, *see* EMOTION.

choice, 84, 86-87, 91, 230-2; *see* freedom of the will.

CHRISTIANITY:

the early Church, 305.

the Creeds of, 297-9.

the Fathers of, 141, 301.

A. J. Ayer's view of, 302; and C's unjust criticism of Ayer, 302-3.

C's view of: in *SM*, 298, 303; in *Faith and Reason*, 298, 300-1, 303-4; in *EM*, 278-9, 299, 301; in *NL*, 305-7.

cliché, 132; cf. 127-9.

coincidentia oppositorum, 275-6.

CONCEPT, *see* BEING, concrete ethics, and PROPOSITION.

(1) Conceptual thinking: as predicative, and so universal, 49-50,

55-56, 63; as abstract, 14, 48-50, 54, 282-4; in *SM*, C asserted that all application of abstract concepts is false, 13, 137-8; in *NL*, C repudiated this view, 139-40; C persuaded that conceptual thinking not propositional, 55-56, 92, but mistakenly, 55, 63-64, 66, 92.

(2) Philosophical concepts: in *EPM*, C implied that philosophical concepts are not abstract, 14, 260-2, 281-2, and that this was the view of traditional ontology, 262, 281; in *EM*, C repudiated this view, 14, 263, 280-1.

(3) Frege's theory of first-level and second-level concepts, 255-9, 283.

concrete ethics, *see* ETHICS (4).

Confucianism, 85, 298.

CONSCIOUSNESS, *see* ATTENTION and EXPRESSION.

(1) Nature of: 27; and heeding, 27; and preconsciousness, 37-38, 40-41, 107-8; brought about by attention, 39; has objects, 28, 30-31, *see* Intentionality, Principle of; involves expression, 108.

(2) Orders of consciousness; First Order (of a whole here-and-now), 43-46; 91; Second Order (conceptual thinking), 47-54, 63-65, 91; Third Order (interrogative thinking), 66-67, 82-84, 91; Fourth Order (free choice, or liberation from desire), 84-86, 91; Fifth Order (rational thinking), 86-89, 91; higher Orders, 91-92.

(3) Functions of: *see* function of consciousness.

Conspiracy Theory of Society, 207.

Contingency, Law of, *see* PHILOSOPHY OF MIND.

stated, 29.

convention, linguistic, 51-53.

corruption of consciousness:

defined, 127.

bad art as, 127-8, 130, 132.

the true *radix malorum*, 94, 132-3.

craft (τέχνη), *see* ART (4).

defined, 103.

false theories of art as, 102-3.

critical history, *see* HISTORY (2).

criticism, *see* ART (2).

Dark Ages, 240.

deduction, *see* LOGIC (2).

desirable, 83–84.

desire, *see* CONSCIOUSNESS (2) Fourth Order.

and appetite, 83.

true and false, 83–84.

determinism:

scientific, 228–35, 293–7.

speculative, 234–5.

difference, and identity, 220–1.

economics, 170, 205, 207, 232–5.

'emergent' characteristics, 296–7.

EMOTION:

(1) Defined: 105; a charge upon any object of feeling or consciousness, 44, 105–6.

(2) Varieties of: (*a*) preconscious (or 'psychic'): 44–45, 107–8; (*b*) conscious: upon objects of any order of consciousness, 105–6; upon the higher orders of consciousness, 106, 130–1; 'emotions of consciousness', 106; 'the aesthetic emotion', 109, 111.

enactment, *see* act.

ens realissimum, 253–5, 258–61, cf. 282–4.

epiphenomenalism, 295–6.

ETHICS:

(1) Nature of ethical inquiry: rational, not dogmatic or intuitive, 242–3; C considers realist ethics to be anti-rational, 289.

(2) Utilitarian Ethics: abstract, 246; defines 'good' in terms of happiness, 83–84, 241; C's definition of 'good' naturalistic, 83–84; C derides Nietzsche's attack on English utilitarianism, 84; pursuit of one's own good not psychologically necessary, 84–86; C wrongly considers utilitarian ethics the basis of teleological physics, 246, cf. 87–88.

(3) Regularian Ethics: abstract, 242, 246; a theory of moral law, 241–2; 'low-grade' because does not prescribe an act *omnimodo determinatum*, 242, 244; C wrongly considers regularian ethics the basis of regularian physics, 246, cf. 87–88.

(4) Concrete Ethics: non-abstract, 242, 244; C's exposition of in *A* and *NL*, 242–5, presupposes that not all conceptual thinking is abstract, 242–

3, which C denied in both *PA* and *NL*, 14, 243; refutation of, 245–7; C wrongly considers concrete ethics the basis of scientific history, 246–7.

'exist, to':

P. T. Geach discriminates three senses of, 256–8.

existential propositions, *see* PROPOSITION (1), 'exist, to'.

EXPRESSION, *see* ART, EMOTION.

(1) Nature of; in general, 107–11; an achievement, not a psychological process, 107–8; both of emotion and of objects upon which emotion is a charge, 109–10; distinguished from (*a*) betrayal, 114, (*b*) description, 109–10, (*c*) evocation, 109.

(2) 'Preconscious' (psychic): defined, 44; not strictly expression, 114, cf. 106; identical with betrayal, 114, cf. 45–46; not confined to preconscious (psychic) emotions, 115.

(3) Imaginative or conscious: defined, 114; emotional charges on any object of consciousness can be imaginatively expressed, 108, and also those on any object of feeling, 115, although in *PA*, C inconsistently denied the latter, 114–15; expression of emotional charges on objects of theoretical reason, 106, 130–1.

(4) Conscious expression as art: artistic expression not confined to specific emotions, 108–9, 129–30; dramatic expression distinguished from expression proper, 110–11, 119–20; major art consists in the expression of emotional charges on what matters in the human condition, 131–3; expression and *cliché*, 132, cf. 127–8; artistic expression 'only altered by a man of genius', 132.

expressionism, 129.

externalization, 116, 118.

failure, *see* success.

in *A*, C inconsistently declared a scientific history of to be impossible, 4, 16, 267–8, cf. 246.

possibility of a scientific history of, 202–6.

falsification, *see* VERIFICATION (1).

fear, 64, 66, 91, 106.

feeling:
  defined, 30, 105–6.
  emotional element in, *see* EMOTION.
  sensory element in, *see* SENSATION.
  first-level concept, *see* CONCEPT (3).
  forms, scale of, 6–8, 260, cf. 281–2.
  freedom of the will, *see* CONSCIOUSNESS
    (2) Fourth Order.
  as freedom from desire, 84–85.
  wrongly alleged to imply determinism, 230–2.
  and causes of human action, 231.
  C wrongly asserted to be presupposed by scientific history, 232.
  function of consciousness:
  defined, 28.
  functions recognized by C, 91, 105.

geography, 170, 205.
gloves-off philosophizing, 90–91.
God, *see* religion.
good, C's definition of, 83.

heeding, 26–27.
historical propositions, *see* PROPOSITION (1).
historicism, 10–11, cf. 276–7.
HISTORY:
  (1) Pre-scientific history: mythical and theocratic, 211; 'scissors-and-paste', 177–8; and authorities, 177–8.
  (2) Critical history: defined, 178; examples of, 178, 181; and scientific history, 178, 181–2.
  (3) Scientific history: defined, 179–80; (*a*) its subject-matter ('history as the history of thought'), 176–7, 192, 201, 212; objections to C's view from historical knowledge (i) of physical facts, 201–2, and (ii) of failure and success, *see* failure, success; (*b*) explanation in, 200–9: rests not on laws but on reconstructions of the thoughts of historical agents, 191, 200–2, i.e. of their *causae ut, causae quod*, and their practical reasoning, 192–5, 204–6, 208–9; C's theory applies to processes in groups as well as to individual acts, 207–9; but not, unless supplemented, to success or failure, 202–4; (*c*) method of: Baconian, 179–80, 182–3, 191, 196; not intuitive, 214–16; distinct from that of natural

science, 173–6, 182, 190; (*d*) presuppositions of, 210–14, *see* PHILOSOPHY OF HISTORY (1).
hunger, 47–48, 64, 91, 105, 305–6.

IDEALISM, *see* REALISM.
  (1) At Oxford: 3 n., 56.
  (2) Influence on C: (*a*) in ethics, 242–6, 289; (*b*) in *EPM*, in metaphysics, 18, 260–2; (*c*) in *SM*, in natural science, 137–8, in *EPM* also, 154–6; (*d*) in *IH*, in philosophy of history, 225; (*e*) in *SM* and *A*, in theory of knowledge, 285–7.
  (3) Idealist views repudiated in C's later work: (*a*) that abstraction falsifies, 139–40, 286; (*b*) that all experience is a flux, 226–7, existing only in the present, 223–4; (*c*) that thoughts occurring in different contexts cannot be identical, 225–7.
identity and difference, *see* difference and identity.
IMAGINATION, *see* EXPRESSION.
  (1) In art: *see* ART (3) and (4).
  (2) In history: in Inaugural Lecture, C argued that historians construct imaginary pictures of the past from their *a priori* idea of such a picture, 210–11; in *IH* and *A*, C implicitly substituted a theory of absolute presuppositions for the theory of such an *a priori* idea, 211–13.
imaginary picture of the past, *a priori* idea of, *see* IMAGINATION (2).
indeterminism, *see* determinism.
inner sense, *see* introspection.
intention and action, *see* action.
intentional fallacy, the so-called, 119–21.
Intentionality, Principle of, *see* PHILOSOPHY OF MIND (1).
  stated, 27–28.
interactionism, 289–91.
interrogative thinking:
  defined, 66–67.
  confounded by C with propositional thinking, 55, 64, 66–67.
introspection, 25, 41, 82, 108, 159–60.
Islam, 298.

James-Lange theory of emotion, the, 106.

knowledge, *see* REALISM (1).
C's analysis in *NL* mistaken, 92–93.

LANGUAGE, *see* ATTENTION, CONSCIOUS-
NESS.
(1) In general: defined, 41–42; not a
merely physical phenomenon, 49; not
preceded by consciousness, 41–43;
attention only possible by means of,
41–42, 85; as expressive, 44–46, 108,
110–31; inexpressive use of common
languages, 126–9, 132.
(2) Orders of: orders of language
correspond to orders of consciousness,
41–43, 46, 66; (*a*) unlearned languages: first-order (non-abstract),
43–46; second-order (abstract and
'intellectualized'), 50–51, 64–65;
(*b*) learned languages: second-order,
51–54; third-order (interrogative),
66–67, 82–83; fourth-order, 84–86;
fifth-order (rational), 86–87.
law, scientific, *see* NATURAL SCIENCE (3).
liberation from desire, *see* freedom of the
will.
LOGIC, *see* PROPOSITION.
(1) Deductive Logic: distinct from
methodology, 57, cf. 253; divided by
modern logicians into the propositional calculus, the predicative calculus, the calculus of classes, 57–58; all
three are in C's sense 'propositional',
56, 58; invalidity of C's objections to,
58–61.
(2) C's 'Logic of Question and
Answer' as expounded in *A* incoherent, 59–62, inconsistent with his
later views in *EM* and *NL*, 62–63.
logically proper name, 256.
love, 64, 305–6.

magic:
and art, 101–3.
and religion, 303.
and science, 142, 277.
METAPHYSICS, *see* BEING, PRESUPPOSI-
TION.
(1) C's conception of in *EPM*: place
of metaphysics in philosophy, 7–8,
251–3; as the science of Being itself,
253–5, 259–60; as concerned with
categorical universal propositions, and
so distinct from history and natural

science, 13, 255, 259, 261–2; incompatible with view in *PA* and *NL* that
all concepts are abstract, 14, 282.
(2) C's projected reform of metaphysics: in *A* and *EM*, C asserted that
metaphysics has been converted into
history, 10, 262–3; *EM* in part a
reversion to C's 'juvenile' views, 12,
262–4; C's reformed metaphysics inconsistent, 267–73; and involves a
coincidentia oppositorum of scepticism
and dogmatism, 11, 276–9.
(3) The future of metaphysics:
283–5.
methodological individualism, 206–9.
mind, *see* CONSCIOUSNESS, PHILOSOPHY
OF MIND.
defined as consciousness, 25.
properly studied by scientific history,
30, 291, 293; cf. 171–2, 176.
MIND-BODY PROBLEM:
(1) C held the classical solutions to
rest on a category-mistake, 290–2; and
to be demonstrably false: (*a*) interactionism, 289–90; (*b*) parallelism, 290.
(2) In *NL*, C's solution a 'two-
language' theory, which is similar to
Ryle's, 292–4, and incompatible with
C's denial that history can be supplanted by natural science, 294–7.
music, 2, 124–5.

natural history, 173–7.
NATURAL SCIENCE, *see* VERIFICATION.
(1) C's early idealist criticism of:
in *SM*, declared false because abstract,
137–8; in *IN*, retracted this conclusion
139; in *NL*, retracted his reason for it,
139–40.
(2) Method of: Baconian, 150–4,
see Baconian method; presupposes
historical knowledge, 174–6; absolute
presuppositions of, 140–50, 269–70
273–5.
(3) Explanations in: rest on general
laws, 144–6, 190–1, 228–9; in *EM*, C
uses 'law' in two senses, 143–4; sense
of 'law' in *NL* and modern natural
science, 143, 186–7.
(4) Realms of: in *IN*, C recognized
two (the physical and the biological
or physiological) as having 'come to
stay', 143, 149; but in *NL* he left such